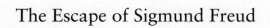

The Escape of Sigmund Freud

ALSO BY DAVID COHEN

Freud on Coke
Psychologists on Psychology

THE ESCAPE OF
SIGMUND FREUD

David Cohen

THE OVERLOOK PRESS
New York, NY

This edition first published in hardcover in the United States in 2012 by
The Overlook Press, Peter Mayer Publishers, Inc.

141 Wooster Street
New York, NY 10012
www.overlookpress.com
For bulk and special sales, please contact sales@overlookny.com

Cataloging-in-Publication Data is available from the Library of Congress.

Book design and typeformatting by Bernard Schleifer

Printed in the United States
10 9 8 7 6 5 4 3 2 1
ISBN 978-1-59020-673-7

This book is dedicated to two people. First, to Zoltan Gruber, my Austro-Hungarian uncle, who had to flee the Nazis. "My boy, I always carry twenty thousand dollars in cash in my pockets in case the Gestapo come back," he once said to me. He survived the war and went to live in Paris. My uncle was no psychoanalyst but a very astute money smuggler. He was a survivor like Freud and would have understood many of the dilemmas the founder of psychoanalysis faced during the 1930s.

Second, to my dear son Reuben who taught me so much about Freud and writing about him.

"States of conflict and turbulence alone can further our knowledge."
—SIGMUND FREUD, *An Outline of Psychoanalysis*, 1940

Contents

Author's Note

In 1925 Edward Bernays wanted his uncle, Sigmund Freud, to write an autobiography. He had had, he said, a good offer from an American publisher. Bernays, too, was a pioneer. In the 1920s he was called the first "public relations consultant," and he had an acute sense of how to influence public opinion.

"What deprives all autobiographies of value is their tissue of lies," Freud shot back to his nephew. "Let's just say parenthetically that your publisher shows American naivety in imagining that a man, honest until now, could stoop to so low for five thousand dollars. The temptation would begin at one hundred times that sum, but even then I would renounce it after half an hour."

Twelve years later Freud's friend Arnold Zweig, the Socialist writer, asked for his permission to write his biography. Freud was as fierce as before: "Anyone who writes a biography is committed to lies, concealments, hypocrisy, flattering and even to hiding his own lack of understanding, for biographical truth does not exist and, if it did, we could not use it." He added a reference to his beloved Hamlet: "Was the prince not right when he asks who would escape whipping were he used after his desert?"

I have chosen to ignore my subject's obvious distrust of biographies, on the grounds that I concentrate on how Freud refused to leave Vienna after the Nazis annexed Austria until it became clear that it was far too dangerous to be at the mercy of the Gestapo.

The British version of this book was published January 2010. In June of that year I received a letter from Anna Freud's former secretary, Gina Le Bon. I went to see her in Zurich and to thank her for some new information included here.

Freud's discoveries did not only stem from analyzing his own dreams or treating his patients; he was possibly the first great artist-scientist to grow up in a now very familiar institution, the extended stepfamily. Modern psychologists speak of the blended or reconstituted family. Freud was born into just such a family and lived in one for most of his life. Those experiences helped shape his ideas to the end of his days.

Appendix 2 details the letters and other material to which scholars still do not have access seventy years after Freud died.

1
The Bureaucracy of Hate
Vienna, July 25, 1947

Anton Sauerwald looked very haggard for a man of forty-two. His doctor, Karl Szekely, had written many times to the court to explain that his patient was suffering from tuberculosis and asked that the proceedings be delayed. Sauerwald had spent a month in the hospital. However, Judge Schachermayr would have no more delays. The accused's wife, Marianne, sat close to her husband. She had told the court that her husband had no secrets from her.

For most of the war Sauerwald had been an officer in the Luftwaffe, not a pilot but a technical expert. In March 1945 he was captured and sent to a prisoner of war camp at Bad Heilbrunn run by the Americans, but in June he was released and returned to Vienna. The Nazi defeat had shattered a long-treasured private dream. Throughout the war he had looked after fifteen allotments belonging to a group of Nazis who planned to build a small estate for like-minded people. Their slogan had been *Miteinander Füreinander* (Together for Each Other), but that dream was now over.

Sauerwald was an extremely well-educated man. When he was only twenty-four years old, he had published four learned papers in the influential *Monatsheft der Chemie* (*The Monthly Journal of Chemistry*). He had a doctorate from the University of Vienna, where his professor was a distinguished organic chemist, Josef Herzig, who is still remembered for a particular reaction he discovered. Herzig was also a friend of Freud's and regularly visited him in the evening to play cards. Sauerwald always liked and respected "Herr Professor Herzig."

Once in Vienna, a city in ruins and a city of betrayals, Sauerwald could not find his wife. Three months before the war ended, she had abandoned her factory job and fled west, not wanting to be captured by the Russians. Sauerwald spent a night at the house of his mother-in-law, Anna Talg, but in the confusion at that time, Anna did not know where her daughter was to be found. Sauerwald then went to his wife's grandmother's house in Kritzendorf, but his wife was not there, either. While Sauerwald was searching for her, someone else was looking for him. Harry Freud, Sigmund's nephew, was an officer in the American army and insisted that Sauerwald be tracked down. Harry Freud had excellent contacts: one of his cousins was Edward Bernays, who had worked for Woodrow Wilson, the president who took the United States into the First World War. Harry Freud believed that Sauerwald had robbed his family and destroyed the family business, the psychoanalytic publishing house that had started in 1919. He forced his way into the Sauerwalds' old flat to seek documents that would prove the man's guilt. No one would stop an American officer.

A few days later, when Anna Talg was asked by the police to describe her son-in-law, she found it hard to say anything much about him. His nose was normal; his ears were normal; his mouth was normal. His eyes were blue-gray. He had absolutely no distinguishing characteristics apart from his blond hair.

At the end of October 1945, at Harry Freud's insistence, Sauerwald was arrested and the police started to investigate his past in detail. The archives of the city of Vienna make it possible to follow the police inquiries that led to Sauerwald being imprisoned, first in Gefaengnis 1 and then in Gefaengnis 2. He lost the flat on Witterhauergasse, in Vienna's Eighteenth District, where he and his wife had lived since the mid-1930s. He had to go to the civil courts to be allowed even to set foot inside his old home. The city had given his flat to a new tenant, Frau Leidersdor, and Sauerwald claimed she had robbed him of the contents of a wardrobe and chemicals, including gold and some catalysts, worth 50,000 reichsmarks.

Frau Leidersdor had a good grasp of publicity and told the press that she was being harassed by the man who had robbed Sigmund Freud. In 1946 the Vienna papers published two stories portraying Sauerwald as a vicious Nazi who was trying to boot a defenseless woman out of her home.

The *Neues Österreich* (*New Austrian*) even managed to obtain a letter that Matthias Goering, the cousin of Hitler's deputy, Hermann

Goering, had written to Sauerwald. It seems likely that Frau Leidersdor found the letter in the flat and "leaked" it. Addressing Sauerwald as a fellow member of the Nazi Party, Matthias Goering asked Sauerwald to send a book by a non-Jewish psychoanalyst, August Aichhorn, but to remember to rip out the foreword by Freud because Goering didn't want anyone to think he was reading Jewish "filth." In a superb Freudian slip, Goering mistyped Freud's name as Frued. Then, as Sauerwald must have collected money from the sale of goods belonging to Freud, Goering asked for at least 1,600 marks to help with some expenses. Finally, Goering signed off with a cheery "*Heil Hitler.*"

The publication of this letter seemed damning. Sauerwald's lawyer, Franz Petracek, who had been his friend since their schooldays, told Sauerwald he would no longer represent him.

Sauerwald was sent to be tried in the new Volkesgericht, or People's Court, which was set up as soon as Germany surrendered in June 1945. The records of the People's Court are now housed in Gasometer D, a once elegant Victorian brick building whose interior has been developed into a tacky shopping mall. Sixteen percent of the defendants in the People's Court were accused of financial fraud, as Sauerwald was. Sauerwald was also charged with having been a member of the Nazi Party, which had been outlawed in Austria after civil disturbances in 1933 and 1934. The specific charge was of having been an "illegal," meaning an "illegal" Nazi.

The People's Court trials were not as high profile as those at Nuremberg, but the Allies were still keen on proper legal processes. They wanted to show that the Nazis had been defeated by civilized people who followed rules. As a result, everything took a great deal of time. In fact, Sauerwald's trial lasted longer than any trial at Nuremberg.

The prosecution's case against Sauerwald was simple. As soon as they seized power in Germany in 1933, the Nazis passed decrees to limit the personal and financial freedom of Jews. All Jewish holdings of over 5,000 marks had to be declared. The Nazi Party paper *Der Angriff* (*The Attack*) made it clear that "all Jewish assets are assumed to have been improperly acquired."

The Nazis appointed a trustee or *Truehandler* to every Jewish business. The *Truehandler* was supposed to ensure that these improperly acquired Jewish assets were used for the greater glory of Germany and the Nazi project. In Austria, after the Nazis annexed the country, there were at least nine thousand such trustees, who were also called *Kommissars*. Anton Sauerwald was better qualified than most, having studied medicine and law, as well as chemistry.

On March 15, 1938, Sauerwald was appointed trustee to the Freud family and controlled both their assets and their destiny. By then the psychoanalytic publishing house was being run by Freud's son, Martin. It had a stock of several thousand unsold books in Leipzig. Despite Freud's international reputation, the company was a financial disaster. But the Freud family did have money. The prosecution claimed Sauerwald had abused his position to seize the money, as well as assets, including manuscripts, artwork, books, and much else of value.

The People's Court asked Sauerwald whether he pleaded guilty or not guilty. "Not guilty," he replied. Over the next eighteen months, he insisted on his innocence in many statements. He repeatedly told the court it was incredible that he should be so charged.

Sigmund Freud had died in London in September 1939, the court was told, but many other members of his family had also suffered at the hands of the accused. Harry Freud, Freud's nephew, felt he had every reason to press for the arrest of Sauerwald, but Harry tended to be flamboyant. He managed, for instance, to get hold of some of Hitler's personal headed notepaper and wrote a note on it to the Freuds' housekeeper, Paula Fichtl—not that he said anything of importance in it. The housekeeper, who revered the family, said that Harry Freud was the only one of them who was not really clever.

As the case against Sauerwald proceeded, with many delays, the prosecution failed to draw attention to one crucial fact. After Sauerwald was reunited with his wife, Marianne, she wrote to Freud's widow, Martha, who was then in her late eighties and living in Hampstead. In July 1947 Marianne Sauerwald explained her husband's plight; she did not know whom else to turn to, she said in desperation. If the Freuds were honorable, she said, they would rescue Sauerwald from the terrible difficulties Harry Freud had created for him. Martha did not reply herself but handed the letter to her daughter, Anna. Anna Freud did respond, but the copy of her letter is not signed by her or, indeed, by anyone else. The copy is in the papers relating to Sauerwald's trial, which are in the Vienna archives.

Sauerwald also asked for letters of support from Freud's lawyer,

Dr. Alfred Indra; from the well-known psychoanalyst, Dr. August Aichhorn (whose book Matthias Goering had wanted); and from Princess Marie Bonaparte of Greece, Napoleon's great-grandniece. Marie Bonaparte was also an analyst and Freud gave her the exceptional privilege of having two-hour sessions with him.

Anna Freud's letter was clear, if unsigned. She said it was wrong for Sauerwald to be charged with harming the Freud family. Dr. Alfred Indra and Princess Marie Bonaparte also wrote to the court in Sauerwald's favor. They all agreed that Sauerwald had actually helped the family in very difficult circumstances. Many who might have been expected to help Freud and his family in their hour of need had not done so. Carl Jung, for example, did nothing, even though he was very influential in Germany.

Anton Sauerwald was hardly the only German or Austrian to help Jews. The most celebrated "helper" is, of course, Oskar Schindler, the subject of Thomas Keneally's *Schindler's Ark* and Steven Spielberg's film *Schindler's List*. At Yad Vashem, the Holocaust memorial in Jerusalem, there is a list of Gentiles who took large risks to help Jews. Schindler is remembered with honor, as is Albert Goering, Hermann Goering's brother.

Sauerwald's name is not inscribed at Yad Vashem as one of the righteous Gentiles, but he did help at least one Jewish family. In fact, without Sauerwald's help, it is unlikely that Freud, his wife, his sister-in-law, his daughter, his son—and a total of sixteen relatives, associates, and "servants"—would have managed to escape. Four of Freud's five sisters stayed behind in Vienna; all died in concentration camps.

This book will explain why a Nazi—and Sauerwald was a sincere Nazi—had every reason to expect that Sigmund Freud's daughter and his friends would come to his rescue. For a variety of reasons, it is not a story that Freudians have tended to explore.

2
Biographies and Restricted Archives

The Library of Congress houses 153 boxes of correspondence among Freud and his family, friends, and patients, as well as clinical notes and other papers, but not all of these can be read. Nineteen boxes cannot be opened until 2020, 2050, or 2057; eight are closed in perpetuity. One box contains an envelope marked TOP SECRET.

It is natural that Freud should wish to protect the confidences of his patients, even for fifty years after they died. The restrictions go well beyond this, however, and it is far from clear that all of the closed items deal with confidential medical matters. In contrast, Carl Rogers, the founder of humanist psychotherapy, gave the Library of Congress all of his papers with no restrictions. Appendix 2 contains a detailed list of materials in the Freud Archives that are restricted, but some need to be highlighted from the start.

Not to be opened until 2050 or 2057 are the following folders:

Till 2050, correspondence between Freud and his nephew Harry Freud, the man who had Sauerwald arrested. No other correspondence with a nephew or niece is restricted.

Till 2056, correspondence relating to the Bernays family, with whom Freud became doubly linked by marriage. He married Martha Bernays, while his sister Anna married Martha's brother, Eli. One of Martha and Eli's sisters, Minna, lived with the Freud family from 1892 after her fiancé died. Freud and his sister-in-law traveled together to Rome in 1913. Freud historian Peter Swales claims Sigmund Freud and Minna Bernays were lovers and that she had to have an abortion after she became pregnant by him.

The papers relating to Minna Bernays are restricted in perpetuity. If she and Freud had a sexual relationship, that would not be surprising.

The papers relating to Anna Freud, Freud's daughter, are also restricted in perpetuity. Freud called her "Anna Antigone," because of her devotion to him. Antigone was the daughter of Oedipus in Greek mythology. Her friends denied Anna was a lesbian, though she had a fifty-year-long intimate friendship with Dorothy Burlingham, whose grandfather, Charles Tiffany, founded the famous jewelers, Tiffany & Co.; Burlingham had a husband, too. Despite her close relationship with his daughter, Robert Burlingham was analyzed by Freud. It was a web of entanglements. In his biography of Anna Freud, Robert Coles, the distinguished psychiatrist and historian, merely says the relationship between the two women was "complex." When I asked Anna Freud's last secretary, Gina Le Bon, whether the two women were lovers, she replied, "Does it matter?" They were discreet if they were.

The papers relating to Edith Jackson are also never to be opened. She was a wealthy American who worked with Anna Freud and Dorothy Burlingham setting up nurseries for poor children in Vienna and London. She knew a good deal about the relationship of her two close friends.

Freud's own pocket books are also closed in perpetuity, though I found two of them in Box 50 in the Library of Congress. They offer some of Freud's meticulously kept notes on his patients, the drugs he prescribed, and the fees they paid.

In 1952, an American psychoanalyst, Leslie Adams, was planning a biography of Freud. Adams wrote to the British Library, which passed his letter on to Manchester City Library. Adams wanted information about Freud's British relatives and had gotten nowhere by asking fellow analysts. Adams was challenging in his letter to the British Library. He wrote:

> It will guide you somewhat that the Freud family are morbidly reticent about the family history and that any work which must be done in this direction must be in spite of their cooperation. This indicates that behind this history is some disillusioning truth.

Adams never published his biography. Curiously, some of his notes have ended up in the archives of Manchester City Library where they have languished, unseen.

There have been bitter, sometimes melodramatic disagreements about access to the Freud Archives. In 1964 the Manuscript Division of the Library of Congress received a gift of the papers of Princess Marie Bonaparte on condition that no one read them until 2020. In 1982, the historian Phyllis Grosskurth was not just denied access to these papers, but she was not told that she might be able to consult copies of them in Paris. When she found out, Grosskurth went on the attack in *The New York Review of Books*. The Librarian of Congress, Mr. Wilkinson, America's senior librarian, had to defend the reputation of his institution: "Although some say that great secrets about Freud are being kept by these restrictions, I have examined most of the sealed material, for administrative reasons, and can say that no great horrors will be revealed by any of these documents." It's a lovely phrase, "administrative reasons"; the use of the word "horrors" is, of course, intriguing, but the Librarian of Congress did not specify how he defined "horrors."

Even more dramatic were the disagreements that centered on Jeffrey Masson, an archivist who claimed Freud had suppressed facts about the seduction of children in order not to shock people too much. Masson's aggressive study *The Assault on Truth* charted this "suppression" and how the Freud Archives sacked him. A good view of the Masson saga, which ended in litigation, can be found in Janet Malcolm's *In the Freud Archives*.

Given the extensive scholarship on Freud, it is surprising to come across some strange omissions. No one had tried to get access to the archives of the school Freud attended from the age of ten. The files matter because one of his friends at school was Josef Herzig, one of Anton Sauerwald's teachers. Very few scholars have consulted the Sauerwald files in the Vienna and the Austrian state archives. The exception is Dr. Murray Hall of the University of Vienna, who is concerned with the history of publishing rather than the history of psychoanalysis. Hall has done valuable work on the publishing company Freud helped set up in 1919, the company that Sauerwald would eventually control. Harry Freud's letters, records, and unpublished autobiography also seem to have been rather neglected; they form a separate collection in the Library of Congress.

Two books that have never been published in English are also relevant to Freud's last years. The first is by Freud's sister Anna. She wrote an article about her brother after he died and then expanded it into her memoir, *Eine Wienerin in New York*. It took fifty years for this memoir to be published; it gives insights into what it was like to grow up in the Freud family, and it puts some of Freud's work in a subtly different light. The second book comes from "below stairs" and was written by Paula Fichtl. Fichtl joined the Freud household at the end of the 1920s as a maid and then became their housekeeper. A book about her life, written with her full cooperation, appeared in Germany in the 1980s. The author first met Paula Fichtl when he came to have tea with Anna Freud in London, and Paula Fichtl provided a different view of the family.

After Paula Fichtl had been with the Freud household for two years, a patient told Freud that it was a pleasant surprise to discover that his fees included refreshments. This was the first time Freud heard that his housekeeper often offered coffee and cakes to patients while they were waiting for their session. He was amazed—a doctor did not offer snacks. Paula had the courage to tell the "Herr Professor" (to whom she was devoted) that as the patients were about to face a stressful session of analysis, she thought it only polite to fortify them with caffeine. Her memoir provides many details Freud scholarship has tended to skim over or suppress. These range from the fact that Freud ate a soft-boiled egg every day to how much he charged per analytic hour in the 1930s. For one hundred hours of Freud, you could buy a house in a good area in London. He was expensive, incredibly so.

Freud was an avid correspondent and there are two sets of revealing letters that have been drawn on very little. The first were written in 1938 by Freud to his sister-in-law, Minna Bernays, while he was arranging to leave Vienna. These letters have only been published in German. There is also a neglected collection of 238 letters between Freud and his nephew Sam, who lived in Manchester. The correspondence lasted twenty-five years, up to 1939, and helps explain why Freud fled to London. It, too, has never been published in English.

The psychoanalyst Fritz Wittels wrote the first biography of Freud in 1924 but Freud hated the book. It was indeed something of a hack job. Stefan Zweig then included one hundred pages on Freud in *Mental Healers*, a book published in 1932, in which he also wrote about Mesmer and Mary Baker Eddy, the founder of Christian Science. Zweig offered a good outline of Freud's ideas, efficiently introducing readers to the works that had made Freud famous: *The Interpretation of Dreams*, which was based on Freud's pioneering analysis of his own dreams (1899), *The Psychopathology of Everyday Life* (1903),

Jokes and Their Relation to the Unconscious (1905), *Three Essays on the Theory of Sexuality* (1913), *Beyond the Pleasure Principle* (1923), and *The Ego and the Id* (1924).

There was no other biography in Freud's lifetime because he disliked the idea. Freud argued that the relationship between a biographer and his subject was strange and almost corrupting. Many biographers idealize their subjects and so "forgo the opportunity of penetrating into the most fascinating secrets of human nature." Freud appointed Ernest Jones as his biographer, though he knew that Jones would find it hard to be objective. Snide critics have said that was precisely why Freud gave him the job. Jones was inclined to hero worship and wrote that by the time Freud was forty-five years old, he "had attained complete maturity, a consummation of development that few people really achieve." Freud managed this guru-like marvel by triumphing over his neuroses when he analyzed his own dreams.

Knowing that he could be criticized, Ernest Jones claimed that his own "hero worshipping propensities had been worked through" before he met his subject. Jones was susceptible to flattery, however, and Freud had encouraged the Welshman from 1908 onward. Freud was honest about his motives, though not to Jones's face. Jones was a Methodist boy from Wales. Fearful that psychoanalysis would be seen as a Jewish sect, Freud was delighted to recruit a Christian doctor, even one who had a few skeletons in his closet. Most of the skeletons were female. Jones was incidentally an excellent figure skater, perhaps the only analyst of importance to shine at any sport. Jones's three-volume *Life and Work of Sigmund Freud* was published starting in 1953.

Ernest Jones nearly always presented Freud as a crusader fighting the demons of ignorance, so he made little of events like those of October 13, 1902. That day, Freud had an audience with Franz Josef I to thank the kaiser for conferring on him the rank of Professor Extraordinarius at the hardly ancient age of forty-six. Freud wrote to his friend Wilhelm Fliess, admittedly with a certain irony:

Congratulations and bouquets keep pouring in as if the role of sexuality had been suddenly recognized by His Majesty, the interpretation of dreams confirmed by the Council of Ministers and the necessity of the psychoanalytic therapy of hysteria carried by a two thirds majority in Parliament.

There were many other examples where Ernest Jones either ignored or even falsified the positive. For example, he suggested that one psychiatrist, Wilhelm Weygandt, had refused to discuss some of Freud's shocking ideas, saying such notions were "a matter for the police." In fact, Weygandt had written a glowing review of Freud's *The Interpretation of Dreams*.

While Freud's theories might have been cutting edge, even scandalous, Ernest Jones insisted there were no improprieties on the couch because his subject was almost a monk. Freud had lost interest in the "passionate side of marriage after he turned forty." In reality, Freud slept all his life in a double bed with his wife. The two seem, at least, to have been physically quite affectionate, according to Paula Fichtl.

Ernest Jones's most startling omission concerned Freud's use of cocaine, which Freud first took in April 1884. Jones claimed Freud only used cocaine for two years. The truth was that Freud took the drug regularly from 1887 to 1900 to cope with depression, lack of energy, and stomach troubles, and as an aphrodisiac. In his enthusiasm, Freud prescribed it to one of his teachers, Ernst Fleischl, to wean Fleischl off morphine. The treatment failed, Fleischl became hooked on huge doses of cocaine and morphine, and he died a junkie's death. It was a tragedy and a scandal for which Freud was partly responsible. Jones never mentioned it or the fact that Freud wrote four papers praising cocaine that Freud excluded from any collection of his works.

Many people who knew Freud were still alive when Ernest Jones published, so discretion was required and Jones himself played a part in many of the dramas he described. He was too close for it to be easy for him to be objective. He dealt with Freud's last years in the third volume and sometimes wrote as if he were rather tired of his subject. He listed a series of events that happened each year and drew few conclusions, even dismissing the year 1935 as one where nothing much happened.

There have been at least twenty substantial biographies since Jones's, but most tend to concentrate on how Freud achieved his "breakthroughs" so his last years have been studied less than any other period of his life. Yet Freud was not inactive. He still had patients, he still wrote, and his work after 1934 is far more than a mere coda to his career. He discussed important subjects—the nature of monotheism, Moses, whether psychoanalysis could be terminable or was bound to be "interminable," and the effects of the frailties of Woodrow Wilson on the negotiations for the Treaty of Versailles.

When he was well over seventy, Freud could still contemplate, and enjoy contemplating, causing trouble. Three of his late books—*The Future of an Illusion*, *Woodrow Wilson*, and *Moses and Monotheism*— were bound to shock. Ernest Jones said Freud was a seeker after truth, but he was also a seeker after trouble. He got bored otherwise. One of Princess Marie Bonaparte's friends said that Freud had so many thoughts in his quick mind that he could not follow all of them.

In *The Future of an Illusion*, Freud argued that if our Stone Age ancestors had reclined on a Neanderthal couch, they would have soon realized there was no God, but they could hardly do that, so their unconscious fabled up God, a useful "projection" to cope with the reality that they were small, insignificant creatures who could die any minute. Insecurity made human beings need God or gods.

Then, if Woodrow Wilson had understood his own obvious neuroses, he would never have allowed Lloyd George and Clemenceau to bully him into agreeing to a punitive Treaty of Versailles. The treaty ruined Germany and led to hyperinflation and social unrest in the 1920s. If the treaty had been fairer, as Wilson wanted, Hitler would have remained a rabble-rouser at the margins of power. If only Woodrow Wilson had had a good therapist, world history would have been different.

Moses and Monotheism provoked fierce hostility, too. Both Orthodox Jews and many Christians felt the book was blasphemous, partly because Freud described God as a deity with an identity problem. Yahweh was sometimes a tribal god, ready to advance in His Ark on the tribe next door and beat them to a pulp if they didn't bend the knee and offer sacrifices of "sweet-smelling spices pleasing to the Lord," while, at other times, God was a truly higher being, offering love, peace, and forgiveness. Freud went further and argued that Moses was not Jewish at all but an Egyptian prince who believed in one God rather than the traditional menagerie of divinities. To the end of his life, Freud enjoyed provocation.

Only one book that Freud published after 1930 was uncontroversial. In the eighteen months before his death, he wrote his *Outline of Psychoanalysis*, which some commentators think gives the clearest summary of his ideas. One might have expected biographers to consider these last works in detail but, for a number of reasons, they tended not to.

The somewhat sparse literature on Freud's last years includes *Freud in Exile*, published in 1988 and edited by Edward Timms and Naomi Segal. It is a book of essays whose title is misleading. Only *The Death of Sigmund Freud*, published in 2007 and written by Mark Edmundson, focuses on Freud in the 1930s; for much of it the author intercuts between Freud preparing to leave Vienna and Adolf Hitler annexing Austria. The aim is to draw parallels between the dictator and the analyst. Anton Sauerwald, the key figure in allowing Freud to escape Vienna, is mentioned on four pages only. Ernest Jones, too, makes just one mention of Sauerwald, even though Jones met Sauerwald.

Freud loved detective novels, including Agatha Christie's. Some of her mysteries take place around archaeological digs; Freud was also fascinated by archaeology. He and Christie were both diggers. In her novels and in his case histories, the past had to be excavated and explained; only then could we know the truth and be at peace.

Freud had an ambivalent attitude toward total honesty, as he admitted in the preface to *The Interpretation of Dreams*. If he laid bare every detail—and every interpretation—of his own dreams, he would have to "reveal to the public gaze more of the intimacies of [his] mental life than [he] liked, or than is normally necessary for any writer who is a man of science and not a poet."

The intimacies mattered. For readers to understand his theories properly, they had to know the personal details, palatable or unpalatable. That led to a "painful but unavoidable necessity." Freud arrived at a compromise that made sense, to him at least. On the one hand, he was extremely frank, while on the other, he held back some of the secrets of some of his dreams. He knew the compromise was flawed because he wrote:

> Naturally however I have been unable to resist the temptation of taking the edge off some of my indiscretions by omissions and substitutions. But whenever this has happened the value of my instances has

been very definitely diminished. I can only express a hope that readers
. . . will put themselves in my position and treat me with indulgence.

Freud deserves our indulgence. In *The Interpretation of Dreams*, he
revealed many dark feelings and wild wishes. In one dream, he pissed
on a mound of feces and his urine flushed it away down the hill. He
called this "the dream of the outside toilet" and interpreted it as follows: he felt, in his unconscious, that he had to wash away the cob-
webs of the mind and soul so every man and every woman could face
the world with self-knowledge.

In the middle of his self-analysis, Freud wrote to his friend Wilhelm Fliess that "being entirely honest with oneself is a good exer-
cise." Freud knew honesty did not come easily. Twice in his life he
burned some of his letters to keep some secrets away from future
biographers. In 1925, in a letter to his half nephew in Manchester,
Freud admitted he was willing to hide difficult truths. He told Sam
how his mother had turned ninety but admitted that her family had
been less than frank with her, saying, "We had made a secret of all the
losses in the family." He then outlined a distressingly long list of all
the deaths she would never discover and be upset by: "my daughter
Sophie, her second son Heinz, Teddy in Berlin, Eli Bernays [Martha's
uncle], and your parents. We had to use many precautions not to be
discovered."

The question of how many of Freud's relatives killed themselves
and the effect it had on him has not been studied at all—and that is
a worrying omission. There were too many of them. Freud was not
ashamed of deceiving his mother; he wanted to protect her, even if she
was in robust physical and psychological health, he said. In the light
of this, it's interesting that he did not attend her funeral.

Freud was always very modest—he had a good sense of historical
perspective—but he was also a little vain. The last years of his life reveal both his courage and his ambivalences. Freud was brave,
provocative, and a great pioneer, but he was human, with limits and
secrets. Seventy years after he died, it is hardly improper to reveal the
last of these secrets.

3
The Making of a Psychoanalyst

Our experiences as children shape us, Freud argued. On May 6, 1856, he was born into a complicated family, which had what we would now call "stepfamily issues." From his first marriage his father, Jacob, had two sons, Emanuel and Philipp. After the death of his first wife, Sylvia, Jacob remarried. Very little is known about his second wife, Rebecca, but that marriage lasted only two or three years. There do not appear to have been any children.

Then, in 1855, Jacob Freud married Amalie Nathanson, who was nineteen years younger than he was. Sigmund was their first child. Jacob had been brought up as an Orthodox Jew, but his marriage took place in a Reform synagogue. He noted in his diary that Sigmund "joined" the Jewish community on May 13, 1856, by which he meant that his son had been circumcised, as the Torah commands that every Jewish boy should be on the eighth day of his life.

Soon after Sigmund was born, Amalie became pregnant again. She and Jacob called their second son Julius; they adored him, but the baby was sickly and died when he was eight months old. Freud "discovered" during his self-analysis that he had been delighted by the death of his little brother. He had not wanted to compete with another male child.

Jacob Freud's children from his third marriage played together with his grandchildren. Emanuel's oldest son, John, who was a year older that Sigmund, was Freud's first friend and "the companion of my misdeeds between the ages of one and two years. . . . The two of us seem occasionally to have behaved cruelly to my niece, who was a year younger," Freud wrote to Wilhelm Fliess. "Until the end of my third year we had been inseparable; we had loved each other and fought each other." This close friendship influenced all his later relationships with people of his own age. He always had to have "an intimate friend and a hated enemy" in his emotional life. Freud told Fliess that sometimes "my childish ideal has been so closely approached that friend and enemy have coincided in the same person; but not simultaneously, of course, as was the case in my early childhood."

The death of Julius may not have been the only drama around Freud when he was a toddler. Marianne Krüll, author of *Freud and His Father*, has suggested that Jacob's son Philipp and his stepmother, Amalie, had an affair. Krüll offers two nuggets of evidence. Freud remembered a dream he had had as a child involving Egyptian bird masks. In *The Interpretation of Dreams*, he suggested it reflected his fear that his mother would die. Krüll argues that the dream was a memory of a moment when the toddler Freud stumbled on his mother in bed with his half brother. Krüll's interpretation depends largely on the fact that the German word for "fucking" (vogeln) is almost identical to the German word for "bird" (vogel). Krüll also stresses that Philipp and Amalie were close in age. What is more certain, though, is that the family moved to Vienna when Freud was four, but Philipp went to live in Manchester. His father never saw Philipp again.

The Freud family lived in an apartment on the Glockengasse in the heart of Vienna's Jewish district, Leopoldstadt. It was a working-class area though some solid tenement-style houses are still standing today. There were fifty synagogues within walking distance. The streets still have a slightly shabby feel compared to the splendors of the rest of the city. In addition to its fifty synagogues, Leopoldstadt also had Jewish butchers, Jewish bakers, Jewish bookshops, Jewish shoemakers, and Jewish secondhand shops that sold Resten, old and damaged goods. Peddlers hawked stuff on most street corners. Leopoldstadt was not a ghetto but its streets belonged to the world the Nobel Prize–winning author Isaac Bashevis Singer described in his Yiddish stories. Many Jews had come from small villages and clung to their traditions, but many were confused at a time of rapid cultural change.

After Julius died, Jacob and Amalie Freud had four daughters. By the time their last son, Alexander, was born, Sigmund was eleven and his position in the family was assured. He was admired for his evident intelligence. His sister Anna complained that he was given a room of his own so he could study, whereas the rest of the children were crammed into one room.

The home, Anna said in her memoirs, was a place of some religious confusion. "I did not know the difference between Jews and Christians." When she was eight years old "in my naivety," she said she did not know whether the kaiser was Jewish, Catholic, or Protestant. Since the kaiser ruled over all of these faiths, she assumed that he was Catholic one month, Protestant the next, and Jewish the next! For a while the family employed a Catholic nanny, Resi Wittek, who sometimes took Freud to local Catholic churches. There were odd prohibitions in the family, though, reinforcing the fact that they were Jewish. Anna noted that her father refused to let them give their teachers Christmas presents, which other families did. Later in life, Freud refused to have a Christmas tree in his home but gave Christmas presents.

In her memoir, Anna says that she never went to a synagogue as a child. Nevertheless Freud was familiar with the stories in the Bible even before he learned to read and he was proud of that fact. He sprinkled his books with references to the prophets and to Jewish stories. His third book, *Jokes and Their Relation to the Unconscious,* is full of Jewish jokes; 46 of the 140 jokes he quotes and analyzes are specifically Jewish. Freud was especially fond of those told by Heinrich Heine (who was also a Jew), a poet he loved as much as he did Goethe. Freud gave as examples jokes about *schnorrers*—Jewish beggars—and matchmakers. He had a collection of Jewish jokes that, it is claimed, he burned. Why he burned them has never been explained.

The confusions in the family were not just religious; they also reflected typical problems in stepfamilies. According to the would-be biographer Leslie Adams, just after he had finished his self-analysis, Freud said that he had "meditated" (Adams's word) on the question "How different would it have been if I had been the son of my brother rather than of my father?" It is hard to be sure Adams's claim is accurate, but it is not totally implausible. Freud's father was rather weak. The young Freud may have felt Jacob was hardly the ideal father.

Until he was nine Freud was educated at home. Then he entered the elite local Gymnasium after passing a tough examination. Throughout his schooldays, he was always at or near the top of his class. One of his first successes was winning a prize for translating thirty-three verses of Sophocles' play, *Oedipus Rex*.

The story of Oedipus would haunt Freud all his life. Many versions abound, but in nearly all the salient details remain the same. Oedipus arrives in Thebes as the city is being ravaged by the plague. King Laius has been murdered. The plague will not cease until someone solves the riddle of the Sphinx, the oracles say. The question is: What walks on four legs, then on two, then on three? The answer is a human being. The baby crawls on all fours; an adult stands on two legs; when we are old, we use three legs because we need a cane.

Oedipus solves the riddle, the plague vanishes, and he is crowned in place of Laius; he also marries the king's widow, Jocasta. Twelve years later, the plague returns. The blind seer, Tiresias, finally announces that Oedipus himself killed Laius. Jocasta now admits to Oedipus (apparently for the first time in their twelve years of marriage, so they clearly do not talk much) that it was foretold that her son would kill his father and have children by his mother. To prevent such a calamity, she gave her baby son to a trusted shepherd and ordered him to leave the child exposed to the elements. But the shepherd was softhearted and brought Oedipus up as his own child.

The truth becomes obvious: Oedipus did kill his father without knowing it and married his mother, again without knowing it. The end is appalling. Jocasta hangs herself. Oedipus stabs out his eyes (this was symbolic of castration, Freud argued). Then Oedipus goes into exile.

Forgeries Leave Traces

While Freud was at school, a family tragedy occurred that would affect Freud deeply. Freud's uncle Josef and his half brothers Emanuel and Philipp became involved in a major criminal conspiracy. (Ernest Jones, in his three-volume work on Freud, wrote just one vague sentence about it.)

Sigmund's father was not that impressed with his brother Josef and described him as "not a bad man but a simpleton." After Emanuel and Philipp immigrated to Manchester, Josef often traveled there to deal in hardware and other goods.

In June 1865, when Freud was nine, Vienna's newest paper, the

Neue Freie Presse (New Free Press) reported that the police were on the track of counterfeiters of Russian rubles. This was something of an obsession with the kaiser. Vienna's Criminal Museum, located on Sperlgasse, very close to the street Freud's school was on, still has cabinets of forged banknotes and much material devoted to a famous forger whose banknotes fooled everyone. Fake money was an outrage against capitalism, so the kaiser ordered the police to make sure there was no fake money in his capital.

The *Neue Freie Presse* provided its readers with lurid accounts of evil from New York to St. Petersburg. On June 26, 1865, the paper reported that a Viennese man who had been touting forged 50-ruble notes had named a number of accomplices. One of those arrested in the subsequent inquiry was Josef Freud.

The case was heard by Judge von Schwartz a year later. The prosecution outlined an international conspiracy. Josef Freud often went to visit Emanuel and Philipp Freud in Manchester. When they searched Josef's apartment, the Vienna police found two very suspicious letters sent by Philipp and Emanuel. The first said that "there is as much money as there is sand by the sea and that if we are wise fortune will not fail to smile on them." The second letter asks if Josef can find a bank for the "merchandise" where the turnover would be "larger, faster and more profitable." The letters are obviously incriminating.

The prosecution alleged that Josef Freud had met a certain Osiah Weich in 1864. Weich told Josef that he could offer him a good deal because he had bought some forged notes from a man in England. They had only cost him 25 percent of their face value. Josef Freud rejected the deal, but the two men continued to meet. A few weeks later Weich made it clear that he was in financial difficulties. The "simpleton" Josef Freud lent him 300 florins. He claimed Weich then gave him as security an English envelope containing fake rubles that came from London and Manchester.

By 1864 Josef Freud was at the center of the forgery, the prosecution claimed. He asked another accomplice, Simon Weiss, to help him find a buyer for four hundred 50-ruble notes. Weiss promised he could do this, but the two men had a falling-out. Weiss then contacted the police.

On June 20, 1865, Weiss took Josef Freud to the Hotel Victoria in Vienna and introduced him to a "client" who appeared to be willing to buy four hundred of the rubles notes at 10 percent of their face value. Josef said he would fetch more of the notes. While he was gone, Simon Weiss and the police prepared the trap.

Josef Freud returned after an hour and counted out one hundred 50-ruble notes. At this point, the police (some of whom had been disguised as waiters) arrested him. They took him to his apartment, where they found a further 259 ruble notes as well as the letters from Emanuel and Philipp. In all Josef Freud had 349 fake ruble notes whose face value was the considerable sum of 17,450 rubles.

The police sent the fakes to the Russian Imperial Bank in St. Petersburg. Its directors commented that they were produced by copper engraving and lithographic print on ordinary paper. They were excellent forgeries.

Simon Weiss was not prosecuted, presumably because he had helped the police. In court Josef Freud and Osiah Weich gave different accounts of what had happened. Weich accused Freud of having set him up. The prosecutor added that the motive behind this forgery was political in nature, for which there is no evidence, since none of the plotters seem to have had any interest in either reform or revolution. Simple greed was their ideology.

The judge found Josef Freud and Osiah Weich guilty of aiding and abetting the issue of counterfeit banknotes. Each man was sentenced to ten years in prison. But the judge handed over Freud's case to the Supreme Court, with a view to seeking leniency. It is not clear why the judge would do that, but the case received attention in the highest circles. The Austrian police minister, Belcredi, even wrote an account of it to the Austrian foreign minister, Count Mensdorff.

At the time of his uncle's arrest, news of which made the papers, Freud had just started attending the Gymnasium. His school friends must have known that he was the nephew of the wanted man. Vienna was an anti-Semitic town. To be the nephew of a Jew accused of forgery cannot have been easy. The Freud family was shamed. Freud noted that his father's hair turned gray from the grief.

Freud was ten when his uncle was jailed, and Uncle Josef haunted him for the rest of his life. Sigmund recorded nine dreams about him in *The Interpretation of Dreams*. Freud often had these Uncle dreams when he was under stress. One involved a telling pun, as it included the words Für Uncle—"for uncle." In German, *furuncle* means a "sore" or a "carbuncle."

Freud was not very frank about the forgery or the trial, merely writing that his uncle had "allowed himself to become involved in a transaction of a kind that is severely punished by law and he was in fact punished for it."

The notes in Manchester City Library left by Leslie Adams include a copy of a letter about a conversation Adams had with Freud's son Oliver, who lived in Williamstown near Boston and who died in 1969. Oliver told him, Adams claims, that Philipp was in financial difficulties when the family left Freiberg in 1860, and that explained why he and his brother went in for the forgery. They were not arrested because the fake rubles were not circulated in Britain.

Leslie Adams argued that the "disillusioning truth" the Freud family tried to hide was simple poverty. Freud's uncle and half brothers had been peddlers who barely eked out a living selling *alte sachen*, any old rubbish. Freud himself wrote that he was always afraid of poverty. He had read that a horse that had been lassoed once always feared the lasso for the rest of its life. Freud had been humiliatingly poor once and he was haunted by the fear of poverty for the rest of his life.

Only one book, *Questions for Freud*, considers the impact the conviction of Uncle Josef had on Freud. The authors, Nicholas Rand and Maria Torok, suggest that it made Freud wary of outlining his theories in any detail because detail would allow the theories to be tested and, therefore, proved false or "forgeries." It was wiser to keep it all a bit vague and muddled. This was not, of course, a conscious decision, the authors argue. Freud's unconscious fears made him imprecise.

Ernest Jones trumpeted that Freud was always a seeker after truth, but Rand and Torok suggest that this was only so "as long as what he finds will obey his control." They claim that "Freud is 'the architect of a paradox' and that his 'flawed methods of investigations derive from the need to foresee his results.'" Only that way could Freud be certain he would not be exposed as a peddler of forgeries or false ideas.

Emanuel Freud did not ever again become involved in crime, but it is harder to be sure about Philipp. The brothers concentrated on their small textile business, though it was obviously precarious at first. According to Manchester City records, they set up at 26 Market Street in 1861. It was one of the best commercial streets in the city, so they could not afford to rent a shop but took one room on an upper floor. In 1863, they moved and the firm of Freud and Co. was described "as importers of foreign fancy goods." By 1865, they described themselves as importers of London, Birmingham, and Sheffield goods. Three years later, they established themselves in the more glamorous trade of jewelers, which suggests they had more money than before.

By 1871 Emanuel Freud was listed as doing business on his own and his home address was given as 12 Green Street in Ardwick. He was now a respectable citizen. Manchester City Sessions even record that Mary Callaghan, aged thirty-five, was imprisoned for six months for stealing a quantity of twine and "fents" belonging to him. "Fents" is a word for cloths and fabric used in the northern English counties of Yorkshire and Lancashire.

Half-truths

Biographies of Freud have stressed his intellectual brilliance, not his capacity for getting into trouble as a young man. When he was fourteen, he became involved in a scandal at his school. Some of his school friends were accused of going to brothels—and Freud had to give evidence against them. An unpublished essay about Freud's schooldays written by the son of one his fellow pupils, Hugo Knopfmacher, gives some details, though it does not reveal whether Freud actually went to the brothels himself or merely sat in the cafés outside.

In 1875, when he was nineteen years old, Freud visited his half brothers in Manchester. The most dramatic news was that Philipp had married Matilda Bloomah, from Birmingham. They had one child when Freud went to see them. Pauline Mary (Poppy also known as Polly) was born on October 23, 1873. In 1897 she married Frederick Oswald Hartwig, who would run a successful company called Scientific Glass Blowing. She preserved the letters between Freud and Emanuel's son, Sam. Philipp's second child, Morris Herbert Walter, was born on April 2, 1876. He immigrated to South Africa as a young man.

Freud described his Manchester family to his friend Eduard Silberstein. "The unfavorable turn their business took caused them to move to England, which they have not left since 1859. I can say that they now hold a generally respected position, not because of their wealth, for they are not rich, but because of their personal character.

They are shopkeepers, the elder selling cloth and the younger jewellery, in the sense that word seems to have in England." The baubles that were passed off as English jewelry clearly did not impress Freud.

Freud described his two sisters-in-law and reminded Silberstein that he already had met John, "an Englishman in every respect, with a knowledge of languages and technical matters well beyond the usual business education." There were also two charming nieces, Pauline, "who is nineteen, and Bertha, who is seventeen, and a fifteen-year-old boy by the name of Samuel—which I believe has been fashionable in England ever since Pickwick—and who is generally considered to be a 'sharp and deep' young fellow." Freud said nothing to his friend about his half brothers' criminal history.

The fate of John Freud remains a mystery. The only mention of him after this letter is when Poppy's husband, Frederick Hartwig, said that John had left his parents when he was quite young. John Freud is, like Jacob's second wife, Rebecca, one of the missing Freuds.

Freud also stayed some days in London in 1875 and was to remember this visit fondly. It has often been assumed that the two branches of the family stopped communicating, but there is a photo of the Freud clan in 1876; Emanuel Freud stands in the back row. He is next to Sigmund but has turned his back to him. The twelve others in the picture are facing outward, but Emanuel is looking down and to the side. His right hand protects his midriff. He draws one's attention because he strikes a very odd pose for a Victorian family photograph where everyone usually faces the camera.

The complicated family had many sides to it. One story makes very clear that Freud's father was no patriarch but far weaker than one might expect the head of a Victorian family to be. In her memoir, Freud's sister Anna tells a romantic teenage story. When she was sixteen years old an uncle from Odessa on the Black Sea came to visit. (Amalie Nathanson, Freud's mother, had lived in Odessa for a few years; the city had a large Jewish population.) The uncle was smitten with Anna and took her to see *William Tell* at the opera. Amalie had to come as well, to act as chaperone. The uncle showered young Anna with chocolate and sweet talk, preludes to a proposal of marriage. Her would-be husband can't have really been an uncle, as that would make the marriage incestuous, but he was clearly a close relative. Stepfamily issues again!

Anna spent a sleepless night dreaming of becoming a rich wife in

Odessa. In the morning she went to talk to her mother, who was quite excited by the idea but insisted she discuss the proposal, not with her husband but with her son, who had not yet turned eighteen. The form of course was for a suitor to ask the father if he could have the daughter's hand in marriage. Papa ruled but clearly not in the Freud household.

"Sigmund was less than delighted," Anna recalled, "and explained to mother and me what was involved when a man of fifty-nine wanted to marry a girl of sixteen." Freud won the argument and the cradle-snatching "uncle" was sent back to Odessa in disgrace. Anna then became infatuated with Freud's friend Eduard Silberstein. He was her first true love, but they were so innocent that they never even kissed.

Freud's Jewish Identity

At the age of thirteen, Jews boys are bar mitzvahed. They read a portion of the Torah in synagogue and become full members of the congregation. No biographer has pinpointed whether or not Freud had a bar mitzvah, as would be perfectly normal for a Jewish boy even if his family were not devout. Freud himself is silent on the subject. Anna's statement that she never visited a synagogue suggests there was no such ceremony, and Freud once complained that "[his] education was so un-Jewish" that he could not even read Hebrew. Yet in a letter written to Eduard Silberstein, just before he was to take an examination, Freud refers to an event that took place on "erev" examination. "Erev" in Hebrew means "the eve of." Jews celebrate the eve of Passover, the eve of Yom Kippur, the eve of Rosh Hashanah, the New Year. Freud, who knew no Hebrew, drops the Hebrew word casually into a letter and uses the word correctly.

Whether he was bar mitzvahed or not, Freud made it clear that from his teens on he did not believe in God. Writing in the *American Mercury*, Anna said of her brother: "He grew up devoid of any belief in God or immortality. He had no need of it." As we shall see, this would be a source of friction between Freud and Jung.

Freud may have decided he could do without God, but that did not mean he did not learn, and absorb, a great deal about Judaism. His teacher of religion at school was Samuel Hammerschlag, who was a practicing Jew. When Hammerschlag died, Freud wrote an obituary for him:

A spark from the same fire which animated the spirit of the great Jewish seers and prophets burned in him and was not extinguished until old age weakened his powers. But the passionate side of his nature was happily tempered by the ideal of humanism which governed him and his method of education was based on the foundation of the philological and classical studies to which he had devoted his own youth. Religious instruction served him as a way of educating towards love of the humanities and from the material of Jewish history he was able to find means of tapping the sources of enthusiasm hidden in the hearts of young people and making it flow out far beyond the limitations of nationalism or dogma.

One of Hammerschlag's other pupils at the Leopoldstädter "Communal -Gymnasium" on Taborstrasse was Josef Herzig, who was three years older than Freud. The two young men were good friends—and nearly more. Freud asked Herzig for advice on some aspects of his first papers, which dealt with physiology and involved a little chemistry, Herzig's speciality. In 1884, when Herzig was nearly thirty, he started to court Freud's sister Rosa. The two went on holiday for three weeks to Oberswaldorf but the relationship did not blossom. Freud and Herzig stayed friends, though, and often played what is reputed to be one of the oldest of card games, Tarok. Herzig became a successful academic chemist and taught at the University of Vienna from the mid-1880s until his death in 1924. Like Freud, he was Jewish.

The young Freud may have rejected God but he remained more involved with the Jewish community than he sometimes admitted. Herzig was the first of many Jews Freud worked with all his life.

As a young doctor, Freud struggled and failed to get a proper position at the university. In 1885 he applied for a grant to study in Paris under Jean-Martin Charcot, who was called the Napoleon of neurosis and was the most dramatic "mind doctor" of the time. Charcot used to present his patients to his students almost as music hall acts and even had "star patients" like Augustine, whose bizarre behavior illustrated various forms of insanity.

After Paris Freud decided that his future lay in studying hysteria. Psychiatry was less closed to Jewish doctors than were other areas of medicine because it was a less respected branch of medicine. When Freud returned to Vienna in 1885, he worked closely with two Jews,

Dr. Josef Breuer and Dr. Wilhelm Fliess. Both men were crucial in his intellectual development. No non-Jew ever played such an influential a role.

The view that Freud played down his sense of Jewish identity comes partly from his authorized biographer, Ernest Jones, who shared much of the casual anti-Semitism of Britain's upper middle class in the 1920s. There was a more personal reason, too. Jones sensed that Freud always felt closer to Jewish analysts, and that made Jones a little jealous. Other commentators, like Sandor Gilman, find it hard to accept Freud's loyalty to Jewishness. Freud suffered from "internalised anti-Semitism," Gilman suggests, and looked down on the religious Eastern European Jews as ignorant, superstitious peasants with long beards that were probably teeming with lice. Paul Vitz in *Freud's Christian Unconscious* claims that some of Freud's dreams have associations to the Crucifixion. In some guilty corner of his soul, Freud wanted to convert, Vitz suggests. Immanuel Velikovsky, who is best known for his book *Worlds in Collision*, made the same point, but perhaps with more authority. Velikovsky was a practicing psychoanalyst and a Zionist who moved to Palestine.

There is no evidence, however, that Freud looked down on religious Jews. It is true that he had his moments of ambivalence toward his father, which did sometimes lead to some ambivalence about his heritage. But Freud always felt Jewish.

A Very Jewish Wife

Freud never seems to have considered marrying out of his faith, as many Victorian Jews did. He courted and married Martha Bernays, who came from a pious and well-connected Jewish family. They were engaged for four years, from 1882 to 1886, and wrote constantly to each other. Their letters show the young Freud as ambitious, passionate, driven, but also anxious and insecure, often the charming, even humble lover, but also forceful. He admits many anxieties to her, especially the fact that he cannot manage financially and has to borrow money. Two of his teachers, Samuel Hammerschlag and Ernst Fleischl, who taught anatomy at the University of Vienna, often provided loans. Freud bemoaned the fact that no one was willing to lend money to a young doctor without charging exorbitant interest rates. He was not frugal; he bought books, ate out in restaurants, and took

French lessons even when he could afford none of these things. In his letters he shared with his fiancée his scientific ideas and reflections on being Jewish.

Martha Bernays's grandfather had been a famous rabbi in Hamburg. Her uncle, Jacob Bernays, was one of the foremost classical and biblical scholars of the mid-nineteenth century; Freud knew his work well. In one of Jacob Bernays's books, *Ein Lebensbild in Briefen* (roughly translated as *A Portrait of a Life in Letters)*, Bernays described how he refused to convert to Christianity. One of his friends, Christian von Bunsen, the Prussian ambassador to London, wanted to help Bernays get a professorship but he knew Bernays could never get a chair in Prussia because he was a Jew. Bernays should convert, von Bunsen suggested, but not merely to gain such lofty academic status. The ambassador was a subtle tempter. Jews were consigned to the margins of history, von Bunsen told his friend. A great scholar like Bernays should convert and be "in the mainstream." Bernays was never even tempted to convert and told von Bunsen that his "inner core" was Jewish.

Freud's inner core was also Jewish. And he liked talking about it more than one might expect. In one letter, Freud described meeting an old Jew, Nathan. Nathan had no doubts about the romance of his religion. Freud seems to have approved, for he told Martha. Nathan said the Jew is the finest flower of mankind. The Jew is made for joy and joy for the Jew. Nathan then explained how his teacher, Martha's grandfather, the famous rabbi, used to explain how various Holy Days brought with them particular degrees of joy. The most joyous was Simchat Torah when Jews celebrate the fact that God has given them the Torah and drink a good deal. [In biblical times it was wine, but once Jews lived in Eastern Europe, they toasted the Torah in vodka.]

Then, Freud told his fiancée, a customer walked into the shop and Nathan dropped the elegiac tone and "became a merchant again." Freud reassured her with surprising intensity:

> And as for us, this is what I believe; even if the form wherein Jews were happy no longer offers us any shelter, something of the core, of the essence of this meaningful and life-affirming Judaism, will not be absent from our home.

After four years, and much opposition from her mother, Sigmund Freud and Martha Bernays married, in 1886. The wedding was not conducted in a synagogue. Emmeline, Martha's mother, did not want her daughter to marry a poor young doctor. She had seen what poverty could mean. She and her husband had had to come to Vienna because Berman, Martha's father, was in desperate financial difficulties. Berman worked selling advertising but he was financially chaotic. In 1866 he was put on trial for keeping false accounting records. He was made bankrupt and served a year in prison at exactly the same time as Uncle Josef did. In 1867, devastated, the Bernays family moved to Vienna.

So when Freud married Martha Bernays, they both had seen people they loved imprisoned. The nephew of the forger married the daughter of the embezzler. It's hardly surprising that Martha's mother had wanted her daughter to marry someone who offered security. We owe to Freud's grandson, Anton, the details of his great-grandfather Bernays's inglorious business career.

The first son of the marriage was born in 1887 and named Jean-Martin in honor of Charcot. The law required births to be registered according to religious faith. The old registers for Jewish families are still held in the offices of Vienna's main synagogue, on a cobbled street near the city center. There is a kosher restaurant nearby. To see the register, you have to go through strict security, submit to a search, and pass through a metal detector. The Jews of Vienna still feel under threat.

The Jewish archive is run by Dr. Walter Eckstein. He smiled as he brought out the huge books and pointed to the entries that recorded the birth of Jean-Martin Freud, mother Martha Freud, and father Sigmund Freud. Looking at the fine copperplate handwriting, I wondered whether Freud had his own sons circumcised, as he himself had been. On this point, I can find no information, and two men who might have been able to answer, his grandsons, Clement and brother Lucien Freud, did not answer my questions. Sadly both men are now dead.

Late in life, Freud wrote that he had been exceptionally happy in his marriage but that it was not a simple one. His wife's sister lived with them for forty-six years. Minna Bernays moved in after her fiancé died. Consciously or unconsciously, Freud re-created a situation much like that of his childhood stepfamily. Minna had to walk through her sister and brother-in-law's bedroom to reach her own. Carl Jung has been accused of starting the rumor that Freud and his sister-in-law slept together. The two certainly spent holidays together on their own while Freud's wife stayed in Vienna to look after the children; author Peter Swales claims to have found a hotel register that suggests Freud and his sister-in-law shared a room.

The Hat in the Gutter

The Freud family tradition that has been much written about is far less intimate. Freud himself told the story of how a Gentile knocked Jacob Freud's hat off his head deliberately when Freud was still a child. Jacob did not dare respond to the insult. He just bent down into the gutter and picked his hat up without saying a word. Vienna was an anti-Semitic city in the 1860s. A sensible Jew did not provoke a fight with a Christian. But Freud felt his father should have stood up to the bully.

It did not make Freud admire his father more when, in his teens, Freud found out that not all Jews were so timid. Even before he went to see his half brothers in Manchester, Freud would have heard of Moses Montefiore. Montefiore had made his fortune by the time he was forty and devoted the rest of his life to improving the lot of Jews from Ramsgate (where he lived) to the Middle East. He had some stirring successes. In 1840 in Damascus, the "medieval blood libel," claiming that Jews used the blood of a Christian for making their Passover matzo, flared up again. Syrian Jews were arrested and persecuted. Sir Moses, as he was by then, got the support of the British foreign secretary, Lord Palmerston, and descended on the khedive of Egypt. The khedive was informed of what his obligations were; if he did not comply, one of Palmerston's gunboats would start bombing. Camels raced across the desert to tell the Ottoman authorities to release the imprisoned Jews, or else.

Sir Moses then sailed to Istanbul and would not leave until he got a *firman*, a royal order, from the sultan of Turkey, guaranteeing protection to all the Jews in his lands against similar false charges. The Gentile who dared touch Sir Moses's hat would have been quickly surrounded by British warships.

The position of the Jews in the Austro-Hungarian Empire was totally different, Freud knew. A Jew could never have become an important politician in the Hapsburg Empire, let alone prime minister, as Benjamin Disraeli had become in Britain. Disraeli represented Britain at the Congress of Berlin in 1878 and became friendly with the German chancellor, Otto von Bismarck, during the Congress. "Der alte Jude, das ist der Mann" ("The old Jew, he is the man"), Bismarck said, being more enlightened than the archduchess Maria Teresa, who financed an anti-Semitic journal, the *Oestrreicher Volkspiel* (*Austrian People's Digest*). In 1893 a boy was murdered in Xanten in Silesia, and the paper trotted out the blood libel again; Jews had to sup on Christian blood for the Passover "sacrifice." The 1890s also saw pogroms in Russia, which caused thousands of Jews to flee west. The new century did not make for new attitudes. In 1913 a Jewish brick maker, Mendel Beiliss, was tried in Kiev for the ritual murder of a thirteen-year-old boy.

The reality was stark; Jews suffered, were hated, and were the "Other." In 1900 Vienna elected a rabid anti-Semite as its mayor, Karl Lueger; Lueger would be admired by the young Hitler, who said that Lueger's work taught him that anti-Semitism was the correct "policy." There is still a huge Karl Lueger Platz in the middle of Vienna.

Some of the most virulent anti-Semites were professional men, even fellow psychiatrists. Hans Blüher, in his *Secessio Judaica*, argued that Jews should "secede" from society whether they wanted to or not; a psychiatrist, Wilhelm Dolles, claimed that the Jew and the Christian were such different psychological types that they should not try to mix. After he broke with Freud, Carl Jung adopted a similar view, as did Matthias Goering, Hermann Goering's cousin. All were deeply influenced by the ideas of Houston Chamberlain, the son of an English admiral, who developed the theory that Aryans were the superior race engaged in a titanic struggle against Jews. Chamberlain wrote a number of immensely popular books, including a biography of Wagner. Chamberlain met Hitler in 1923, and the two men admired each other.

It seems that Freud was not ambivalent about being Jewish, nor was he a self-hating Jew, but he did not believe in God. Freud believed that God was a man-made delusion and that Judaism, like every other religion, was an illusion neurotic Neanderthals had needed and that human beings now needed to evolve beyond.

Freud made his feelings about being a Jew clear in his preface to the Hebrew edition of *Totem and Taboo.*

No reader of the Hebrew version of this book will find it easy to put himself in the emotional position of an author who is ignorant of the language of holy writ, who is completely estranged from the religion of his fathers—as well as from every other religion—and who cannot take a share in nationalist ideals, but who has yet never repudiated his people, who feels that he is in his essential nature a Jew and who has no desire to alter that nature. If the question were put to him: "Since you have abandoned all these common characteristics of your countrymen, what is left to you that is Jewish?" he would reply: "A very great deal, and probably its very essence." He could not express that essence in words, but some day, no doubt, it will become accessible to the scientific mind.

Freud tried to express that "essence" of Jewish culture. Its roots are most obvious in the Talmud with its commentaries about biblical texts as well as its commentaries about commentaries. The Talmud encourages the asking of questions. So did some books in the Bible, such as the book of Job. Job cross-examines God and God does not respond, as if such questions were impertinent. Freud said:

It was only to my Jewish nature that I owed the two qualities that have become indispensable to me throughout my difficult life. Because I was a Jew I found myself free of many prejudices which restrict others in the use of the intellect: as a Jew I was prepared to be in the opposition and to renounce agreement with the "compact majority."

In talking of his difficult life, incidentally, Freud was *kvetching*, to use a Yiddish expression, complaining, throwing up his hands to the heavens, demanding compensation from the Almighty in whom he did not believe. One might ask if in 1925, when Freud wrote this, he had much reason to *kvetch*. He had a devoted mother, a devoted wife, a devoted sister-in-law, devoted followers, and devoted children, and he was about to be interviewed as a world celebrity by Chaplin's friend, Max Eastman, for *Heroes I Have Known*. The only reason that Freud didn't have a devoted rabbi was that he never went to synagogue. Freud was not a perfect man but in his kvetching, he was perfectly a Jew. He claimed he had the necessary "degree of readiness to accept a situation of solitary opposition—a situation with which no one is more familiar than a Jew."

Historian Diaz de Chumacerio has suggested that Freud was so enraged by anti-Semitism that he ignored Wagner's contribution to the study of dreams. The composer had developed his own dream theory half a century before Freud. Freud knew of Wagner's writing on dreams when he wrote *The Interpretation of Dreams*, de Chumacerio claims. *The Interpretation of Dreams* discusses previous writers on dreams without devoting a word to Wagner, and that seems an "inexplicable case of omission." Freud, consciously or unconsciously, blotted out the influence that a hater of Jews had on him, according to de Chumacerio.

In an anti-Semitic town, Freud had the sense to see that psychoanalysis would suffer if it seemed to be a Jewish monopoly, so he rejoiced when two Christians, Ernest Jones and Carl Jung, joined the "cause," as psychoanalysis was sometimes called. Freud even asked one of his first followers, Karl Abraham, to forgive the fact that he had to pay so much attention to these *goyim* (the Yiddish term for Gentiles), but they found it harder to accept the unconventional ideas of psychoanalysis. Christians were not used to "solitary opposition."

Living in a Jewish neighborhood

In 1891, after five years of marriage, the Freuds moved to the mezzanine floor of 19 Berggasse. The street slopes upward, which may be why it is called Mountain Street. Today 19 Berggasse houses Vienna's Freud Museum. Two doors away from its entrance there is a Café Freud where someone has put up a number of portraits of Freud including a very pointillistic picture in which he twinkles covered in sequins. Freud belongs to us all now, even the sex industry. Across the road is a sex shop called *Boudoir* whose window has a number of balloons with Freud's face on them as well as copies of books by the Marquis de Sade. Few sex shops try so hard to achieve intellectual respectability.

When Freud and his wife moved to 19 Berggasse, they were not far from the Jewish quarter. If Freud turned left out his front door, he could amble down to the Donau Canal in five minutes. If he walked across the bridge, it would take ten minutes to reach the end of Taborstrasse, one of the main streets of the Jewish quarter. Taborstrasse was the obvious route to take to the Prater, the park Freud had liked ever since he walked there as a small boy with his father. His sister's memoir describes many days when they strolled through the Prater as a family and Freud's father, Jacob, enjoyed a beer in its café. The great analyst never moved far from his Jewish roots.

In 1891, when Freud turned thirty-five, his father gave him a fine Bible and said he hoped he would return to the faith of his fathers. Freud did not ever become religious, but in one simple way he did what his father wanted. Freud lived for forty-seven years in an apartment block where nearly all of the other residents were Jewish. The ground floor was occupied by Kornmehl, a kosher butcher.

Husband and wife had their separate spheres. Freud certainly did not interfere with her housekeeping. Decades later, when their youngest daughter, Anna, wanted to change her bedroom, Freud said it was fine with him, but that hardly counted: her mother ruled the domestic sphere, and the twenty-year-old daughter had to ask her mother for permission. Anna also complained that her mother was a stickler for punctuality and that they always had to have the main meal of the day at 1:00 p.m. That raises the question of what food Frau Freud served.

Given their marriage "contract," which stated that the wife should rule the home, it is possible that Freud hardly ever set foot in the kitchen. That would have allowed his wife to keep a partially kosher home. She may have bought kosher meat from the kosher butcher downstairs, without her husband ever knowing. Freud had no time for the intricacies of Jewish law which include 613 rules a good Jew must adhere to. His good Jewish wife keeping a good Jewish kitchen prompts an unanswerable question: Would he have been amused or annoyed that she made him eat kosher?

In her memoirs, the maid, Paula Fichtl, provided a copy of the recipes that were the favorites in the Freud household from 1929. There was ox tongue, stewed carp, and many kinds of soufflés, but not one recipe for pork. Herr Professor's great treat was caviar at Christmas. One of his grateful patients brought him a huge pot of caviar once. (For much of his career, Freud was too poor to afford such luxuries.)

The death of Freud's father—
and its consequences

In 1896, Freud's father, Jacob, died. He had lived to be eighty-one years of age. Freud may have dismissed religion as a kind of superstition born of insecurity, but he was not always rational himself. In the 1890s, some of his letters written to the physician Wilhelm Fliess reveal anxieties about how long he would live. Fliess's bizarre "laws of periodicity," based on the numbers like 23 and 28, were also used by Freud to calculate the precise date of his death. Freud called Fliess "a great astrologer"; the number 81 would stick in Freud's mind for the rest of his life.

Freud said that his father's death freed him to pursue his radical ideas. For the next three or four years, Freud recorded his own dreams and tried to understand what they meant. "Wise" men had been interpreting dreams since biblical times, but no one had attempted a scientific analysis of their own dreams. They were the basic evidence for his "shocking" theory, which claimed that children were sexual.

Freud presented some of his early "shocking" ideas to the B'nai B'rith Jewish Society, the Viennese branch of a fraternity set up in New York in 1843 to promote communal help. In Vienna, the lodge held meetings where Jewish intellectuals presented and discussed their ideas. Freud felt he would get a more sympathetic hearing from his coreligionists who knew something about what he called "solitary opposition."

The idea behind solitary opposition concerns seeing things from a new perspective. When Jews left their small, and small-minded, agricultural settlements where the rabbis were usually dominant, many Jews stopped keeping the 613 commandments or, at least, most of them; they peered at the world and unpeeled their eyes; they blinked and their blinkers were lifted. They saw the world with the insight of the outsider who had no status to lose and so could take intellectual risks. It was not the meek who would inherit the earth, but the risk takers. It is a splendid argument, grand, sweeping, and very romantic.

The theory is not without problems, however. Charles Darwin, who Freud greatly admired, developed the theory of evolution and outraged the Church. The Bible was not the literal truth or word of

God, he said, and the world had not been created in six days in 4004 BCE, as Bishop Ussher had calculated by working out the precise year in which one ancient begat another. Darwin was no outsider, however. He came from a well-established English family, trained to become a clergyman, and married a young woman who was a devout Anglican.

It could be argued that the roots of Freud's creativity had less to do with being able to cope with the fact that he was Jewish and could glory in "solitary opposition" than he imagined. Freud exposed hidden tensions between children and their parents. He had grown up in a complicated family and had sensed those tensions as a little boy. (It seems more plausible that his mother only flirted with her stepson Philipp, and did not have an affair with him, but that could have been enough to make her husband, Jacob, furious.) When Freud analyzed his dreams, memories of these tensions flooded back and gave him the material on which he built his theories.

Anti-Semitism and "La Chose Genitale"

Long before the Nazis came to power, Freud believed he understood the deep reasons for anti-Semitism, which came down to "la chose genitale," to use neurologist Jean-Martin Charcot's phrase—specifically, the rule that Jewish boys had to be circumcised when they were eight days old.

The roots of anti-Semitism, Freud claimed, lay in "remotest past ages" and had nothing to do with differences in public appearance. Jews did not look weird and were not of a different color, and jibes about hooked or Hittite noses were silly—Julius Caesar had had a very hooked nose, after all. Jews were not "fundamentally different"—they were "essentially Mediterranean." Freud also dismissed the idea that anti-Semitism was due to the fact that the Church blamed the Jews for betraying Christ.

Anti-Semitism was so emotional and ran so deep that it had to have unconscious roots. Freud's analysis in the 1930s was based on his treatment of the only child he ever saw as a patient, which had taken place some thirty years earlier. Little Hans was the five-year-old son of his Jewish friend, Max Graf, a composer and historian of music who attended some of the Wednesday psychoanalytic meetings at Freud's house. Hans had been growing up normally and then suddenly developed a crippling phobia.

Little Hans would not leave the house. He would not step into the street. When his father asked why, the boy said that he was afraid a horse would bite him. The boy was brought to Berggasse. Freud soon realized that the horse reminded Hans of his father. There were two visual details Freud made much of—Max Graf had a mustache and wore glasses. Those were very significant, Freud argued, because to his son, they made Graf look like a horse. If Freud could have painted, he would have become a surrealist. Little Hans's phobic fear that a horse might bite him was a desperate compromise to try to solve the Oedipal conflict.

Hans loved his father but his father was also a rival for his mother's love. Such thoughts were forbidden, Little Hans knew unconsciously, so the little lad was a stew of guilt, repressions, and fears. The lid would blow off his inner kettle any moment so the child developed acute castration anxiety. When Hans's sister was born, the anxiety got worse because he was jealous of her. The boy did say he wanted her dead, but he could not say anything of the sort about his father. He had to repress his anger and aggression, and that repression made him fear that his father wanted to castrate him.

At the age of five, Little Hans was, in his unconscious mind at least, a subtle strategist. It was not hard to avoid horses because Little Hans did not have to go out into the street. But the real monster, Dad wielding the castrating knife, was at home. By being frightened of the horse, Little Hans could ward off the greater anxiety, that his father would cut off his penis. The horse phobia helped the boy manage his terrors. It is a view of phobias that remains influential today.

To understand why Gentiles hated Jews, Freud wrote in a footnote to his paper on Little Hans, one also had to look to Genesis. God promised Abraham that the Jews would be the Chosen People. The mark of that covenant was that every male child should be circumcised when he was eight days old, as Freud had been. But the snip reminded men of their primal fear—castration.

Freud wove this into a complex theory. Jews made themselves "separate" and, of all their practices that made them so, "circumcision has made a disagreeable uncanny impression." Christians hated the Jews not because the Jews had Christ crucified but because Jews reminded Christians of the traumatic fear that makes men wriggle with discomfort. It was canny of Saint Paul to argue that Christ demanded circumcision of the heart, which is rather less traumatic than the physical cut for adult converts. As Jean-Martin Charcot said, it was all down to "la chose genitale," the genital thing.

Freud also blamed Jewish pride. Genesis and Exodus constantly emphasize the covenant between God and Israel, the Chosen People. So the Jews do not just evoke unconscious fears of castration; they also have the impertinence to claim a privileged relationship with God the Father. "I venture to assert that jealousy of the people which declared itself first born, favourite child of God the father has not yet been surmounted among other people even today; it is as though they had thought there was truth in the claim." Freud believed this before the Nazis came to power, but he did not dare utter these thoughts for many years.

Moses and Rome

Freud had a lifelong interest in Moses, but his attitude toward the prophet was complicated by his ambivalence about Rome. Freud adored the city, yet, by the time he was forty, he had never visited it, even though he had managed to get to London, Manchester, Paris, Nancy, Hamburg, and Berlin. He even got to Trasimene, some eighty-five miles from Rome, but he did not press on. There was a reason for that, of course.

In 217 BCE Hannibal brought elephants over the Alps and defeated the Romans on the shores of Lake Trasimene. Freud identified with the general, and in *The Interpretation of Dreams* he wrote in a spirit of confession:

> I had actually been following in Hannibal's footsteps. Like him, I had been fated not to see Rome; and he too had moved into the Campagna when everyone had expected him in Rome. But Hannibal, whom I had come to resemble in these respects, had been the favourite hero of my later school days. Like so many boys of that age, I had sympathised in the Punic Wars not with the Romans but with the Carthaginians. And when in the higher classes I began to understand for the first time what it means to belong to an alien race, and anti-Semitic feelings among the other boys warned me that I must take up a definite position, the figure of the Semitic general rose still higher in my esteem. To my youthful mind Hannibal and Rome symbolized the conflict between the tenacity of Jewry and the organization of the Catholic Church.

Hannibal's father, Hamilcar Barca, made his boy swear that he would take vengeance on the Romans. If Hamilcar had had a hat, the Roman who dared knock it off his head would have found his throat slit. "Ever since that time, Hannibal had had a place in my fantasies," Freud wrote. For Hannibal, Rome meant the capital of the Empire; for Freud, Rome meant the Catholic Church, which often humiliated Jews. In December 1897, Freud told his friend Wilhelm Fliess, "My longing for Rome is, by the way, deeply neurotic."

After four years of self-analysis, Freud finally overcame his resistances. Ernest Jones reports this visit rather grandly, saying Freud "triumphantly entered Rome," as if Sigmund marched into the city with a band of armed analysts. In fact, Freud and his younger brother, Alexander, traveled on the overnight train from Vienna and, once in Rome, got a cab to the Hotel Eden, much like ordinary tourists. "The visit was a high point of my life," Freud wrote to Fliess. Freud was about to see a work of art he had studied in detail in photographs for years.

If you walk up the hill that overlooks the Coliseum, you snake up through lanes leading past a magnificent yellowing building, the School of Engineering of the University of Rome. Past the school, the lane opens out onto a modest piazza, but the church that dominates the piazza is anything but modest. The entrance to the Church of San Pietro in Vincoli, Saint Peter in Chains, is protected by wrought-iron gates. Inside, the church is dramatically white; it is supported on either side by ten white marble columns. The columns lead the eye to what looks like a giant four-poster bed that covers the altar.

Lavish paintings and sculptures decorate the walls; there is a particularly macabre skull and a strange sculpture of a lobster. Just in front of the giant four-poster structure, a few steps lead down to a small alcove. This is what the devout come to see, a box that contains the chains in which Saint Peter was held. The chains gleam; no rust has ever tarnished them.

The chains are not the most remarkable trophies in the church. An alcove to the right houses a huge monument with seven life-size statues. There is a marble statue of Pope Julius II lying down, as well as of the Old Testament heroines Rachel and Leah. In the middle is the magnificent, imposing "Moses" by Michelangelo. This statue is more than life-size. "Moses" measures 2.35 meters (7 feet 8 inches). The prophet is seated and holds the Tablets of the Law God gave him on Mount

Sinai. Moses's beard is a spectacular flowing tangle of locks. The prophet looks slightly manic, partly due to the fact that two horns protrude from his head. They look remarkably like stunted cucumbers but, of course, they are not. According to Exodus 34:29–35, Moses had *korein or panav* or "rays on the skin of his face" because he was bathed in the Divine Light. The Hebrew is ambiguous, though. The root *k-r-n* can be translated either as "radiated (light)" or "grew horns."

Michelangelo felt Moses was his most lifelike creation. According to one tradition, when he finished it, the sculptor hit Moses's right knee and said, "Now speak!" A scar on Moses's knee is thought to be the mark Michelangelo made with his hammer.

The tomb of Pope Julius II was designed for St. Peter's Basilica in the Vatican and was supposed to contain forty statues, but there were financial issues as the rebuilding of St. Peter's ran over budget. The negotiations about the size of the tomb took years. Finally, in 1542, Michelangelo agreed to reduce his forty sculptures to seven. As a result, Moses dominates the structure even more.

Freud had read and reread Vasari's *Life of Michelangelo*, which was published in 1568. Vasari described the "Moses" wonderfully:

> Michelangelo finished the "Moses" in marble, a statue of five braccia, unequalled by any modern or ancient work. Seated in a serious attitude, he rests with one arm on the tables and with the other holds his long glossy beard, the hairs, so difficult to render in sculpture, being so soft and downy that it seems as if the iron chisel must have become a brush. The beautiful face, like that of a saint and mighty prince, seems as one regards it to need the veil to cover it, so splendid and shining does it appear, and so well has the artist presented in the marble the divinity with which God had endowed that holy countenance . . . The Jews still go every Saturday in troops to visit and adore it as a divine, not a human thing.

Freud found this last phrase interesting enough to underline it in his guidebook. The statue awed him, and sometimes he "crept cautiously out of the half gloom of the interior as though [he himself] belonged to the mob," by which he meant the mob of rebellious Jews who exasperated Moses by dancing around the Golden Calf. Freud expected to see it "start up on its raised foot, dash the Tablets of Stone to the Ground and let fly its wrath."

Michelangelo caught Moses just before he gets up to smash the tablets, Freud argued. The marble bristles with tension. Moses stares to one side; the veins on his hands bulge. Freud went beyond Exodus, however, and claimed that Moses managed to control his anger and stopped the Tablets of the Law from slipping out of his grasp. So when he smashed the Tablets, he was in control of himself. That was an achievement to salute, as Exodus paints the prophet as a man given to anger, and even violence.

Freud visited Rome seven more times after 1901. He usually stayed at the Hotel Eden and he seems to have had no problems going back to the city. The last visit he made was in 1923 with his daughter Anna.

It would take Freud thirteen years after his first visit to publish any of his ideas on Moses, and then he did so anonymously. The paper was published in *Imago*, a psychoanalytic journal Freud controlled. There was even some effort to suggest the writer was not an analyst. The paper reads more like a response to a great statue rather than an attempt to put Michelangelo's masterpiece in any analytic context; it reads more like art history.

Ernest Jones was rather cavalier in failing to explore why Freud identified so deeply with Moses, according to psychoanalyst and professor of English Patrick Mahony. A great dream interpreter like Freud would, one might expect, identify rather with either Joseph or Daniel, the Bible's main dream diviners. There was one key difference between Moses and these other two prophets, however: only Moses encountered God face-to-face and spoke with Him, not in a dream but on top of Mount Sinai.

In *From Oedipus to Moses,* Marthe Robert argues that, in his writings on Moses, Freud was battling with his ambivalent feelings about his father. Jacob was not the strong father a clever boy was entitled to expect, so Freud looked for nobler father figures, picked some distinguished ones, and identified with them.

4
Freud and Jung:
A Battle for Supremacy

Five years after he first set foot in Rome, Freud met the most important of his "disciples," although Carl Jung did not see himself as one of them. If two men were destined not to have an easy relationship, they were Freud and Jung; each was a prima donna, each had problematic parents, and each had a tendency to faint under stress. It is tempting to suggest that both great therapists needed a great therapist.

Carl Jung's father was a poor pastor in the Swiss Reformed Church. His mother came from a rich family and it seems likely she was allowed to marry the pastor because she suffered from depression. Emilie Jung lost three children when they were small, so it is not surprising that she looked for spiritual consolation. Her son remembered that she usually slept in a separate bedroom where she waited for the ghosts. One night she saw a glowing and indefinite figure emerging from her room; its head was detached from the neck and the body floated through the air.

Jung's mother had to spend several months in the hospital, and Jung was sent to live with her sister in Basel for three years. His father then applied for a different parish, which made it possible for his wife to return home. Jung responded to these domestic tensions in an imaginative way. He decided—and it was a conscious choice—that he had two personalities, one that of the schoolboy living in his own time and a second personality, an eighteenth-century man of some importance.

Jung also remembered that as a boy he carved a tiny mannequin out of the end of his wooden ruler and placed it in his pencil case. He added a stone, which he had painted into upper and lower halves, and hid the case in the attic. He would often take the mannequin out and add tiny sheets of paper with messages inscribed on them in his own secret language. This gave him a feeling of security, he wrote later. Jung's behavior is similar to that of children who devise imaginary worlds or paracosms.

Jung also had troubles at school. In his first year at the Humanistisches Gymnasium in Basel, another boy pushed him to the ground. Jung briefly lost consciousness but he remembered thinking, "Now you won't have to go to school anymore." He then fainted a number of times when he was going to school or had to do homework. Later, he managed to control his urge to faint, but the fainting, Jung wrote later, "was when I learned what a neurosis is."

Freud's complex family influenced his thinking, and the same was true for Jung. Jung's doctoral dissertation included the case of S.W., who was really his cousin Helene Preiswerk. She had visions and hallucinations at séances Jung attended with his mother. Jung may not have told the truth about the timing of these séances; in his thesis he said the séances took place between 1899 and 1900, when Helene was fifteen and he was twenty-four. A contemporary account by one of her other relatives claims, however, that Jung helped organize these sessions as early as 1895, when Helene was eleven years old and he was a nineteen-year-old first-year medical student. Jung was frank about his purpose, though, which was "to pursue his profound curiosity about occult and spiritualistic matters." The family had "discovered" that Helene was an excellent medium when she was nine years old.

Freud, the teenager who knew that God did not exist, and Jung, the precocious organizer of séances, were not likely to find it easy to work together.

After studying medicine at Basel University, Jung went to work under Eugen Bleuler, who made major contributions to the study of schizophrenia. While at the Burghölzli, the hospital Bleuler ran, Jung read Freud's *The Interpretation of Dreams* soon after it was published and it inspired him in a number of ways, of which the most unexpected perhaps was creating the Word Association Test, a test that is far more scientific than spiritual.

Subjects were shown a card with a word on it and then had to produce an association.

The words might be neutral, like the color red, or have some emotional charge, like MOTHER. Subjects responded differently to neutral and emotional words. Sometimes subjects hesitated in producing the association. Jung attached his subjects to a galvanometer to measure the electrical resistance of the skin and watched where the needle peaked. A spike in electrical activity when a subject was asked to associate to the name Mary showed there was something to investigate about what Mary meant to the patient. Delays or hesitations suggested where the psychoanalyst should probe. The "psychogalvanometer," as Jung called it, was like those instruments prospectors used to locate buried treasure.

Jung's study points to another difference between the two psychoanalysts. Jung carried out a number of experiments to prove his theories. Freud had been trained as an anatomist and his first three papers were conventional anatomical descriptions of the sexual organs of the eel. They were well received but they were not experiments. In fact, Freud never conducted an experiment apart from one brief study of one subject. That subject was Josef Herzig, Sauerwald's teacher. In 1884, Freud gave Herzig cocaine and measured how this affected his muscle power and physical endurance. The drug improved both, but that would not have surprised either man. As early as 1876 in the respectable *British Journal of Medicine*, Sir Robert Christison, the president of the Scottish Medical Association, enthused that he was not remotely tired after climbing a number of hills in the Highlands under the influence of cocaine. Christison even had the energy to collect samples of his own urine and stools while doing so. What made the feat unusual was that Sir Robert Christison was seventy-eight years old at the time.

In 1906, Jung sent his work on word association to Freud, who sent Jung a collection of his essays in return. They started to write to each other on a regular basis. They agreed on many issues; both believed that below the conscious mind, there is another realm of the psyche, which both called the unconscious. At first neither man shared anything about their profound religious differences. Quite apart from his spiritual leanings, Jung shared the casual anti-Semitism of his day. He sniped that Jews were different from other people and even needed to be dressed differently, because otherwise "we mistook them for people like ourselves." This is, of course, a wounding description of the Jew as "Other."

Jung did not reveal these views to Freud in their letters. If Jung had done so, one can only wonder how it would have affected their relationship. It seems doubtful that Freud would have decided to call Jung his "son and heir." Despite his views on Jews, Jung did not object when Freud called him Joshua, who would enter the Promised Land. Moses was not allowed that privilege. Both analysts saw themselves as prophets and neither could be said to suffer from low self-esteem or lack of ego, though at times they often proved rather vulnerable.

In his book *Memories, Dreams, Reflections*, Jung claimed that he was always worried by Freud's hostility to the spiritual and by his stress on sexuality. He claimed Freud would become obsessional about sex and pronounce that it was "a bulwark against occultism." Freud, on the other hand, claimed he stressed sexuality because of his experiences with patients. "When I insist to one of my patients on the frequency of Oedipus dreams in which the dreamer has sexual intercourse with his own mother, he often replies, 'I have no recollection of having had any such dream.'"

These denials did not last long, since Oedipal material kept forcing its way through the denials and defenses. The conscious mind screened, censored, softened, deceived, fiddled, faddled, and fudged, but it could not change the raw truths of the unconscious. "Disguised dreams of sexual intercourse with the dreamer's mother are many times more frequent than straightforward ones," Freud claimed. Jung commented that "Freud was emotionally involved in his sexual theory to an extraordinary degree. When he spoke of it his tone became urgent, almost anxious and all signs of his normally critical and sceptical manner disappeared." For Freud, on the other hand, Jung was a repressed Swiss Protestant who could not admit the importance of sex because the Christian tradition demonized the body.

Jung does not say if he told Freud about his fainting fits at school. Freud also had a tendency to faint. He fainted twice in Jung's presence, once in Bremen when they were discussing bodies that had been drowned in peat bogs. Jung said Freud was "convinced that all this chatter about corpses meant I had death wishes towards him." The second time Jung saw Freud faint was when they were speaking about the Pharaoh Akhenaton, who had apparently destroyed inscriptions that had related to the pharaoh's father. Jung wrote that both these episodes revealed that Freud wanted to kill his father. Naturally, Freud saw it differently. He claimed he fainted after he had bested Jung in an argument and that could be traced back to the death of the baby Julius in 1857. That death was Freud's first triumph as he got rid of a rival for his mother's love. Any other triumph, like defeating Jung in an argument, inevitably brought back unconscious guilty memories that the death of Julius had aroused. Ernest Jones accepted Freud's explanation without question.

Other explanations have been offered. One is that Freud felt some homosexual attraction for his Swiss colleague and was embarrassed by that. A second one is that he hated giving up the least shred of control or authority, which is precisely what Jung craved. Jung was a dominant personality, too. To avoid a final battle, Freud fainted.

In 1909 Jung sailed with Freud to America to attend the twentieth -anniversary celebrations of Clark University. Freud had been invited to make a keynote speech. Jung insisted he had not been invited to accompany Freud but had been invited independently, as the Americans recognized the importance of his own work on word association. As they traveled, Jung told Freud his dreams, which Freud duly analyzed. Jung felt that since he had trusted Freud with these dreams, Freud should reciprocate, but Freud seems to have given only very brief accounts, which annoyed Jung; Jung wanted a more personal history in order to interpret the dreams. Freud clammed up, denying "the Crown Prince" any more juicy morsels. The voyage was tense; they were not happy sailors.

Freud prepared the lectures he gave at Clark with great care. He knew how important it was for psychoanalysis to establish itself in America. Suggesting that his patients dreamed of committing incest with their parents did not endear psychoanalysis to the public, Freud knew, and he suspected that this would be especially true in America. So he had the good sense to offer some independent evidence—and even better that it came from an American psychologist who had worked at Clark. Freud quoted a study of twenty-five-hundred observations of infants made by Sanford Bell, who had published in *The American Journal of Psychology* in 1902. Bell wrote: "The emotion of sex love . . . does not make its appearance for the first time at the period of adolescence as has been thought." Freud added: "He [Bell] says of the signs by which this amorous condition manifests itself: 'The unprejudiced mind, in observing these manifestations in hundreds of children, cannot escape referring them to sex origin. The most exacting mind is satisfied when to these observations are added the confessions of those who have as children experienced the emotion to a marked degree of intensity, and whose memories of child-hood are relatively distinct.'"

Skeptics "will be most astonished to hear that among those chil-dren who fell in love so early not a few are of the tender ages of three, four, and five years," Freud said, and then he added that Bell was an American and that "it would not be surprising if you should believe the observations of a fellow-countryman rather than my own."

Bell was not the only expert who backed Freud's ideas. Eugen Bleuler, Jung's superior at the Burghölzli, "said a few years ago openly that he faced my sexual theories incredulous and bewildered, and since that time by his own observations had substantiated them in their whole scope," Freud told his audience. Doctors ignored the Oedipal complex because they had "forgotten their own infantile sex-ual activity under the pressure of education for civilisation and do not care to be reminded now of the repressed material." His audience should analyze their own dreams, which would soon lead them to "an interpretation of [their] own childhood memories" simmering with sexual thoughts. The audience was more impressed than shocked.

Though Freud received an honorary doctorate at Clark, he did not take to America. It was almost a visceral reaction. He blamed rich American food for intestinal troubles that had, in fact, started long before he set foot in the United States. "I often said to myself," he once wrote, "that whoever is not master of his Konrad should not set out on travels." Konrad was the nickname he used for his bowels. The Americans had no understanding of the need for public toilets. Freud suffered from prostate troubles by 1909 and had to urinate often. But in America men were expected to have heroic bladders. "They escort you along miles of corridors, and ultimately you are taken to the basement, where a marble palace awaits you—only just in time." Freud never seems to have forgotten how uncomfortable not finding a convenient toilet could be. Or forgiven America for the inconvenience, so to speak.

Jung's attitude toward America was more positive. After the lectures, he went to St. Elisabeth's Hospital in Washington, D.C., to research the dreams of African American patients, more like an anthropologist might than an analyst. He discovered patterns that seemed to him to be like those of Greek mythology. The dreams showed the existence of a "universally human characteristic," Jung argued—and that led to the development of his theories of archetypes.

Jung returned to America in 1912 and lectured at Fordham University in New York. Five years after starting to work with Freud, he was not shy about explaining their differences, even on such a central issue as how to interpret dreams. Jung said: "I did not reduce them to personal factors, as Freud does, but—and this seemed indicated by their very nature—I compared them with the symbols from mythology and the history of religion, in order to discover the meaning they were trying to express."

If Freud ever dreamed of Jung, he did not admit it, but Jung recorded a dream that belittled the older man, turning Freud into a petty customs official. Jung was puzzled as Freud's friendship "meant a great deal to me," but he deduced that his unconscious was telling him not to believe Freud. The dream then continued in a blaze of medieval glory as the shabby customs man was confronted by a magnificent knight. The customs man was a petty bureaucrat; the knight was brave and bold. He inspired Jung to study alchemy, a subject Freud thought was perfect nonsense. Both analysts dreamed perhaps a little too easily of themselves as heroic. Freud wrote that his mother's love gave him the confidence to be a conquistador; Jung saw himself as the perfect warrior. No wonder they jousted for supremacy—and fainted when they felt in trouble.

Jung was also sentimental in his attitude to the German *Volk* in a way Freud could never be. German myths help us realize who we are, as they are "first and foremost psychic phenomena that reveal the nature of the soul." Freud thought the soul was a psychological relic of the neuroses of the Neanderthals.

By 1913, Jung had decided he could no longer work with Freud. By then Freud had already expelled a number of analysts from the Vienna Psychoanalytic Society. These expulsions bolstered his authority. Only he could decide who was, and who was not, an analyst.

As the split loomed, Jung experienced a horrible "confrontation with the unconscious." He saw visions and heard voices. He worried he was "menaced by a psychosis" or was "doing a schizophrenia." Though he might be more fragile, Jung had no intention of being bested and he decided to use this descent into madness and to see it as a gift. In private, he induced hallucinations, or "active imaginations." He recorded these in small notebooks and began to transcribe his notes into a large, red, leather-bound book. Over sixteen years, he refined this material into the now famous Red Book. But just as Freud refused to let some material be published, Jung never made this public in his lifetime.

In May 1914, Jung resigned as the chairman of the International Psychoanalytic Association. The two men never spoke again and never even exchanged a letter.

The differences between them would have profound consequences when the Nazis came to power in 1933.

5

A Treasure Trove of
Family Letters

Given the amount of material the Freud Archives have restricted, it is fortunate perhaps that some interesting material was not originally controlled by the archives. The John Rylands University Library at the University of Manchester was given 248 letters, postcards, and telegrams in 1958 after the death of Polly Hartwig, the daughter of Philipp Freud, Freud's half brother. The letters included those written by Sigmund Freud to Polly Hartwig's cousin, Sam (Solomon) Freud, as well as Sam's replies.

After they moved from Vienna to Manchester in 1860, Emanuel Freud and his full brother Philipp had a memorable telegraphic address, Freud Manchester. Emanuel returned to Vienna a number of times. In 1900, Freud told his friend Wilhelm Fliess that Emanuel "brought with him a real air of refreshment because he is a marvelous man, vigorous and mentally indefatigable despite his sixty-eight or sixty-nine years, who has always meant a great deal to me."

The letters between Sam and Sigmund Freud reveal some touching aspects of the latter's personality, his affection for his extended complicated family, his worries about money, nice trivia such as his fondness for cheese, and, crucially, information about Freud's "secret" bank accounts. Sigmund Freud Copyrights—a fund that controlled the ownership and publication of his works—was unaware for some time that these letters existed and so could not stop scholars from consulting them. The letters to Sam go back as far as 1914; the last one was written in 1938. Many of the issues that would concern Freud in his last years are reflected in them.

In 1953, Polly Hartwig deposited 234 letters written by Freud and her cousin, Sam, in the University of Manchester Library. There were also four letters by Anna Freud and a telegram. After Sigmund visited Manchester in 1875, Emanuel came to Vienna. There is no record of any family reunion until Sam came to Vienna with his father in 1900. Freud also spent four days in Manchester and Southport in 1908. He and Emanuel planned to go to the Isle of Man but the sea was too rough. Emanuel traveled down to London with him and they then crossed the Channel together.

Given that and Freud's fondness for writing letters, it is hard to believe there were no letters written between 1876 and 1914, especially given evidence that some other documents are missing. Leslie Adams discovered that Emanuel Freud had taken out a British passport, but the documents relating to this appear to have been lost. The archives at the University of Manchester have a photograph of two men who could be Freud's brothers in their thirties. One is dressed as an army officer and has a handlebar mustache; the other is wearing a cowboy hat. Unfortunately the photographs are not properly labeled so it is not possible to be sure. Neither man is Sigmund Freud.

The first letter between Freud and his nephew Sam dates from 1914, but it may not be the first, in fact. It does not start with an apology or a polite reason for resuming writing after years of silence. Freud had excellent manners—except when it came to dealing with some fellow analysts perhaps—and would in all likelihood have made some apology. Letters among Freud and his half brothers may be restricted in the Library of Congress or, perhaps, not correctly cataloged. Two letters to Sam had slipped into the Harry Freud collection and were therefore not properly filed.

In his letters to Sam, Freud seemed able to say things he could not say to analytic colleagues, apart perhaps from Fliess. The letters are quite emotional at times. In one, for example, Freud wrote that his son Martin was in some difficulties over his marriage; he had an "unreasonable abnormal wife." The material is a rich and untapped resource that also reveals his unhappiness about a number of family tragedies. In one letter he tells Sam that there are many "weak spots" in the family.

The letters also show frequent anxieties over money. In one of the first letters Freud talks about his family as Sam's "poor relatives" because the 1914 war meant they lost so much. The letters also shed light on Freud's secret bank accounts, which would become extremely important when Freud wanted to leave Vienna in 1938.

The first letter is dated July 7, 1914, and Freud had a very specific reason for writing. His daughter, Anna, was going to spend time in England to learn the language better. Her father sent Sam £20, which she could draw on as she needed. "I hope you will do the kindness to play the role of her banker," he wrote. Sam agreed.

Freud added, "I am glad to have learned by his handwriting that the great older man [which can only be Sam's father, Emanuel]—an old one I am myself—is unchanged and I hope that the ladies and your dear person are all right." The ladies were Sam's aunts, who also lived in Manchester.

It was lucky the letter got through because, on June 28, the archduke Ferdinand was murdered in Sarajevo, starting the confusion of events that led to the First World War. During the war, the Freuds of Manchester and the Freuds of Vienna could not communicate because they were on different sides.

Not long after the archduke's assassination, an event occurred that is still shrouded in mystery. The offices of Freud and Co. in Manchester by now were at 61 Bloom Street, then in the middle of the textile district. Freud's half brother Emanuel had moved by then to Southport, an elegant suburb by the sea. He had not retired and still commuted to and from work. The following note appeared in the *Southport Guardian* on Wednesday, October 17, 1914: "On Saturday afternoon just as an express train from Manchester to Southport passed Parbold station, it was noticed that one of the carriage doors had opened and a man lay on the line. He had apparently fallen out of his train." When authorities reached his body, he was already dead. "He was identified as Emanuel Freud aged 82, residing at 21 Albert Road Southport."

Parbold is still a small village with a tiny unmanned railway station next to a level crossing. The platform is not long enough to accommodate a train of more than three carriages. It is just possible that Emanuel Freud opened the door thinking he was stepping out onto the platform and just fell out onto the track. However, he did the journey every day. He must have known the platform was short. Ernest Jones mentioned Emanuel Freud's death but wrote nothing about its dramatic circumstances. Equally, he wrote nothing about any of the later untimely deaths in Freud's family.

Freud just said to Sam, "Your father died leaving the train." Sam's father was eighty-two years old. Jacob Freud had died at eighty-one.

The length of their lives made Freud believe he would reach at the very most eighty or eighty-one years of age. He never again raised the topic of how his half brother had died.

Emanuel Freud died just as the First World War started and it took some toll on the entire family. Hermann, Freud's nephew, was killed in action in 1917. Freud's sons fought in the war and saw the horrors. Some doctors who were analysts went to the front to treat casualties. Like many Austrians, the Freuds went hungry and were grateful for food parcels. Some food was sent by Max Eitingon, a wealthy analyst who helped Freud and his family in many practical ways during the hard times of the First World War.

The war made Freud reconsider a fundamental aspect of his theory. The slaughter of millions in the trenches made him realize that the libido, the life-giving, life-making pleasure principle, was not the only motive for human behavior. The libido had a dark mirror image, the Nirvana principle or death instinct, as it has come to be called. Life is hard. We want to stop struggling; we escape into sex, drugs, and booze; we lose ourselves in books or movies; we sleep. At the most extreme, we flirt with taking our own lives and every year thousands of human beings commit suicide. Apart from lemmings, we seem to be the only species capable of self-slaughter. Freud would set these ideas out in *Beyond the Pleasure Principle*, which was first published in German in 1920 by the company he set up with backing from a wealthy patient, Anton von Freund.

Jung, however, saw the war very differently. It was the consequence of the "death of God," as Nietzsche put it in the 1890s. Jung claimed that his European patients told him dreams that showed that the "beast" was ready to break out "with devastating consequences" as "the Christian view of the world loses its authority." In his German patients, he found "peculiar disturbances"—images of violence, cruelty, and depression—that could not be ascribed to their personal psychology, but appeared to represent something in the collective German psyche. The powers of darkness were rushing into the void created by the death of God.

Religions were "psychotherapeutic systems in the truest sense of the word, and on the grandest scale. They express the whole range of the psychic problem in mighty images; they are the avowal and recognition of the soul," Jung argued. Religions helped create an integrated personality. Loss of the spiritual connection to the soul made a "psychic split" or neurosis. For Freud, of course, the war had no spiritual causes.

The war made it impossible for Freud's correspondence with Sam to continue, and the next letter in the archive is dated October 27, 1919. Freud outlined the difficult situation in Vienna and the fact that the fall in the value of money had most affected "the middle class and those who earn their living by intellectual work." A month later, Freud announced that his son Martin had gotten married—"a courageous deed in these times"—and also that they were freezing since it was impossible to get coal. Sam asked if there was anything he could do.

Bureaucracy was the problem, Freud explained. One needed a permit to receive parcels and he had not "procured one because I have not the time to procure it." The customs procedure was very slow and tedious. "My time at least is still precious," he said. Sam said that he was "deeply pained" to hear of the privations Freud faced in Vienna.

In January 1920 Freud told Sam, "I assure you it is not money we are in need of, we have plenty of this bad stuff and good sterling money cannot be brought here by post."

On the twentieth, there was a tragedy. Freud's second daughter, Sophie, died of pneumonia. Her mother was distraught; Sophie was only twenty-seven years old, had been happily married, and left two sons. Freud knew Sam would feel for them "in our mourning." Sam replied that he remembered meeting Sophie in 1910 and that he did not know what to say. He could imagine nothing worse than losing a child.

It is a little shocking that about three weeks after his daughter died, Freud was thinking about suits. His next letter, dated February 15, 1920, reveals Freud the sharp dresser. He needed a new outfit, according to his wife, and managed to send his nephew £4 to buy him the cloth to make one. She wanted him to have a "salt and pepper" one or a "tête de nègre." Freud also lamented that you could send anything to Vienna except tobacco. Luckily, he had another source for that, a young cavalry officer who had analytic ambitions.

The letter also introduced a theme that would recur often during the next twenty years. Freud hoped he might visit Manchester again.

"I am assured of a good reception in England were I to come over but business is very brisk now and you will have to wait," he wrote.

In a separate letter to Sam, Anna Freud asked if Sam might be able to send her six tennis balls as she and her cousin wanted to learn the game. She wrote to him three weeks later to say that the convoluted bureaucracy had failed to provide the permit to allow the balls into the country. She apologized to Sam for putting him to the trouble.

On April 22, Freud told Sam of another marriage. His second son, Ernst, was engaged to a "Jewish girl of good family." Also Eli Bernays, the father of Edward Bernays, was coming to Vienna. Freud added that Sam's "pa," as he called Emanuel, would have made the crossing to Austria to see Eli. In November there was cheerful news. His niece, who called herself Tom, was marrying a clever Hebrew scholar, Jankel Seidmann. That would not turn out well, however.

Freud was a master of *kvetching*, and now he had much to *kvetch* about. He told Sam: "As for me you know I have a big name and plenty of work but I cannot gain enough and am eating up my reserves." The economic situation in Vienna was "so bad." The financial prospects of psychoanalysis got even worse when one of Freud's first benefactors died. Austrians might need therapy, but there was no way they could afford to pay for it.

Sam asked what food they needed because he could send parcels of provisions. Freud was not too proud to reply that they needed "corned beef, cocoa, English tea cakes and cheese." He was very fond of good cheese and was dismayed that it could not be found.

In a letter of October 15, Freud said he had hoped to come to Manchester because he had to attend a congress in The Hague and it would be easy to get a cross-Channel ferry from there. At the last minute, however, he sent Sam a telegram from the Hotel Paulez to say he would not be coming. There had been another death, that of Morris, whose name was sometimes written as Moritz or even Maurice, his sister Mitzi's husband and Freud's brother-in-law as well as a distant cousin. Morris had a weak heart. He had recovered from a period of heart strain but, it seems, then killed himself. Money was the cause, Freud suspected. Morris had been unable to pay his debts. Freud had to return to Berlin to console his sister and her children. He was sorry he had to cancel the trip to Manchester because "it was an opportunity to come to Britain which is not likely to recur soon."

Sam replied tersely: "Poor Maurice, it is all very sad." His own business was going through hard times, too, because the price of cotton had fallen so much.

Three weeks later, on November 5, 1920, Freud worried about how Sam might have taken some of his remarks about his uncle's reputation. He did not want his nephew to think he was arrogant. "I am anxious that you could misconstrue my question about my renown in England; I wanted to know how much of the noise has reached your quiet home. Popularity is utterly indifferent to me, it must be considered at the best a danger for more serious achievements."

On July 22, 1921, Freud felt bothered by how much he was costing his nephew. He told Sam he had ordered the bank of Lippmann, Rosenthal & Co. in Holland to send £8 to pay for the provisions Sam had sent. This is the first specific mention of the foreign bank accounts that would play such a big part in Freud's last years.

Freud could reimburse Sam because his practice was in better shape. "I have somewhat recovered by the treatment of foreign patients and am in possession of a deposit of good money in The Hague." He was treating patients in English most of the time and it made him aware that he should have learned the language better. Life in his apartment with his wife was depressing. "We live together, old people in a big dwelling. Grandma is very old." It was upsetting that Morris had left a financial muddle after his suicide. "The conditions in Berlin after Morris' death are so intricate that nobody can see how rich or rather how poor they are." And he and his wife were suffering "the whims of old age."

Freud asked Sam to give his love to all his Manchester family and then added, "Are they aware that my name in the world at large and in England too is far more respectable than riches?" Shortly after that, Freud again reassured his nephew. "I am accumulating money in Amsterdam and can send you from there any amount you spend for me." He regretted not to have crossed to England as he had been expected in Cambridge "where they take great interest in my work." The University had a psychology laboratory whose director, Frederic Bartlett, became the first British psychologist to be knighted. He wrote a significant book entitled *Remembering* as well as a charming but less weighty one called *The Mind at Work and Play*. He often cited Freud as an influence on his work.

Sam often told his uncle how proud they were of him. He had seen a poem about Freud and Jung in *Punch*. He had also read an article on his uncle in a magazine called *Jack London*.

Some of the comments about Freud were not flattering, but Sam does not seem to have known that. D. H. Lawrence, who later wrote *Lady Chatterley's Lover*, published a small book, *Psychoanalysis and the Unconscious*, in which he made fun of Freud's ideas. Lawrence was exuberantly rude. "Oh, damn the miserable baby with its complicated ping-pong table of an unconscious," Lawrence wrote. If children were inclined to be in love with their parents, parents should not encourage them too much. Lawrence snipped:

> Oh, parents, see that your children get their dinners and clean sheets, but don't love them. Don't love them one single grain, and don't let anybody else love them. Give them their dinners and leave them alone. You've already loved them to perdition. Now leave them alone, to find their own way out.

Shortly thereafter James Thurber and E. B. White published a wonderful satire called *Is Sex Necessary?* which included a section on "Six Day Bicycle Racing as a Sex Substitute." The title says it all. Pedaling was even better than masturbation. Thurber poked fun at Freud over the next twenty years. He wrote a number of spoof reviews of therapy books for *The New Yorker* including *Be Glad You're Neurotic, How to Worry Successfully*, and *Growing into Life*. Millions of Americans were psychologically blocked and didn't understand the Science of Happiness. Thurber knew the jargon of analysis and joked that, for most wives, the latent content of their husbands' minds was manifest enough—especially at breakfast. He made fun of an analyst called Bisch, who suggested that people like Mr. C. who got run over had unconscious motives. Sexual hunger made Mr. C. leap out in front of cars and also led to frightening dreams in which automobiles "unquestionably have sex significance." Thurber would never have targeted analysis, of course, if it had not been influential and in the news.

What Thurber and White would have written had they been aware of Freud's cigar addiction is delicious to imagine.

The Cigar Is a Nipple

On one of the landings in the Freud Museum in London, a mummified half-smoked cigar perches on the lip of an ashtray. It is a Montecristo but of less gargantuan size than the cigars Churchill smoked. Tobacco was an indispensable prop to Freud as he worked; he wrote and smoked, smoked and wrote. In 1920, Freud offered his nephew Harry a cigarette and a lecture: "My boy, smoking is one of the greatest and cheapest enjoyments in life, and if you decide in advance not to smoke, I can only feel sorry for you."

Freud often went through twenty cigars a day and was unwell if he did not get his daily nicotine. Even after he was diagnosed with cancer of the jaw, Freud continued to smoke. Without cigars his writing would not flow. He made no effort to stop.

Ernest Jones never asked why Freud smoked. A conventional analytic interpretation would be that cigars and cigarettes are "nipple substitutes." A man who can't do without them is fixated at the oral level of development, which is the most infantile. Freud wrote that the pleasure he got from being in the company of his daughter Anna could be compared to the pleasure he got from smoking a good cigar. As a cigar is a rather obvious phallic symbol as well as a nipple substitute, this was a truly odd statement for a father to make. Ernest Jones did not mention this comment in his three-volume work about Freud, let alone attempt any analytic interpretation. If he had, he would have had to raise the bizarre issue of whether, at some symbolic level, Freud saw his own daughter as a nipple!

But there were more serious issues.

Untimely Deaths

Often in his letters to Sam, Freud mixed in conventional family news. "I am sorry to hear that Ma is losing her sight," he consoled. His own mother, whom he called "Grandma," was nearly deaf. "There is no blessing in old age. I am ready to resign my claim on the longevity of our family," he said stoically.

Families were all about growth and decay like plants, a comparison that "old Homer" had made. If "Grandma" was aging, Alexander's son was doing well. This is the first mention of Harry Freud, who was then twenty-five years old. "Harry is growing nicely. He is good and clever," Freud told Sam. Harry was also learning the joys of smoking from his uncle. But Freud's brother Alexander was often very depressed because he had lost so much money after the war.

There was no good political news, Freud complained to Sam. "You will have gathered from the papers how desperate our public conditions are. As long as I continue working I am sure to be free of financial cares."

The Freud finances were being kept in good order by his British and American patients; the Austrians could not afford therapy. On July 25, 1921, he told Sam, "I listen and . . ." Freud's next word is hard to read. It looks like "talk," although Freud has neglected to cross the t, so it looks at first like "lick." Those to whom he listened were "Englishers four to five hours a week." Freud knew that "*Englishers*" was not the right word, but it was part of his game of using some inappropriate words. "I will never learn the d—d language correctly."

Then, the family had more devastating news. Freud's sister Pauline had to face the tragedy that her only daughter, Rose, who was twenty-five years old, had suffered "a nervous collapse" and had to be sent to an asylum. So a year after his daughter died and his brother-in-law committed suicide, Freud had to cope with the fact that his niece was sent to an institution. He seems not to have intervened, perhaps because he thought "Rose was gifted but half crazy." The use of the very casual "half crazy" is surprising given Freud's usually careful definitions of various psychiatric conditions.

There is then a sad sentence. Freud had gone to Hamburg to see Sophie's widower and her two small sons. He held Heinz, the baby, "all that is left of Sophie."

Freud commented on the mood in Vienna where "the general depression is felt in every household." He was never able to quite relax about money, even when he had plenty of patients. "I can earn foreign money and am free of cares," he told Sam. The wider family was still "dependent on Eli," who had gone into advertising and sales and was now doing so well in New York.

The fees patients paid made it possible for Freud to arrange for Sam to get some money again. Freud was always nagging his nephew to ask how much he had cost him. Eventually Sam said he had spent £40 on provisions and had received £12. It did not matter. Nevertheless, on December 27, 1921, Freud told his nephew that he had sent him £28 through James Strachey, who translated many of Freud's books. The Manchester files include a letter from Strachey in which he confirms that he had sent Sam a check for £28. Sam joked to his uncle, "Your credit is good."

Throughout, Sam does not seem to have asked Freud for anything, but now he wanted Freud to check the value of some old Austrian bonds he had found among his father's things. Their value was tiny and the act of realizing their value required going through much bureaucracy, Freud learned. On November 30, 1921, he wrote that the effort would hardly be worth it because, at most, they would produce a few shillings.

One of the reasons Freud sent Sam the £28 becomes clear in a letter dated February 5, 1922. Freud asked Sam if Sam could send him a pair of strong boots. "My feet are normally configured but when I tried a new pair bought in Vienna I spoiled them. Nothing good can be obtained here." Three months later, on May 13, Freud told Sam he had an account at yet another bank, the Bank of Lissa and Kann in The Hague; he could send Sam some money from there to reimburse him for the cost of the boots.

Six months later, Freud wrote to Sam about another suicide. His favorite niece, Cäcilie, had had an unhappy love affair and had become pregnant. "The poor girl was passionate, yet obstinate, and very secluded so we don't know what the exact motive is." It did not help that she could not call on her family in the crisis as they were on holiday outside of Vienna. She could not face the shame and took an overdose of Veronal. She died on August 18, 1922. Sam replied that it was "a pitiable ending."

Freud had some consolation, life in the midst of death. He was very moving in describing how he adored his small grandson. Sophie's second son, Heinz, was a "charming devil of a boy."

On December 14, 1922, Freud wrote, "I am still earning foreign money," even though Vienna was "left quiet and lonely. All eyes are turned to Germany and the impending collapse there." He had ordered three new volumes of the Encyclopaedia Britannica because they were the ones in which "psychoanalysis is first fully mentioned."

Another relative now was causing concern. Lucy, the daughter of Freud's sister Anna and the creditor-fleeing-turned-millionaire Eli Bernays, was "as crazy and unreliable as ever," Freud told Sam.

Good news followed bad when, seven weeks later, Freud announced that his third son, Oliver, was getting married and that he had another grandson, Lucian. Lucian Freud would become one of the major artists of the twentieth century. "You may wonder what a thriving tribe we are," Freud rejoiced on February 9, 1923. He was perhaps accentuating the positive to convince himself after the deaths and suicides.

The optimism was short-lived. A few months later, Freud announced another untimely death; he wrote more about this one than about any other apart from the death of his father. His grandson Heinz, Sophie's son, died. "The boy was the cleverest, sweetest child I have met." Freud mourned the boy and once said it had been the last time he had fallen in love. In addition, Freud was in poor health; he had had to have a growth removed from his soft palate.

The year saw another family tragedy. His nephew, Mitzi's son Theodor, drowned while swimming in Berlin. "The mother bears it with silent resignation," Freud wrote to Sam. Within six years Freud had to cope with a death in combat, two suicides, and two accidental deaths, as well as the deaths of his daughter and his grandson.

Six months later, Freud referred to the Nazis for the first time. "The situation in Berlin is a very threatening one," he told Sam. By 1923 Hitler had become self-confident enough to stage the famous putsch in Munich. When it failed, Hitler was sent to jail, but he had many supporters and he was kept in some luxury; he used the time to dictate *Mein Kampf* (*My Struggle*), in which he set out his philosophy and his anti-Semitic program. Hitler's colleague Hermann Goering, who was a brilliant pilot in the Luftwaffe during World War I, was less lucky. He had to flee Germany and ended up addicted to morphine. Goering was placed in a lunatic asylum in Austria and often had to be restrained in a straitjacket.

Freud told Sam that grieving for Heinz was still agonizing. They had Heinz's older brother staying with them, but Freud "did not find him a consolation to any amount." He had bad medical news, too, as he had not overcome the effects of his last operation to stem the cancer. His mouth hurt dreadfully, which made swallowing excruciating.

On October 25, 1923, Freud told Sam that when he had returned from the sanatorium the previous day, "very much broken and enfeebled," it had cheered him to find Sam's letter. The operation removed the greater part of the buccal mucous membrane and a skin graft was put in its place. Freud told Sam, "If I recover and become movable, to see all three of you would be an enjoyment I would try to attain."

Freud did not tell Sam the whole story. He was furious when he discovered that his physician, Felix Deutsch, and his surgeon, Hajek, had not told him that cancer of the jaw had been found. "By what right?" he demanded when he realized he had been kept in the dark. He dismissed his doctors at once. For the next four years the only doctor he would see was his oral surgeon, Hans Pichler.

After the operation, Freud had to wear a prosthesis in his mouth. It was painful, but if he did not wear it, he would not be able to speak or eat properly. If he kept it in all the time, it hurt, but if he took it out for long periods, there was a serious risk that the device would shrink and not fit back in properly. A small antiseptic room was set up in the apartment so that his daughter Anna could take out the prosthesis, clean it, and put it back in every day. Freud always hoped someone would build a better prosthesis. For a while he could not write with a pen, so his letters for the next six months were typed. Freud told Sam that his speech "may be impaired but my family and my patients say it is intelligible."

Freud could not give up smoking, however. In the next sixteen years, he had to have thirty operations to excise precancerous lesions. He was lucky to have in Hans Pichler a brilliant and devoted surgeon who kept up with the latest technology. Nevertheless, "the result was a life of endless torture," Max Schur, who became his physician in 1927, noted in *Living and Dying*.

A second operation, Freud told Sam, had left him drained of nearly "all confidence." It had been costly, too. "I have lost a great deal of money, spent a great deal of money and expect to pay a high but well-deserved fee to my physician," he wrote on December 19, 1923. That physician was Hans Pichler.

Freud underwent another medical procedure on November 17, 1923, a peculiar "rejuvenation" treatment that had a certain vogue in high society. Steinbach, an endocrinologist, had discovered that the interstitial cells of the testicles produced the male sex hormones. Tying these sperm ducts up would atrophy the cells that produced the male sex hormone. Because cancer was thought to be at least partly the result of aging, rejuvenation treatment was considered to help because it delayed the aging process. The whole thing was, of course, a bizarre fantasy. Many years later, Max Schur asked Freud whose idea it was that he should go in for this treatment. His own idea, Freud insisted. He also revealed that he hoped it might revive his sexuality a little.

Some family details were not covered in the letters between Freud and his nephew. In 1923, Dorothy Burlingham, the granddaughter of the man who had founded Tiffany's, came to Vienna. She wanted help for her four children. There is a touching photograph of her, a tall elegant woman, her hair parted in the middle, gazing at a baby on her lap. She had married a surgeon, Robert Burlingham, but they often spent long periods apart because he remained in America. He was depressed and the marriage was in trouble. Dorothy first met Anna Freud because Dorothy wanted Anna to help her "naughty" children. The two women became close friends and then life partners, though many Freudians deny the relationship ever became a sexual one.

The next letter to Manchester asked how Sam's life had "changed since Ma died." At least her death was "in time." Eli Bernays, however, had died at the relatively young age of sixty-one after a sudden attack of appendicitis. The man who had left Vienna to escape his creditors left an estate worth $1 million. Freud wondered whether Eli had made any provisions "for his indigent sisters for this time."

Two days before his sixty-eighth birthday, on May 6, 1924, Freud was given the freedom of the city of Vienna. Sam congratulated him. This honor, which can be compared to being given the keys of the city, would make him all the more reluctant to leave the city when the time came.

On August 21, 1925, Freud's mother celebrated her ninetieth birthday. He rejoiced in her strength but his sister-in-law, Minna Bernays, was ill, he told Sam. Freud was approaching his seventieth birthday himself. He felt rather inadequate compared to his own father, Jacob, who was "journeying over the Continent after he was 70 years old." Freud was, at least, happy to note, "I am considered a celebrity." Jews all over the world were "pairing me with Einstein. I have no reason to complain. After a long period of poverty I am earning money without hardship." Freud also told Sam how proud he was of his daughter Anna, who was "treating naughty American children earning lots of money." She had passed her thirtieth birthday and "does not seem inclined to get married and who can say if her momentary interest will render her happy when she has to face life without her father." The momentary interest seems to have been Freud's way of describing Anna Freud's work in child therapy.

In the end, Sam did not manage to come to Vienna for Freud's seventieth birthday in May 1926. If Freud was offended, he did not show it. He sent Sam a special proof copy of his 1925 autobiography and inscribed it for his nephew. The copy is in the Manchester archives.

Sam could not make it, other relatives did, however. Perhaps the most interesting one who came to visit Freud was Edward Bernays, Eli's son, who arrived from New York to wish his famous uncle well. He was, Freud told Sam, "a clever boy and a rich man and good-natured but truly American." Edward Bernays was more than clever. If his uncle invented psychoanalysis, his nephew could be said to have invented public relations. After leaving Cornell University, he worked in the entertainment business. When he had to give a character reference for the famous tenor Enrico Caruso, Bernays was asked his profession and he replied, "Counsel in public relations"; some historians say that was the first time anyone used the term "public relations."

Bernays had more serious ambitions than getting film stars on the front page, though. In his early twenties, he became an adviser to Woodrow Wilson. Bernays founded the Committee on Public Information, which aimed to influence public opinion to support American participation in World War I. He published *Crystallizing Public Opinion*. Basing himself partly on his uncle's work, he wrote: "If we understand the mechanism and motives of the group mind, is it not possible to control and regiment the masses according to our will without their knowing about it? The recent practice of propaganda has proved that it is possible, at least up to a certain point and within certain limits." He called this scientific technique of opinion-molding the "engineering of consent."

Crotchety Genius

By the mid 1920s. Bernays' uncle was so famous that Max Eastman decided to include Freud in a book of interviews with twelve modern celebrities. Chaplin and Einstein were among the others. Freud was smaller than Eastman had imagined. "Slender limbed and more feminine apart from his nose," Eastman called him. The Freud hooter looked "as if somebody with brass knuckles had given him a good poke in the snoot."

In Freud's study the two men sparred about the state of America.

Eastman joked that American intellectual leaders had stopped thinking at all.

"Why?" Freud asked.

"You know why people stop thinking," Eastman said. "It's because their thoughts would lead them where they don't want to go."

That amused Freud, and "the whole of his gentleness came back including the delighted little crinkles at the corners of his eyes. He put his head back and laughed like a child." Eastman added that Freud "waggled his head and hands about all the time looking up at the ceiling and closing his eyes or making funny little pouts and wry faces when he was trying to think of a word or an idea." Eastman continued, "I never ceased feeling that underneath it all was an obdurate hard cranky streak but I also never ceased feeling his great charm."

Freud loved jokes and puns. He even revised his book on jokes when he was seventy-two years old. His interest was not just frivolous. Like dreams, jokes allowed dangerous taboo material to erupt into consciousness. Humor was like a blowtorch blasting its way through resistances. Yet every portrait or picture of Freud shows him as a stern sage—never a man with a twinkle in his eyes or laughing. It is a shame that no such picture was recorded for posterity.

Eastman asked why Freud hated America so much. A. A. Brill, who translated some of Freud's books, believed that Freud felt that he had not been that well received during his 1909 visit. "Hate America?" Freud said to Eastman. "I don't hate America. . . . I regret it." He threw his head back and laughed hilariously. "I regret that Columbus ever discovered it."

Eastman laughed with Freud, a good journalistic move because that "rather egged him on." Freud went on to say that America was an experiment that had gone bad.

"In what way bad?" Eastman asked.

"Oh, the prudery, the hypocrisy, the national lack of independence." Eastman countered that the young did show some spirit.

"Mostly among the Jews, isn't it?" Freud said.

"The Jews are not so free from prudery and hypocrisy," Eastman replied. To that Freud made no reply but changed the subject.

Freud even had a crack at John Watson, the founder of behaviorism. "Perhaps you're a behaviourist. According to your John B. Watson even consciousness does not exist. But that's just silly. Consciousness exists quite obviously and everywhere except perhaps in

America." In accusing Watson of denying that consciousness existed, Freud was making a common mistake. Watson argued not that consciousness did not exist but that it did not matter very much because human beings had no choice in how they behaved. Our actions are the result of conditioning, the rewards and punishments we get, not the result of any conscious choice.

Finally Freud asked what Eastman's plans were. Eastman said he meant to write.

"I'll tell you what I want you to do," Freud said. "I want you to go home and write a book on America and I'll tell you what to call it, Misgeburt." He then paused and they debated how to translate the word properly. They rejected "abortion" and then wondered about "monster." Freud finally hit the right word. "The word is miscarriage. The Miscarriage of American Civilisation—that shall be the title of your book.

"That book will make you immortal. You may not be able to live in America any more but you could go very happily and live elsewhere." Freud laughed. Eastman was delighted he had got a good quote. Freud made Eastman promise to send him the book and said he would await it "with happy memories of this conversation."

Eastman returned to America but never published the book Freud had dreamed up for him. But Eastman had drawn a very vivid portrait of Freud at seventy.

Two months after he celebrated his birthday, Freud told Sam of his worries about his three sons. In a July 18 letter, Freud wrote, "None of them can boast a satisfactory position or a good income." Anna was the star among his children. Ten days later, he noted starkly to Sam, "Work is easer for me than enjoyment."

Meanwhile, while Freud was finding fame, Jung was finding himself.

"Dreams Are No Longer Necessary": Jung in the Wild

In 1924 Jung visited the Pueblo Indian chief Ochwiay Biano, who called himself Mountain Lake. Jung recorded their discussions in *Memories, Dreams, Reflections*. The whites, Ochwiay Biano complained, "are always seeking something. What are they seeking? The whites always want something; they are always uneasy and restless.

We do not know what they want. We do not understand them. We think they are mad."

"Why is that?" asked Jung.

"They say they think with their heads."

Jung was surprised and asked Ochwiay Biano what he thought with.

"We think here," the chief replied, indicating his heart.

Jung added, "What we from our point of view call colonialization, missions to the heathen, spread of civilization, etc., has another face—the face of a bird of prey seeking with cruel intentness for distant quarry—a face worthy of a race of pirates and highwaymen."

"The Americans want to stamp out our religion," Ochwiay Biano added. "Why can they not let us alone? What we do, we do not only for ourselves but for the Americans also. Yes, we do it for the whole world. . . . If we did not do it, what would become of the world?" The chief pointed out, "We are a people who live on the roof of the world; we are the sons of Father Sun, and with our religion we daily help our father to go across the sky. We do this not only for ourselves, but for the whole world. If we were to cease practicing our religion, in ten years the sun would no longer rise."

Our Christian belief, Jung noted, is "permeated by the idea that special acts such as certain rites or prayer or a particular morality can influence God." Why should that not also be true of so-called savages who felt they had a living relationship with Creation?

In 1925, Jung went to Kenya where he was deeply impressed by the landscape and the gazelles, antelope, zebras, and warthogs grazing, "moving forward like slow rivers." This was the "stillness of eternal being," the world as it had been before humans achieved a conscious state. The stillness inspired Jung. "Man is indispensable for the completion of creation, for it is man alone who gives the world its objective existence." Mountain Lake had complained about the spiritual vandalism of white Americans and Jung now met a medicine man who complained about the damage the British caused. When Jung asked the medicine man, he got this answer: "In the old days, the medicine man had dreams, and knew whether there is war or sickness or whether rain comes and where the herds should be driven." But since the whites were in Africa, he said, no one had dreams anymore. "Dreams are no longer necessary because now the English know everything."

Though Freud said he was "a conquistador," he never traveled outside Europe apart from his one trip to the United States. The idea that he would discuss things of the spirit with an Indian chief is inconceivable. Jung saw the rise of psychology, however, as a regrettable response to the death of God. Freud hoped psychology might cure people of the need for religion; Jung lamented that. "Formerly, people felt no need of psychology as does modern man."

Freud and Jung were opposites, like yin and yang, oil and vinegar, salt and pepper.

Two years after Jung was in Kenya, Freud met a woman who would play a decisive role in his final years.

A Princess for a Patient

Princess Marie Bonaparte was genuine royalty—Napoleon had been her great-granduncle. Her paternal grandmother, Princess Pierre Bonaparte, was ruined at the time of the Paris Commune in 1871 and suffered the humiliation of opening a dress shop. She soon managed to restore her family fortune, however, by an old aristocratic trick. She arranged for her brother to marry an heiress whose father owned most of Monaco. The girl had money; the boy had class. Their only child inherited a vast fortune.

A month after Princess Marie was born, her mother died. Her father was very often absent—he was more interested in glaciers than in his daughter. In fact, he was one of the world's experts on the subject of glaciers. Princess Marie hardly ever saw him because he was always up an Alp. She was brought up her grandmother, who was acutely aware of her social position. It was out of the question for a girl who could trace her descent from Napoleon to play with ordinary children. So the child princess was lonely. She developed night terrors, a morbid fear of illness, and enough obsessional anxieties to keep an army of therapists fully occupied. She was also sure that, like her mother, she would die young.

Marie Bonaparte was formidably neurotic but also formidably intelligent. When she was seven, she started to write stories and draw pictures that expressed her problems. If she had been a boy, someone would have realized how talented she was and she would have received a proper education as a matter of course. But she was a girl with a harridan for a grandmother.

Napoleon's great-grandniece was as unlucky in love as she was in her immediate family. As a teenager she became infatuated with one of her father's assistants; the man promptly blackmailed her, threatening to publish the love letters she had written to him.

When she was twenty-five years old, Marie Bonaparte's father chose Prince George of Greece as a suitable husband for her. As a result of the marriage, she became related to the British royal family. Prince George was about as suitable as a deck chair; he was a tangle of neuroses, one of which was rare: he suffered from an erotic fixation, infatuation with his uncle Valdemar. The uncle meant more to him than any woman. On their wedding night, Prince George apologized to his new wife. "I hate it as much as you do. But we must do it if we want children," he said. But they were aristocrats and went through the motions.

Unlike her husband, Marie Bonaparte did not hate sex and she had the common sense to take lovers, including Aristide Briand, who was prime minister of France. None of her lovers, however, managed to excite her. Her problem was that "she had a marked virility complex," a French psychiatrist, René Laforgue, told her. He suggested she see Freud. She went to Vienna at once.

Freud chose his patients with care, but it was inconceivable that he would not see a princess who was descended from Napoleon, had a prime minister for a lover, and was fabulously rich. The princess and the analyst adored each other from the moment she walked into 19 Berggasse. Marie Bonaparte had the presence of mind to keep notes about their sessions. She wrote that Freud looked a bit tired when she first met him. He immediately accepted her as a patient and said her analytic hour would start at eleven o'clock.

Freud sensed that Marie Bonaparte would become very dependent. She reported that he told her: "I am sixty-nine years old and there are a few things that don't work so well. You must not get too attached to me." She started to cry. Celia Bertin, her biographer, describes the start of the analysis much like the start of a great love affair. In many ways it would become one.

Within a few days, Marie Bonaparte admitted she loved Freud. It was not all one-way. He replied that although they had known each other a mere three weeks, "I have told you more than I tell most people in two years." He repeated that she should not get too attached. She wept and said she could not bear to be let down by a man yet again. She held out her hand behind her—she was lying on the couch—and Freud took it. He promised not to let her down and doubled her analytic time so that she had two hours a day. There is no record of any other patient being so privileged.

Within weeks Freud became convinced that as a small child, Marie Bonaparte had witnessed the "primal scene." She hurried in her Rolls-Royce to interview her wet nurse, who confessed that she and a groom had indeed made love in front of the baby Bonaparte. Freud had not let her down.

Freud discovered that his intellectual patient was interested in female sexuality and it was to her that he wrote his much-quoted confession, "The great question that has never been answered, and which I have not yet been able to answer, despite my thirty years of research into the feminine soul, is 'What does a woman want?'"

As they shared so much, Freud told Marie Bonaparte he felt it was time he had a new physician. Since the argument with Felix Deutsch, he had relied just on Hans Pichler, his oral surgeon. The Princess had found a good young doctor, Max Schur, and recommended him to Freud.

Freud invited Max Schur to meet him and was quite impressed. Before Freud appointed Schur, however, he insisted that he would always be told the truth. Schur wrote, "My response must have reassured him that I meant to keep such a promise." Freud then added searchingly, "Promise me when the time comes that you won't let me suffer unnecessarily." Freud said this "without a trace of pathos but also with complete authority." Schur knew perfectly well what the seventy-two-year-old man who had been diagnosed with cancer meant. These two relationships, with Schur and with Marie Bonaparte, would be vitally important as Freud got older and faced physical and political uncertainties.

On August 3, 1927, Freud told his nephew Sam, "I am not very confident of the near future." He was losing two American patients and two English patients who had been paying him in dollars and sterling, respectively. "I expect an easier but a poorer life," he wrote.

Ernest Jones, in his three-volume biography of Freud, said virtually nothing about Freud's frequent worries about money. Freud was, in fact, often very generous and loaned and even gave money to some young analysts. But like most people in central Europe, he found the period after the First World War financially stressful and borrowed or simply accepted money from friends.

At the end of 1927, Freud wrote Sam a touching tribute to the women in his family. "Whatever bodily power I save from this debacle, I owe to the tender affection of my wife and my two daughters." He was moody, though. On his seventy-second birthday, he complained, "I do not enjoy life." He was not "better than a wreck in social respects" but, at least, his brain was still functioning well. He was not clairvoyant, though. Freud could hardly expect that his fate would eventually depend on a young chemist who had been taught by Josef Herzig, Freud's friend from school.

The Young Sauerwald

In 1921, Anton Sauerwald met the girl who would become his wife, Marianne Talg. They were both still in their teens. In his twenties, Sauerwald lived in many different places and often went back to stay at home with his parents in the house where he had been born. He also spent much time with his married sisters, who were older and often put him up in their homes. He was a restless young man.

After Sauerwald left school, he joined a fraternity called *Burschenschaft Germania*, which was anti-Semitic and had fascist tendencies. The fraternity had started sometime in the nineteenth century. Only men were allowed to join and there were some odd traditions. Many of the fraternity members liked fighting duels to prove themselves. The slightest excuse would do. That seems bizarre today, but the youngest man to ever be named a professor in Austria, the economist Joseph Schumpeter (who some people think was more brilliant than John Maynard Keynes), fought a duel over who should be allowed into the University of Vienna Library. In 1886 Freud's friend Carl Koller also fought—and won—a duel as a result of a clinical disagreement over whether or not to remove a patient's rubber bandage. Koller may have been the better swordsman but he had to leave Vienna soon after. Apparently no Jew could be allowed to outfence a Christian.

Sauerwald was admitted to the University of Vienna and, after toying with both law and medicine, settled for chemistry. One relative was a chemist who had published two monographs on the properties of iron. His professor was Freud's friend, Josef Herzig, who had worked out the structure of a number of flavonids including quercitin, fisetin, and chrysin. Herzig became famous among organic chemists for a special determination reaction for methylamines: the Herzig-Meyer reaction. When he taught Sauerwald, Herzig had become interested in some natural dyes, such as galloflavin.

After he stopped courting Freud's sister Rosa, Herzig was still often a guest at 19 Berggasse. Sauerwald liked and admired his professor, who told him that he was a friend of Freud's. By 1923 it was something to boast about; Freud was a celebrity.

When Herzig died in 1924, Sauerwald went to work under Johann Pollak, who had been the professor's pupil. It took four years for Sauerwald to finish his doctoral thesis, "Über die Einwirkung von p-Toluolsulfonsäure auf Dibromparaffin"—"On the Effect of p-Tolulosulphate on Dirbromparaffin." Sauerwald then published four papers in the reputable *Monatsheft für Chimie* in one year, a tribute to his energy. Two were shortened versions of ideas he had developed in his thesis, a third one examined how nickel could be a catalyst at a high temperature, and the last one was a synthesis on hexamethylamines. The study of catalysts interested Sauerwald most of all.

After getting his doctorate, Sauerwald could expect a successful academic career, but that did not happen. In all his statements after 1945, Sauerwald did not explain whether he left the university by choice or whether he had simply not been offered a position. Whatever the truth, Sauerwald did not leave the university embittered. That would turn out to be lucky for Freud.

In the autumn of 1928, Sauerwald went to the Academy for Horticulture, not to study but to work as a jobbing gardener. It was a strange choice for a man with his qualifications. After nine months, he got a job as a chemist at the large company Krupp Berndorf. Krupp was an arms manufacturer central to the Nazi war effort. But the company also made knives, forks, and lamps—or at least its subsidiary, Krupp Berndorf, did. Krupp Berndorf had invented a process that made cheap metal look like good silver. (Today, Krupp Berndorf cutlery and tableware are highly regarded antiques.) Sauerwald soon realized, however, that he did not want to spend his life working out the best way to give cutlery a rich-seeming gloss. But there was a Depression. Better jobs were not easy to find.

A New Maid

The year 1929 also saw a change in the domestic arrangements at Berggasse. Paula Fichtl joined the Freud household as a maid. She was twenty-six years old and came from a small village near Salzburg. Her memoirs provide intimate details of Freud's routines, routines he tried to maintain as he got older. At the time, Freud's mother, Amalie, was ninety-four years old.

Freud did not usually discuss his work with his nephew Sam and so did not tell him that he had decided to write a book on Moses. Thirty years after his father had died, it was easier to fulfill the wish that the old man had expressed in 1891, that Jacob Freud wanted his son to return to the traditions of their fathers so that "there will burst upon you the wellsprings of understanding, knowledge and wisdom." For the next ten years, Freud would work on and off at his book on Moses, building on the paper in which he had described Michelangelo's statue back in 1914.

As Freud's reputation grew, some of his friends tried to influence the jury that decided who should get the Nobel Prize. Discreetly Einstein was sounded out, but Einstein said it was hard to be certain that Freud deserved this ultimate distinction. The only prize Freud could be awarded was the prize for medicine and Einstein could not accept that Freud's theories had been scientifically proven. Freud got a significant consolation prize, however. He was awarded the Goethe Prize, one of Germany's most prestigious literary awards. Freud noted to Sam that he was "a celebrity" and added that some people even compared him to Einstein.

In 1929 and 1930, there were two more suicides in the family. Jankel Seidmann, the clever Hebrew scholar, was "an honest, nice and clever fellow" but he had foolishly decided to start a publishing company. He had no backing and soon was in desperate financial trouble. Unable to face it, he killed himself. His wife, who called herself Tom, had been "half crazy before the disaster so you can imagine what she is like now," Freud wrote to Sam. A few months later Tom Seidmann took her own life, the second of Freud's nieces to do so.

The toll was four suicides in ten years among Freud's relatives, as well as a drowning and an unexplained death. The question of how Freud's half brother Emanuel ended up falling from the Southport Express at Parbold cannot be answered ninety years after the event, but it was just the first of many family tragedies.

Since 1981 research has made clear the impact of suicide and sudden death on survivors in the family. Those who are left behind often ask themselves if they failed to see the signs of desperation and if they could have done something to prevent the deaths. Guilt, remorse, even just asking if one could have listened more or listened with more empathy are frequent responses. Freud had been analyzing his own dreams, motives, and anxieties since at least 1896. It is hard to imagine that he never asked himself why close members of his family never turned to him when they were in acute distress. But he never wrote about that, except for the few lines to Sam. There was no evidence of a history of suicide in either Jacob Freud's family or that of Eli Bernays.

Fifteen years after they had started writing to each other, Freud admitted to his nephew Sam that it was not likely they would ever see each other again. The journey was just "too hard," but Harry Freud did arrive in Manchester and went to visit Sam. Freud said his nephew was "a clever boy and affectionate." Sam enjoyed the visit.

Harry Freud still lived Vienna. Paula Fichtl, who had few romantic entanglements, fell madly in love with him. She said that he was one member of the family whose intelligence did not intimidate her. She was as clever as he was, she thought. But the young man did not seem interested in her so she bottled up her love. The new maid believed that Freud did not know how she felt about his nephew.

Anna Freud liked the new maid and Paula Fichtl accompanied her at least once when she and Dorothy Burlingham went on holiday. In her ghosted memoirs Fichtl was asked about the relationship between the two women. Her ghostwriter says that by the time she talked to Paula, Paula was too old to even hear the word "lesbian." But the two women were certainly a couple.

The year 1931 ended well in two ways. Freud and Stefan Zweig had corresponded since 1908. Zweig had become famous as the author of "The Royal Game," *Amok*, *Beware of Pity*, and of biographies of Erasmus, Magellan, and Marie Antoinette. Zweig published

Mental Healers, which appeared in English in 1931. It was flattering, though far from a full biography of Freud, as the book also covered Mesmer and Mary Baker Eddy, the founder of Christian Science. Having explained Freud's ideas and how they had developed, Zweig wrote perceptively that the whole aim of psychoanalysis is "to effect disillusionment and to dispel ungrounded fantasies. . . . It makes no promises at all, offers no consolation and is silent when asked for one or the other." Zweig praised the candor of Freud, which made his work "amazing in its moral significance."

Zweig did not see the twinkling charmer Eastman had seen. Freud had "a dash of Old Testament grimness," but he praised him as an "indefatigable worker." Over fifty years, Freud had seen a procession of "complaining, questioning, eager and excited, hysterical and irate; always the sick, the oppressed, the tormented, the mentally disordered." In his enthusiasm Zweig offered one judgment that feels wrong. He said, "Like Jehovah, he [Freud] is less likely to pardon a lukewarm supporter than an outspoken renegade." Zweig was being tactful given how aggressive Freud was to those analysts he fell out with.

Freud was recognized in the city of his birth. Freiberg, in Moravia, was going to erect a plaque in his honor. "Jacob would have been 116 years old," he told Sam. Anna Freud was sent to represent her father. This accolade did not mean that he could stop worrying about money, though. Freud's son Ernst still "had to rely on an allowance from his father," he told Sam, "and on what he gets from his well-off mother-in-law."

Despite this honor, Freud faced a cash-flow problem. The International Psychoanalytic Verlag had published two of his books in German, *The Ego and the Id* and *Civilization and Its Discontents*. The company also produced the two major journals, *Internationale Zeitschrift für (ärztliche) Psychoanalyse (The International Journal for Medical Psychoanalysis)* and *Imago*. Both lost money, as their circulations were small. Ernest Jones set up an English branch of the company, the International Psycho-Analytical Press, which published authorized translations of Freud's work by C.J.M. Hubback and James Strachey. The British company lost money, too. Finally the Hogarth Press, run by Leonard and Virginia Woolf, started to publish Freud in England, paying him an advance of £50 for each volume. By 1932 there was a serious risk that the German-language publishing company would collapse.

Freud wrote to some of his rich friends, though he did not think that many would help in the middle of a Depression. He was wrong. A. A. Brill sent $2,500 and Edith Jackson contributed $2,000. Both the New York and British societies sent substantial gifts. It is impossible to understand the rest of Freud's life without understanding the economic problems the world faced in the 1930s Depression.

6
The Rise of the Nazis

After the Allies defeated Germany in 1919, France and Britain demanded enormous payments by way of reparation. Germany suffered crippling inflation; money had to be carted about in wheelbarrows when inflation reached its peak.

In *The Gathering Storm*, Winston Churchill's history of the Second World War first published in 1948, Churchill described a "little corporal" who had "been temporarily blinded by mustard gas in a British attack" and whose "personal failure merged with the disaster of the whole German people." As a result "an agony consumed his being." The little corporal left the hospital to find his country in chaos and an "atmosphere of despair and frenzy." The little corporal was, of course, Adolf Hitler; Churchill pictured him as the fog of war turned into the misery of peace in 1919; for Hitler "as in a dream, everything suddenly became clear, Germany had been stabbed in the back and clawed down by the Jews, by the profiteers and intriguers . . . by the accursed Bolsheviks." Churchill's next sentence has a Freudian ring because he imagines Hitler having a daydream that motivates him. "Shining before him he saw his duty, to save Germany from these plagues, to avenge her wrongs. And lead the master race to its long-decreed destiny."

When Churchill wrote this, he would have read confidential reports on Hitler's personality compiled by the American psychiatrist Walter Langer, who had spent some time in Vienna before 1939. In the First World War Hitler was a dispatch rider and had been injured. Langer mentioned that in 1918 Hitler was treated for hysterical blindness at a special military hospital called Pasewalk. World War I saw far more doctors than ever before take an interest in psychiatry as soldiers suffered from shell shock and depression.

Langer, however, did not discover the full truth about the treatment Hitler received. In some ways that is surprising because it had been the subject of a novel, *The Eye Witness*, by Edward Weiss, which explained how A.H. had been treated. But neither American nor British intelligence seems to have realized that A.H. stood for Adolf Hitler. The story has been pieced together largely by David Lewis, an English psychologist. One of the doctors at Pasewalk was a Dutch psychiatrist, Edmund Forster. His methods were not subtle and he would usually bully shell-shocked soldiers into returning to active duty. He dismissed most of his patients as malingerers, but Hitler seemed very different: Hitler did not want to be declared unfit for duty and was eager to get back to the front line. Forster observed Hitler for a week and became certain he had not gone blind out of cowardice. That made Hitler interesting. Forster was familiar with Freud's work and often used hypnosis. He reasoned that Hitler's unconscious had made him blind and that it had done so because Hitler could not bear to see what he would inevitably see, the destruction of Germany.

The most effective treatment, Forster thought, would be suggestion, a method Freud had sometimes used. Forster decided to persuade Hitler that he might play a part in the salvation of Germany and that he had to recover his sight to do that. In *The Eye Witness* Edward Weiss gave a precise account of how A.H. was cured of hysterical blindness because Weiss was given Forster's notes in which he detailed the treatment.

Because of his experience at Pasewalk, Forster also was consulted by Hermann Goering for help with his morphine addiction. The Nazi leader and his deputy both had positive experiences with psychotherapeutic interventions. Goering's cousin, Matthias, was a Jungian. Such medical histories and family connections help explain the particularly tangled nature of the relationship between the Nazis and psychotherapy. Despite such positive experiences, both Hitler and Goering wanted to hide that they had ever been treated by psychiatrists. Forster committed suicide soon after Hitler came to power, but David Lewis believes he was assassinated by the Gestapo to stop him from revealing that the führer had needed psychiatric treatment.

In his biography *Hitler the Pawn*, published in Britain in 1936, Rudolf Olden, the political editor of the *Berliner Tageblatt* (*The Berlin Daily*), did not make the connection between Weiss's novel and Hitler.

Olden did argue, however, that by the early 1920s Hitler knew that he had to construct a good narrative of his early career. Olden discovered that Hitler "came under the spell of an excommunicated man who animated a small circle of friends with messages from a saintly spirit, always ending up with the command to break the fetters of Versailles." Hitler even took part in some dowsing experiments. The search after esoteric wisdom was intellectually fashionable at the time. Arthur Conan Doyle believed in fairies, Houdini thought there might be an afterlife, and there was a fashionable occultist movement in Germany, too. Hitler incidentally told a Paris paper in 1940 that he had been at Pasewalk and that one day he woke up in his bed and realized he had a mission: to save Germany from the Jews and Bolsheviks. He never mentioned Forster, of course.

The Treaty of Versailles, the rampaging inflation of the 1920s, and the Wall Street crash all had a psychological impact. Germany itself could have been diagnosed as neurotic by 1930. Thomas Mann understood why the Nazis had induced a psychotic state in their fellow citizens. He wrote in 1930:

> This fantastic state of mind, of a humanity that has outrun its ideas, is matched by a political scene in the grotesque style, with Salvation Army methods, hallelujahs and bell-ringing and dervishlike repetition of monotonous catchwords, until everybody foams at the mouth. Fanaticism turns into a means of salvation, enthusiasm into epileptic ecstasy, politics becomes an opiate for the masses, a proletarian eschatology; and reason veils her face.

Why War?

In July 1932, when an official of the League of Nations came to see Freud, Freud was unusually diffident. The official, Leon Steinig, believed that Freud and Einstein should have a public exchange on the causes of war, an exchange that might help avoid another one.

Freud listened skeptically and told Steinig that all his life he had had to tell "people truths that were difficult to swallow. Now that I am old, I certainly do not want to fool them." He doubted anyone would want to publish his pessimistic views. The League of Nations "had not paid the slightest interest in our work," Freud complained. But he agreed to work with Einstein. The two men had met briefly in

1927 and Freud had congratulated Einstein when he turned fifty. By 1932, however, Freud knew that Einstein had been against his getting the Nobel Prize.

Why War was an exchange between the great physicist and the great psychiatrist, a major event. Freud was right in guessing that no one would want to listen. The demoralized and incompetent League of Nations printed only two thousand copies.

Freud told Einstein that there was just "one sure way of ending war and that is the establishment, by common consent, of a central control which shall have the last word in every conflict of interests." The League of Nations had "no force at its disposal and can only get it if the members of the new body, its constituent nations, furnish it. And, as things are, this is a forlorn hope." But it would be very "shortsighted" to ignore the League, as it was an experiment that had never before been tried in history.

Freud then discussed his theory of the death instinct and added, "As a rule several motives of similar composition concur to bring about" any action. He cited Professor G. C. Lichtenberg, some-time professor of physics at Gottingen, who had developed a subtle "Compass-card of Motives."

Licthenberg wrote: "The efficient motives impelling man to act can be classified like the thirty-two winds and described in the same manner; e.g., Food-Food-Fame or Fame-Fame-Food." Freud listed the "whole gamut of human motives that may respond when political leaders summon their citizens to war." There was greed and idealism, cruelty and heroism. Idealism was often disguised as a lust for destruction.

"All this may give you the impression that our theories amount to species of mythology and a gloomy one at that! But does not every natural science lead ultimately to this—a sort of mythology? Is it otherwise today with your physical sciences?"

Human aggression was always present. Freud did not credit that "in some happy corners of the earth, they say, where nature brings forth abundantly whatever man desires, there flourish races whose lives go gently by; unknowing of aggression or constraint." No chance! "I would like further details about these happy folk," Freud said. The irony reflects an analytic feud. By 1932, Freud was extremely unhappy with his once favorite young analyst, Wilhelm Reich. Reich was being too literal in arguing that the best cure for sexual repression was to teach human beings how to have better sex lives. Freud dismissed such free love frivolities. The best hope, as he argued in *Why War*, lay not in sex, but in culture.

"On the psychological side, two of the most important phenomena of culture are, firstly, a strengthening of the intellect, which tends to master our instinctive life, and, secondly, an introversion of the aggressive impulse." We might become intelligent enough to avoid conflict as war "runs most emphatically counter to the psychic disposition imposed on us by the growth of culture; we are therefore bound to resent war, to find it utterly intolerable." Freud then described Einstein and himself as pacifists who were simply revolted not just by the atrocities of war but by "the aesthetic ignominies of warfare." This is a curious phrase; war is too ugly. His sons who fought in 1914 told him what conditions were like, as did doctors who were at the front.

Einstein answered on December 3, 1932:

> You have made a most gratifying gift to the League of Nations and me with your truly classic reply. You have earned my gratitude and the gratitude of all men for having devoted all your strength to the search for truth and for having shown the rarest courage in professing your convictions all your life.

The Nazis loathed the pamphlet. It confirmed their views that psychoanalysis polluted the noble Aryan mind and soul. It was typical Jewish thought, with its "degenerate capacity to poison the sources of idealism and feeling for race and nation and, especially, to strike the Nordic races at their most vulnerable point, their sexual life," said *Deutsche Volksegesundheit aus Blut und Boden,* a journal whose title can be translated as *The Health of the German People from Blood and Land.*

Freud's analysis of aggression was being overtaken by events. In October 1932, Hitler took Hermann Goering with him to try to persuade the German president, Hindenberg, to appoint Hitler chancellor. The president thought, as many upper-class Germans did, that Hitler was a puffed-up little corporal. Hitler had a good sense of how Hindenberg viewed him, which is why he took Goering to the meeting. The heroic pilot of World War I could persuade Hindenberg that Hitler was a substantial figure. Hitler let Goering do most of the talking. Goering had thought Hitler was a genius from the moment he first heard him speak, but he failed to convince Hindenberg.

Hindenberg called new elections for the end of November, hoping the Nazis would lose seats in the Reichstag. He had read the country's mood poorly, as Hitler's Nazi Party won 35 percent of the votes, more votes than any other party. Hindenberg had no option but to offer Hitler the chance to form a government.

The French Detectives and the Bankers

Early in 1932 two French detectives entered a hotel near the Champs-Élysées. They had been given a useful tip-off.

The French government faced a huge budget deficit. Édouard Herriot led a coalition government that included a number of Socialist ministers who had a clear program for dealing with the crisis. They wanted to reduce French military spending and to nationalize banks and railways. These measures were too extreme, Herriot thought, and instead he proposed an austerity program. The last thing he needed was a financial scandal that exposed the fact that the rich avoided taxes everyone else had to pay.

The French detectives entered the hotel rooms of the president and vice president of the Commercial Bank of Basel and found incriminating documents. The bank officials had a list of two thousand of their French clients who had gotten money to Switzerland illegally. It did not require much ingenuity. Even today the border near Geneva is guarded by just one custom post at Ferney-Voltaire. In addition, there are now, and were then, many other ways of getting goods into Switzerland.

The French tax "cheats" included senators, a former minister, bishops, generals, and industrialists, the cream of French society. Many who preached public austerity were practicing private greed. After news of the police raid leaked out, there was a furious debate in the Chamber of Deputies. The Socialist Fabien Albertin got hold of a copy of the list of the two thousand cheats and relished reading out some of the names of the "great and good"—and greedy—fiddlers. He told his fellow deputies that France had lost 9 million francs in taxes and called for international agreements with other countries to pursue the cheats and recover the money.

Predictable political posturing followed. The Left called for all the assets of French taxpayers to be declared. The Right denounced this as a cheap ploy to justify passing an austerity budget. The right-wing paper *Le Figaro* oozed morality and reminded readers that the deputies in the Chamber only paid taxes on half their incomes. The Communist paper *L'Humanité* denounced the "2,000 bourgeois compromised in a massive organized tax fraud scandal." Satirists joined in the fun as *Le Temps* joked that "contraband is not something to be reprimanded." Tax cheats should be congratulated for their initiative. The government could hardly refuse to prosecute the tax cheats. It announced the immediate start of negotiations with the Swiss government.

The arrest of two top bankers in Paris was no joke for the Swiss, however. Jesus might have thrown the money changers out of the Temple but, by 1540, many Protestants believed that being rich was a sign of being one of the elect. Heaven beckoned those with a fat purse. The Swiss believed that banks had their God-given duties; the state of one's account was as sacred as the state of one's soul. Priests could not reveal what was said in confession and bankers could not reveal what was in the ledgers. Swiss newspapers complained about the arrogance of the French.

To find a way out of the crisis, Swiss banks turned to the Swiss Federal Court. It ruled obligingly that banks had to keep their clients' files utterly confidential. The battle between the French and the Swiss became bitter. French prime minister Herriot had to pacify his Socialist allies, so he promised to give the tax authorities the right to scrutinize all bank operations. No one would be able to open an account, write a check, rent a safe, or send one sou abroad without a French bureaucrat knowing about it.

The Swiss thought they had won the battle when, on December 18, 1932, the Herriot government fell. The Swiss vowed their banks could never face such embarrassment again and framed a new law. Article 47b of the Swiss Banking Act of 1933 introduced the notion of banking secrecy. Any bank official who revealed the identity of the holder of a numbered account was committing a crime and could be imprisoned. Bank customers could be sure of complete confidentiality.

It was not just French Socialists who complained about Article 47b. A month after Herriot's government fell, Hitler became chancellor of Germany. This new Swiss law would allow Jews and other "enemies of the state" to hide their monies, the Nazis protested. The international Jewish conspiracy was triumphing once again. The Nazis had every intention of taking their revenge.

Jews at this time were under intense pressure, especially mone-tarily. My own family's experience offers a glimpse of what the Freuds endured. My mother's family fled Romania in 1938. The country was ruled by the anti-Semitic General Antonescu. After the war one of my uncles, Zoltan Gruber, to whose memory I have dedicated this book, became a money smuggler. If, for example, you wanted funds in France, you gave money to someone Zoltan trusted in England. There would be nothing written down; no questions would be asked. You would then be told to meet someone in Paris or Rome who handed back your money to you, minus a small commission. The money could also be given to someone you nominated. From 1950 to the end of the 1980s, many countries imposed restrictions on sending money abroad and this informal system usually worked well.

Freud's secret bank accounts were not discussed in the biogra-phies. Thanks to the letters Freud wrote to Sam we now know some-thing of the origin of these accounts. As he treated patients who could pay in dollars or sterling, Freud deposited some of their fees outside Austria. Anna Freud knew of these accounts, as did Freud's other children, especially Martin, who had qualified as a lawyer. But the accounts were a secret, and the kind of secret anti-Semites would say was typical of Jews. There were reasons no one wrote about Freud's accounts even if some evidence existed. It seemed shameful for a dis-tinguished Jew to be too concerned with money. But after the First World War, Freud, like millions of central Europeans, was in financial straits. Money was losing its value. Freud told his nephew Sam that the Austrian schilling had lost 95 percent of its worth.

When Freud asked for contributions to keep his publishing house going, he also urged cooperation between German psychoanalysts and those in the rest of the world. "Let us not be blinded by the apparent lessening of hostility towards our analysis," he wrote. "It is more an improvement in tone than in reality." He concluded, "Yet for some time it will be necessary for the analysts to stick together, more closely together, than the closely related groups of neurologists, psy-chiatrists and psycho-therapists."

One of those who answered the call for funds was Marie Bona-parte. She and Freud had stayed in regular touch. After seeing Freud in 1927, Marie Bonaparte decided to try something different to cure her frigidity. She had an operation that moved her clitoris closer to her vaginal orifice. She believed in Freud's theory of the vaginal orgasm and he did nothing to discourage her. The procedure did not improve her sex life, which continued to distress her. Now she wrote Freud a letter that showed how extreme she could be. She was thinking of committing incest with her son. Did Freud think that was a good idea? He counseled against it. Let Oedipus slumber.

Some scholars have argued that Freud only discovered how Jewish he felt as the Nazis became more powerful. There is much evidence to the contrary, as has been suggested, but Freud himself wrote that he was lukewarm in his attachment to Judaism "until I noticed the growth of anti-Semitic prejudice in Germany and German Austria." The historian Peter Gay argues that in the poisonous atmosphere of the late 1920s and early 1930s he did more than refuse to deny his Jewish origins. He trumpeted them. As he got older, he became more inclined not just to assert his Jewishness against anti-Semites, but also to express a strong positive emotional attachment to it.

Gay suggests that this was partly nostalgia, partly gratitude for the sense of community Freud's Jewish identity gave him in a hostile world. In *Freud's Moses* historian Yosef Hayim Yerushalmi also argues that Hitler's rise to power made Freud feel more Jewish and take more interest in Jewish issues. Jung had a different view, and perhaps a not inaccurate one, as he sniped years earlier that Freud had "the common Jewish sensitivity to the slightest hint of anti-Semitism."

The triumph of the Nazis did lead Freud to discuss with a few other Jews the position Jews found themselves in. He told Stefan Zweig: "And we certainly have our Germanness in common—only it's a Germanness of the past it seems to me." Zweig had thought a great deal about "my relationship to Germany and to my Germanness, and my relationship to the Jews, to the Jewishness in me and in the world, and to Palestine."

On August 18, 1932, Freud answered; he had heard of the Nazi threats against Zweig and encouraged his friend to go on with their correspondence and their regular exchange of manuscripts: "So perhaps the Nazis are playing into my hands for once. When you tell me about your thoughts, I can relieve you of the illusion that one has to be a German. Should we not leave this God-forsaken nation to themselves?"

Freud's approach was historical and psychoanalytic rather than frankly political. He did not dwell much, even in private, on the reasons why the Nazis now attracted so much support. Only two analysts grappled with this issue in political as well as psychoanalytic terms: Otto Fenichel and Wilhelm Reich. Both were Socialists.

Fenichel wrote a paper, "*On Social Anxiety*," which explained the rise of the Nazis as a response to the fear of uncertainty. But Reich was the more glittering character. Freud was so impressed by Reich that he let him treat patients when the young man was only twenty-three years old. Reich was a friend of Anna Freud, who wrote, "Back then in Vienna we were all so excited, full of energy: it was as if a whole new continent was being explored, and we were the explorers, and we now had a chance to change things."

In 1925, Reich became deputy director of Freud's Psychoanalytic Polyclinic and seemed set to become a major figure in psychoanalysis. He was perhaps more practical than other analysts—and more political. In 1928 he joined the Austrian Communist Party. He helped found the Socialist Association for Sexual Counseling and Research. This new group organized centers for psychological counseling that would treat the problems of workers. Reich also organized what we would now call drop-in centers that offered free advice on sex, contraception, venereal diseases, and even homosexuality, to young people.

At first Freud approved but then, not for the first time, turned against a colleague; he started to be annoyed by his prodigy. Freud, who had complained that Jung denied the importance of sex, now complained that Reich overemphasized sex. Reich's ideas seemed too crude and too literal. Reich did not appease Freud by raising questions about the Nirvana principle or death wish. As he reflected on the slaughter of the 1914–1919 war, Freud argued that Eros, the pleasure principle, could not explain all human behavior. Human beings also long for the absence of all struggle, tension and conflict which only comes with death. His beloved Hamlet may have wondered "what dreams may come when we have shuffled off his mortal coil," but Freud assumed that one did not have to deal with any neuroses in one's grave.

Reich's *The Mass Psychology of Fascism* intensified the conflict. Reich could rarely bother to be tactful and suggested that Freud had been unwilling to pursue his own ideas to their logical end. Society suppressed the sexuality of children not in order to socialize them, but to make them docile citizens.

The moral inhibition of the child's natural sexuality, the last stage of which is the severe impairment of the child's genital sexuality, makes the child afraid, shy, fearful of authority, obedient, "good," and "docile" in the authoritarian sense of the words. It has a crippling effect on man's rebellious forces because every vital life-impulse is now burdened with severe fear; and since sex is a forbidden subject, thought in general and man's critical faculty also become inhibited.

The Nazis created "severe fear" expertly, Reich added. "The result is conservatism, fear of freedom, in a word, reactionary thinking. And sexual frustration makes one vulnerable." Nazi parades were almost disguised orgies. "The sexual effect of a uniform, the erotically provocative effect of rhythmically executed goose-stepping, the exhi-bitionistic nature of militaristic procedures, have been more practi-cally comprehended by a salesgirl or an average secretary than by our most erudite politicians." It was inspired of the Nazis to design flashy uniforms for the men and to put the recruiting into the hands of attractive women. Reich recalled that posters for the Royal Navy in the First World War "ran something as follows: 'Travel to foreign countries—join the Royal Navy!' and the foreign countries were por-trayed by exotic women."

Why are these posters effective? Reich asked. "Because our youth has become sexually starved owing to sexual suppression," he answered.

The Left had to understand "why the masses proved to be acces-sible to deception, befogging, and a psychotic situation" and only his mass psychology could explain the question, "Why would millions upon millions affirm their own suppression?"

The Mass Psychology of Fascism had the distinction of being loathed both by the Nazis and by Freud. Anna Freud said that she got along better with Wilhelm Reich than most "because I tried to treat him well instead of offending him. It helps a bit and would help more if he were a sane person, which he is not."

But Reich was far from insane in the early 1930s. He said he had not written about such issues earlier "simply because I feared the con-sequences. Again and again I hesitated to put my ideas down on paper." As the Nazis were in power it might "have a highly dangerous potential as things now stand." He left Germany before the book was published. Today some see it as a classic.

Sauerwald, the Bomb Maker

A year before Wilhelm Reich published *The Mass Psychology of Fascism*, Anton Sauerwald resigned from the cutlery-maker Krupp Berndorf and set up a chemicals business of his own. Sauerwald was twenty-eight years old when he did so, and he had financial help from his parents. This was a brave move, since the German and Austrian chemical industries were suffering in the Depression. Subsidies to academics from large companies like I. G. Farben were being cut. Fewer patents were being registered.

Nevertheless, Sauerwald took premises at 19 Gelbergasse. His company specialized in catalysts, the preparation of patent applications and essence, anything chemical. He employed an old friend, Emil Rothleitner, whom he had known at the University of Vienna and in the *Burschenschaft Germania* fraternity. Rothleitner described himself as someone whose job it was to carry out "practical undertakings" directed by his "chief." Rothleitner was the same age as Sauerwald, but he was not as well qualified academically. But in one respect the employee did much more than carry out Sauerwald's instructions. Rothleitner was heavily involved in Nazi Party activity in Vienna from the early 1930s. There, he led and Sauerwald followed.

After the war, Sauerwald was asked where he had lived after the Nazi Party had been declared illegal. He gave five different addresses. They were:

Vienna. 79 Hauptstrasse, Seventeenth District
Vienna. 41 Semperstrasse, Eighteenth District
London. Kingston Hall
Vienna. 20 Wittehauergasse, Eighteenth District
Rosenheim in southern Germany near the Tyrol border,
    121/2 Aiblingerstrasse. (Rosenheim was a center of
    Nazi activity.)

Sauerwald's time in London is intriguing. Freud's doctor, Max Schur, suggested that the only reason why Sauerwald would have come to England was that he had been sent as a spy by the Nazi Party. The files in the Austrian state archives do not confirm Schur's suspicions. There is no mention of Sauerwald in the British National Archives.

The address Sauerwald gave, Kingston Hall, is also something of a mystery. There was such a place in the London suburb of Kingston upon Thames but it was torn down around 1900. There is still a Kingston Hall Road, however. There was also Kingsley Hall, a kind of superior hostel founded in 1926 where some celebrities lodged while in London. Gandhi stayed there. It had Socialist connections. It is possible that Sauerwald lied about his London address because he was on a Nazi mission, but there is no firm proof of it.

Einstein Leaves

Many Jews, like Stefan Zweig and Einstein, saw that there was no future for them in Germany. In March 1933, Einstein announced that he would never return to Germany. The Nazis confiscated his bank account, his wife's safe deposit box, and his house in Caputh. On March 28, Einstein resigned from the Prussian Academy of Sciences and, four days later, from the Bavarian Academy of Sciences. He also renounced his German citizenship, managing to do this before the Nazis could revoke it. On April 12, 1933, Einstein told the Prussian Academy that he had refused "to put in a good word for the German people as to do so would have been a repudiation of all those notions of justice and liberty for which I have stood all my life." He continued, "I should have been contributing even if only indirectly to moral corruption and the destruction of all existing cultural values."

Einstein made for America. Stefan Zweig headed for Palestine, the first of Freud's friends to try to live the Zionist dream. Zweig wrote to Freud, "This land of religions can, after all, be seen from other points of view than just as a land of delusions and desires." Freud disagreed—for now.

There was one similarity between psychoanalysis and Nazi ideology, however. Both believed human beings could be improved. Freud claimed the purpose of analysis was to heal people so they could "love and work." Some Nazis realized that some type of therapy might be just the tool they needed to produce a more efficient Volk as long as it was clear that the treatment did not owe anything to

Jews or to Freud. Such ambivalences made the relationship between the Nazis and psychoanalysis complicated and controversial.

Nazi hostility could not undo Freud; he remained the most important figure in psychoanalysis. Analysts from Germany, Hungary, Britain, Holland, and Scandinavia visited him. Yet even though the Nazis' behavior toward Jews in Germany became more vicious, Freud remained cautious in public. That did not go unnoticed. Ernest Jones, who was about to become president of the International Psychoanalytic Association, did not denounce the Nazis either. Freud had made bitter enemies—Jung was the most prominent. Jewish analysts like Reich and Adler who had quarrelled with Freud could hardly exploit the political situation but Jung certainly now had his chance to take some revenge. Other analysts succumbed to their own anxieties as well as to Nazi threats.

Historians have debated the reasons why so many analysts were rather meek in this crisis. Historian Geoffrey Cocks, for example, claims that the compromises reached in the extreme circumstances of the 1930s can be understood. Others disagree and argue that some analysts themselves were dazzled by the dictators. Jung attended public ceremonies where Hitler and Mussolini met and suggested that Hitler spoke to the ancient pre-Christian soul of Germany.

The reaction of the analysts to the Nazis was also confused because of their own often bitter infighting. We know more than ever before about their conflicts because Otto Fenichel, the Socialist author of *On Social Anxiety*, circulated letters among some analysts. Few realized that these Rundbriefe, or round-robins, existed until they were published in 1998. They show some analysts in a less than flattering light. Freud had been right to dismiss at least some of his colleagues as "a gang."

The situation was politically, ethically, and psychologically odd. Four different groups were involved in the negotiations that started soon after the Nazis took power in Germany. Members of the International Psychoanalytic Association included analysts from Britain, America, Europe, South America, India, and even Japan. The German Psychoanalytic Society represented all German analysts. Then there were local bodies.

The local Berlin Institute of Psychoanalysis had fewer than a hundred members but ran a major training institute. It had offices on the Potsdamerstrasse and had been founded in 1920 by Ernst Simmel, who was a Socialist, and Max Eitingon. Eitingon provided financial support and nearly all of the state-of-the-art modern furniture. The institute had thirty-six members, twelve teaching staff, and nearly fifty students. Members, mainly Jewish, met every week to hear lectures; many members had been influenced by Marx's ideas. The Berlin Institute made no secret of its ambition to make psychoanalysis, or at least psychotherapy, available not to just the rich but to working-class people who had problems. Freud supported that view.

Several Berlin analysts—most notably Edith Jacobson—took part in "illegal" resistance against the Nazis and were detained by the Gestapo. The best known of these Socialists, Wilhelm Reich and Otto Fenichel, escaped that fate only because they had already left Germany.

The Über Whites

Only two of the Berlin Institute's governing council were not Jewish—Felix Boehm and Carl Müller-Braunschweig. Both men knew Freud well and were part of the analytic circle. Josine, Müller-Braunschweig's wife, was also an analyst who published a number of papers on girls' concepts of the vagina; the fourth important Christian was Karen Horney, who left Vienna in the late 1930s.

When the Nazis took power, Boehm was fifty-one years old. He had studied medicine in Geneva, Freiburg im Breisgau, and Munich. In 1913, he became a member of the Munich regional group of the International Psychoanalytic Association. In World War I he served as a volunteer doctor and acted as a psychiatric expert in a war tribunal held in Germersheim.

After the war, Boehm started a training analysis with Karl Abraham, one of Freud's close friends; it was to Abraham, who was Jewish, that Freud had apologized for devoting so much time to the frailties of the non-Jewish analysts Carl Jung and Ernest Jones. Boehm then taught at the Berlin Psychoanalytic Institute from 1923 to 1933, and while he was there, he put his daughters into analysis with Melanie Klein. He made an interesting study of when girls first become aware of their vagina, a major theoretical issue because Freud believed all women suffered from penis envy. Boehm also studied perversions and had written a major article on the history of the Oedipus complex for the *International Journal of Psychoanalysis*.

No one would have expected Boehm to betray the cause, even though his family had Nazi connections. His father and his uncles knew Alfred Rosenberg, who developed the racist ideas of eccentric thinkers like Arthur de Gobineau and Houston Stewart Chamberlain. It was not only Germans who advocated eugenics. Sir Francis Galton in *Hereditary Genius* (1880) claimed that success ran in families and advocated sterilizing people who had low IQ. That idea became quite popular in America in the 1910s, though many psychologists were not that smart at interpreting IQ tests. They argued that Jews had a low IQ because they did not realize that many of the questions on the tests were not "pure" but required some awareness of American culture.

Alfred Rosenberg argued that there was a hierarchy of human races. Blacks and Jews were at the bottom; the "Aryan" race was at the top. It was not enough to be white to be Aryan. The masters of the master race, the über whites, were the Scandinavians, northern Germans, Dutch, British, and those of pure Baltic stock. Rosenberg couldn't even be consistent in his eugenic fantasies—he argued that the Berbers of North Africa (many of whom both were black and had Jewish ancestry) also belonged to the Aryans. Rosenberg also ranted against homosexuality. His pamphlet *Der Sumpf* (*The Swamp*) claimed it was not just a perversion; it stopped the glorious breeding of the glorious Nordic race.

Carl Müller-Braunschweig was the other key player in the negotiations with the Nazis. After his doctoral thesis on Immanuel Kant, Müller-Braunschweig switched to medicine and also had a training analysis with Karl Abraham. Müller-Braunschweig became a member of the executive committee of the International Psychoanalytic Association in 1925 and regularly wrote in the *Internationale Zeitschrift für Psychoanalyse* (*International Journal of Psychoanalysis*) and in *Imago*. He published a glowing review of Freud's short *Autobiography* (1925), saying that Freud "gives the subject new and fresh applications" and that every psychoanalyst "will take particular pleasure in Freud's pithy phrases." He corresponded with Anna Freud regularly.

The fourth society, the Vienna Psychoanalytic Society, was local, like the one in Berlin. It had grown out of the meetings that had started in Freud's apartment in 1902. Most of the 149 members were Jewish. Freud held an official position only in the Viennese society, but no important decisions about psychoanalysis in Europe were made without his being consulted. In effect, he could stop any development of which he did not approve.

In March 1933, Max Eitingon went to Vienna to consult Freud on the developments in Germany. He left Felix Boehm and Carl Müller-Braunschweig in charge. Behind his back, the two non-Jewish analysts immediately tried to negotiate with the Nazis. They had a simple plan. Because he was a Jew, Eitingon would have to resign as the leader of the German Psychoanalytic Society, as would all of its Jewish members. Only then could the non-Jewish analysts strike a deal with the Nazis to save psychoanalysis.

When Eitingon returned from Vienna, he found that the others had decided that Felix Boehm should become president of the German Psychoanalytic Society. Very soon afterward Eitingon agreed to resign, partly because he had decided, like Stefan Zweig, to immigrate to Palestine. Boehm went to Vienna to discuss this possibility with Freud; even those who were negotiating with the Nazis felt they needed Freud's approval.

Freud was supremely calm to Boehm's face. He said that if Boehm could get a majority of analysts to vote for him, Freud would not stand in his way. But a second version suggests that Freud took the initiative to some extent, as he already knew that Eitingon had decided to go to Palestine.

There is no dispute about the conditions that Boehm had to fulfill if Freud were not to oppose him. First Boehm had to expel Wilhelm Reich from the German society; Freud described his onetime prodigy as a "Bolshevist attacker" and wrote to Eitingon on April 17, 1933, that he wanted Reich removed from the German Psychoanalytic Society and the International Psychoanalytic Association. "I desire it on scientific grounds but have nothing against its coming about on political grounds—I do not begrudge him the role of martyr," Freud said. The scientific grounds had to do with Reich's objections to Freud's death instinct or Nirvana theory.

Boehm would also have to fight against "inside opponents" such as Harald Schultz-Hencke, an analyst who was close to Fenichel. Schultz-Hencke had criticized Freud's libido theory and his ideas on the structure of the unconscious. As a result, Freud forbade him to teach training analysts. In March Freud wrote to Eitingon that he wanted to ensure that Schultz did not take advantage of the "present situation to promote his theories."

The situation was frightening, of course. To the Nazis, Boehm and Müller-Braunschweig intended to argue that it was an accident that psychoanalysis had been invented by a Jew and that the fact that nearly every major analyst was a Jew did not make the enterprise a "Jewish science." Jones did not object; his letters show that he was committed to protecting the interests of German psychoanalysis at least as much as he was to protecting Jewish analysts.

Demonstrations and Murder

One of the less likely consequences of Hitler taking power was that Sigmund Freud started to read *The Manchester Guardian* because German papers did not provide a true picture of events. In Germany many things were not reported, Freud wrote to his nephew Sam, whereas *The Manchester Guardian* provided good coverage. No paper in Germany had reported, for example, that 150 Nazis broke into the house in Trier where Marx had been born. In addition, on Friday, March 10, 1933, *The Manchester Guardian* reported that Nazis had started to picket large shops owned by Jews. The article continued:

> During the busiest shopping hour this evening the following scene could be witnessed outside the Kadewe, the largest department store of the West End. A detachment of Storm Troops marched up to the shop, formed a cordon in front of the entrance, and put up a large notice, "Germans! Don't buy from Jews." The people inside the shop left hurriedly and no others were allowed to go in. The police looked on with apparent indifference. Many people who had assembled outside seemed to be favourably impressed by this demonstration, and talked cheerfully to the Storm Troopers, who assured them that "they would put an end to the Jewish shops."

The Manchester Guardian described similar scenes in front of Rosenheim's, a shop that sold high-class leather goods in Berlin's Kurfürstendamm. "It was closed simply because it belongs to a Jew," the paper reported. Such demonstrations had propaganda value for the Nazi Party, *The Manchester Guardian* added. Anti-Semitism was not just talk; small shopkeepers often supported Hitler and welcomed such attacks on big department stores.

Attacks on department stores were the start of a long campaign of hatred. Anna Freud and Ernest Jones both heard from a Dutch analyst, Johan van Ophuijsen, who visited Berlin and told them, "Germany is at present a hell for German Jews." Only four or five analysts stayed in Berlin. Jones wrote to the analyst Smith Ely Jelliffe in New York. "The persecution has been much worse than you seem to think and has really lived up to the Middle Ages in reputation."

All of this had an effect in Austria. On March 4, 1933, Chancellor Engelbert Dollfuss suspended the Austrian Parliament and blocked all attempts to reconvene it. Dollfuss was concerned by the rise of the Nazis in Austria. He used a 1917 emergency law that had been enacted to protect the state "against the economic dangers associated with a disturbance of public peace, order, and security." Dollfuss said that both the Nazis and the Socialists threatened the country's stability. From then on he ruled by decree.

On June 19, Dollfuss outlawed the German National Socialist Party. The Nazi response was to start a campaign of terror. Six days later, they tried to assassinate ten senior Austrian officials. Crowds of Nazi students gathered in front of the university; mounted police chased them down the Ringstrasse. It was the start of days of rioting. Usually the Nazis targeted Jews.

A huge bomb tore out the inside of one of the Nazis' favorite targets, a department store owned by a Jewish family. In another part of the city, an elderly Jewish woman died: Frau Futterweit was standing in the doorway of her little jewelry shop when a passenger in a car threw an old silk stocking stuffed with newspapers and a hand grenade at her. With great presence of mind, Frau Futterweit tried to throw it back but the grenade burst in her hands and killed her instantly. Eight passersby were wounded; one died in the hospital. *Time* magazine covered the story about Frau Futterweit.

In his book *Living and Dying*, Max Schur offers evidence that Anton Sauerwald was involved in this violence. The company Sauerwald had set up in 1932 also made explosives—and we have seen that his assistant Emil Rothleitner was involved in Nazi cells. Sauerwald told the authorities that he was supplying chemicals to construction companies for demolition. He did do this legitimately, but it has been claimed that the business was also the perfect front for making bombs for Nazi groups. Schur insisted (in a footnote) that Sauerwald boasted to Freud's younger brother, Alexander, that he had played a very subtle game in the 1930s. Sauerwald had been successful as an academic chemist and had four papers published in *Monatsheft der Chimie*. That made him well qualified to work as an explosives expert for the Vienna police. So he became a kind of double agent; on the one hand, he was retained by the police, and on the other hand, he was making bombs for Austrian Nazi groups. Sauerwald would manufacture bombs, the Nazis would plant them, the bombs would explode, and then the witless police would bring Sauerwald the fragments so that he could use his forensic skills to analyze them. It was a black comedy and would have been funny, but for the fact that people died.

The unrest in Vienna continued until June 1933, when the Austrian government arrested 1,142 Nazis. The government suspected Berlin had ordered the violence. The Austrians then refused to grant diplomatic immunity to Hitler's personal envoy to Vienna. The man "was routed out of bed at six in the morning. Police seized numbers of incriminating documents," *Time* reported.

"Berlin replied to this with typical Nazi bumbling," *Time* added. German police called at the house of the Austrian Press attaché in Berlin, Dr. Erwin Wasserback. The doctor picked up the telephone and called Chancellor Dollfuss, who happened to be in London.

"Excellency," Wasserback cried, "the police are knocking at the door. What shall I do?"

"Don't do anything till they threaten force. Then let them in," Dollfuss was reported to have said with some humor.

The Nazis had not chosen their victim cleverly. Wasserbeck was a priest as well as a doctor, which gave Dollfuss a nice opportunity. The chancellor arranged for a formal protest from the papal nuncio in Berlin. Dr. Wasserback was released quickly and Dollfuss transferred him to London, so that the doctor could tell British diplomats how the Nazis behaved.

Dollfuss told a conference in London soon after the riots: "While I do not charge the German Government with any such intention, the danger exists that irresponsible elements might march into Austria from Bavaria. If that happened we would have Czechoslovak and Jugoslav troops marching in to protect the interests of the Little Entente and a virtual war with my poor country as the battlefield. That is what I fear."

Dollfuss returned to Vienna with a substantial prize, a loan for

$29,975,000 from the League of Nations, which had money at least. Dollfuss didn't have long to enjoy his success. Vienna was still in chaos. Nazi sympathizers were throwing grenades at policemen. Freud warned his son Ernst that Dollfuss "probably won't be able to curb the dangerous fools in Heimwehr," the Austrian National Guard.

On May 6, 1933, Freud celebrated his seventy-seventh birthday. It would turn out to be a momentous day—and a very upsetting one.

May 6, 1933, and the Einstein of Sex

On that day the Nazis closed down another institute, some of whose members had links with Freud.

We tend to think that Alfred Kinsey was the first scientist to study human sexual behavior, but it was not just Wilhelm Reich who predated him. From 1919 onward, regular visitors to Magnus Hirschfeld's Institute of Sex and to the Museum of Sex in Berlin were asked to fill in questionnaires about their sexual behavior. Hirschfield was Jewish, had been studying sexology for thirty years, and was nicknamed the Einstein of Sex. He had an international reputation. He had published a book on homosexuality in the German elite, including in the military. Jawaharlal Nehru visited his museum, as did a 1923 commission from the Ministry of Health from Russia. So did W. H. Auden, during his trip to Berlin in 1929.

The institute was affiliated with the University of Berlin. It had a library of twenty thousand volumes, thirty-five thousand pictures, and forty thousand biographies, as well as patients' records and a variety of rare objects and works of art.

On the morning of May 6, trucks drove up to the institute. About one hundred students, all committed Nazis, jumped out. Then, bizarrely, a brass band marched to the front of the building. The students stormed it and took away many of its documents while the band played on. The staff was kept locked up while the students took documents, mainly dealing with "intersexual" or homosexual cases. The band kept on playing. This assault to loud music soon attracted a large crowd.

At noon, the leader of the students made a long speech, and then they left, singing a particularly vulgar song and the Nazi anthem, written by Horst Wessel. In the afternoon a second group of students returned to the institute to loot more patient records. There were bonfires, as usual. Some of the staff at the institute suspected that there was more than "mere" anti-Semitism and homophobia involved. The Nazis feared that the institute "knew too much" about some party officials who had come to be treated for their un-Aryan problem; they were homosexual. More files of so-called Jewish filth were burned in Opera Square.

On May 7, with Freud's blessing, Max Eitingon resigned as president of the Berlin Institute. Three days later, students from the Wilhelm Humboldt University took books from their university library to the Franz Joseph Platz. They also lit a bonfire and, again, a band was playing. The students threw books by fifty-eight authors into a huge bonfire. The writers whose books went up in flames included H. G. Wells, Ernest Hemingway, Karl Marx, Sigrid Undset, Albert Einstein, Thomas Mann, Wilhelm Reich, Jack London, Erich Maria Remarque and, of course, Freud himself. There was some ceremony as students consigned Freud's books one by one to the flames. Freud was one of the most detested of these writers. Many of the other writers were more obviously radical politically, but Freud had described the wild unconscious energies that swirled about in the id, energies that led to violence and unbridled lust. The Nazis did not want to see themselves as being like that.

The event was hardly spontaneous: the propaganda minister, Joseph Goebbels, gave a speech. The students sang Nazi songs around the bonfire. Over the next few days, there were other bonfires. Other university libraries were ransacked and more books were burned all over Germany. The international press was outraged; few international politicians said anything.

"Hundred thousand march here in six-hour protest over Nazi policies," ran the headline of the *New York Times* on May 11. With uncanny prescience, *Newsweek* called the burning "a holocaust of books." Many papers quoted a warning by Heinrich Heine, one of Freud's favorite writers. In his play *Almansor* (1821) about the Spanish Inquisition, one of Heine's characters says: "This is but the prologue. Where books are burnt, people in the end are burnt too." The *New York Times*, in an unusual move, allowed its Berlin correspondent to comment: "This evening a significant part of ancient German liberalism—if that still existed—burnt along with the books."

Walter Lippmann, the liberal journalist, also understood that this violence was the beginning, not the end. He wrote in the *Los Angeles Times* on May 19, 1933:

> The Nazis deliberately and systematically mean to turn the minds of the German people to war. These acts symbolize the moral and intellectual character of the Nazi regime. For these bonfires are not the work of schoolboys or mobs but of the present German Government acting through its Minister of Propaganda and Public Enlightenment. The ominous symbolism of these bonfires is that there is a Government in Germany which means to teach its people that their salvation lies in violence.

With some gallows humor, Freud noted that the Nazi action represented moral progress. In the Middle Ages, they would have burned him but now they were content to burn just his books. Late in May 1933, the Protestant pastor and analyst Oskar Pfister wrote Freud a letter of condolence upon the death of Sandor Ferenczi, one of the early analysts. Ferenczi had been ill for some time and his death was not unexpected. On May 28, Freud replied, "Our horizon has become darkly clouded by events in Germany," and added that "hatred for Judaism is at bottom hatred for Christianity itself." Freud believed that "only this Catholicism protects us against Nazism." But Jews would have to be prudent and "we naturally hesitate to do anything that would be bound to arouse the Church's hostility. This is not cowardice but prudence."

Pfister added that he been infected with "disgust" in Germany and would not easily rid himself of it for a long time. "Proletarian militarism stinks even more rottenly than the blue blooded Junker spirit of the time of the Kaiser," he wrote.

The violence made Freud consider a possibility he dreaded. On May 28 he told Pfister:

"Three members of our family with their families are looking for a new country and still have not found one. Switzerland is not among the hospitable countries. My judgment of human nature, especially of the Christian Aryan variety, has little reason to change." A few weeks later, however, he wrote that "flight would only be justified if there was a direct danger to life." It was the first time he talked of leaving Vienna.

Freud's son Ernst now decided to leave Austria. His younger brother Oliver "was looking for a place to live in France somewhere near St.

Briac." Analysts who wanted to escape Germany did not find it easy to arrange. Britain, for example, was not in a mood to accept refugees and only four analysts went to Britain in 1933. One was Walter Schmideberg. He had been a cavalry officer in the First World War and was the man who had managed to keep Freud supplied with cigars. Schmideberg joined his wife, Melitta, the daughter of the analyst Melanie Klein.

I interviewed Melitta Schmideberg in 1980 when making a film on depression. She was an irrepressible old lady whose house near Marylebone Station was crammed with antiques rather like Freud's had been. She took great pleasure in showing me a spoon that Freud had given her. Life among the analysts made her very skeptical, she said. She had long ago realized that talking and chicken soup were as effective as complicated analytic techniques.

Freud still hoped he could remain in Vienna, but he knew life there was precarious. "We are living here in a Catholic country under the protection of that Church, uncertain how long that protection will hold out," Freud wrote. The Italian dictator Mussolini was doing more than France or England to protect Austria against the Nazis.

"Our bit of the civil war wasn't pretty at all," Freud told Arnold Zweig. "One couldn't go out into the street." All this had an impact on the increasingly worried analysts.

September 1933: Toward a Nazi Psychotherapy

In September 1933, Felix Boehm and Carl Müller-Braunschweig arranged a meeting with the Nazi Ministry of Culture to discuss the conditions under which the German Psychoanalytic Society could continue its work. They hoped to persuade Nazi officials that psychoanalysis did not have to be "Jewish," but that it could be used to help the Reich. Boehm told officials at the Ministry of Culture that it was not especially relevant that a Jew had invented psychoanalysis. The technique had its merits and the Nazis were wrong to believe it was "subversive." "I had never known psychoanalysis to have a destructive effect on love of country," Boehm assured them.

Müller-Braunschweig went even further. He wrote a memorandum on psychoanalysis for the Nazis and published it in a slightly adapted form in October 1933 as "Psychoanalysis and *Weltanschauung*" in *Reichswart*, a "rabid anti-Semitic publication." He claimed it was wrong to see sexuality as the central issue. Rather, psycho-analysis tried to heal the conflicts between our out-of-control instincts and our egos, which struggled to keep everything under control. It was orthodox Freud, but Müller-Braunschweig cleverly framed these ideas in talk of "mastery," which the Nazis lapped up. The uncon-scious could be "mastered," he said; the patient could "master" him-self. He went on to write what some historians see as a passage that was a great betrayal:

> Psychoanalysis works to remodel incapable weaklings into people who can cope with life, the inhibited into confident types, those divorced from reality into human beings who can look reality in the face, those enslaved by their instincts into their masters, loveless, selfish people into people capable of love and sacrifice, those indifferent to the totality of life into those willing to serve the whole. Thus it does outstanding work in education, and is able to give valuable service to the principles, only now mapped out anew, of a heroic, constructive conception of life, at-tuned to reality.

A modified form of analysis, with decent Teutonic elements, could boost psychological health, which he defined "in terms of blood, strong will, proficiency, discipline." Müller-Braunschweig's rhetoric reassured the men at the Ministry of Culture.

But Boehm and Müller-Braunschweig feared fine words wouldn't be enough; it might make all the difference to have a cousin of one of Hitler's strongmen as their ally. Both knew Matthias Goering, the cousin of Hermann Goering, Hitler's deputy.

The Goerings

During the 1923 failed putsch, Hermann Goering was wounded and some accounts say he was saved by a Jewish doctor. Goering had to flee Germany. He was a morphine addict and spent time in an insane asylum, but he loved his wife, Emmy, and she loved him; with her help, he recovered and returned to Germany in 1927. So the Nazi deputy leader knew from all-too-personal an experience that it was possible that psychiatric treatment could help. This created a bond between his cousin, Matthias, and himself.

Matthias Goering studied law at the University of Freiburg and traveled to Palestine, India, and Ceylon. Jerusalem fascinated him. In 1907 he obtained his doctorate and went to work for one of the great psychiatrists of the time, Emil Kraepelin. Goering became interested in psychotherapy and hypnosis. As Freud had once done, Goering believed hypnosis could reveal a patient's repressions and secrets and help heal him or her. Goering was also a practicing Christian and always carried a Bible with him. Photographs taken when he was in his fifties show a man with a long white beard. His patients called him Papi or Father Christmas. Treating the mentally ill seemed to reinforce his sense of the presence of God.

In 1929 Matthias Goering set up a study group of psychotherapists in Wuppertal but he had not become a Freudian. Whereas Freud stressed the libido, Goering emphasized the power of "community feeling," as well as faith: faith in God and faith in the German nation. He does not seem to have seen any contradiction between faith in Christ and faith in Hitler. He wrote:

> External drill does not suffice. The core of man must be grasped as the Führer has repeatedly emphasized, and treated instinctively so that our subconscious is directed on the right path.

Jung was in correspondence with Matthias Goering and seems not to have quibbled at the description of the führer as the theorist of the "core of man."

Matthias Goering once told Werner Kemper, an orthodox Freudian analyst, that it was not just sex that made him object to psychoanalysis. It was also a matter of furniture. Freud made patients lie down while the analyst sat behind them and looked down on them. The unseen analyst had all the power. Eye contact was vital, Goering believed. Helper and helped had to face each other, honestly, in the spirit of Christ.

In his 1933 book on the relationship between Alfred Adler and religion, Matthias Goering wrote: "To love means to be able to merge into another, to understand one's fellow man and to desire to help him in an effective manner."

In *Psychotherapy in the Third Reich*, Geoffrey Cocks cannot decide whether or not Matthias Goering was an anti-Semite. Goering saw Jewish patients though he felt he was unable to help them because of "social differences." Yet it seems likely that, after Anna

Freud asked him, he helped an analyst called Eva Rothmann to escape Germany.

It would not be totally out of character for a member of the Goering family to be sympathetic to Jews. Goering's other cousin, Hermann's younger brother, Albert, hated everything Hitler stood for and left Germany for Vienna in 1928. He spoke out against the Nazis from the beginning. His doctor, Laszlo Kovacs, recalled hearing Albert say: "I defy Hitler, my brother and all the National Socialists." It was not all talk. Alfred Goering gave Kovacs money to set up a secret bank account at the Bank Orelli in Bern, which he instructed Kovacs to use to help Jewish refugees to get to Lisbon. During the 1939 war he was stationed in Bucharest. When two Nazi officers recognized him as Hermann Goering's brother and saluted him with the normal "Heil Hitler," Albert Goering replied, "You can kiss my arse." Despite their different political views, Albert and Hermann Goering got on well. The Nazi often protected his brother loyally and Albert often pressured his older brother to let some Jews escape.

After Albert Goering came to live in Vienna, he took a house in Grinzing where Freud liked to spend his summers. The two men spent weekends and summer months there and had some acquaintances in common. But did the two men meet? There was much café life in the resort, so it is not improbable. The question is intriguing because the Goering family was to have so much influence on the fate of psychoanalysis in Germany from 1933 onward.

With the approval of Ernest Jones, Felix Boehm and Carl Müller-Braunschweig now offered Matthias Goering the leadership of the German "psychotherapists." The pious Christian did not hesitate and had no trouble justifying his decision:

> In the interests of our society I wish to accept your offer, because I am a National Socialist not in name only but wholeheartedly in the spirit of Adolf Hitler, because moreover I bear the name of the Prussian Minister-President and am related to him. Also in the interests of National Socialism I must not refuse, for I believe that we psychotherapists have a great mission in the new state . . . we are called to educate children and adults in the right spirit. From the very start, therefore, the psychotherapists in the Third Reich pinned their colors to a masthead already painted in the Nazi red and black.

The great mission could hardly proceed when so many analysts were Jewish and others were Socialists. Boehm was well aware of the problem. He barbed that "[Wilhelm] Reich had often come out publicly as a Communist and as a psychoanalyst, presenting his opinions as the results of psychoanalysis. . . . I had to fight against this prejudice." Anna Freud, once Reich's good friend, now wrote to Ernest Jones:

> Here we are all prepared to take risks for psychoanalysis but not for [Wilhelm] Reich's ideas, with which nobody is in agreement. My father's opinion on this matter is: If psychoanalysis is to be prohibited, it should be prohibited for what it is, and not for the mixture of politics and psychoanalysis which Reich represents. My father can't wait to get rid of him inasmuch as he attaches himself to psychoanalysis; what my father finds offensive in Reich is the fact that he has forced psychoanalysis to become political; psychoanalysis has no part in politics."

At a board meeting in the summer of 1933, Ernst Simmel, who had founded the Berlin Institute with Eitingon, had proposed that Reich should be expelled. Eitingon wanted this "purge" postponed until the next general meeting at the beginning of October 1933. By that time, he would be in Palestine.

Wilhelm Reich should have been warned of the moves against him and given a chance to defend himself, but he had already fled to Denmark so the board decided it was not "opportune" to contact him. Freud does not seem to have objected. He was always anxious about psychoanalysis seeming too radical, so it is not surprising that he became more hostile as Reich's ideas became more radical. Reich went from Denmark to Norway where he would annoy the authorities again.

Private Criticisms

Anxieties—professional, political, and personal—affected Freud's health. On December 7, 1933, Freud wrote to Marie Bonaparte that he felt "too cold." He was smoking just one "denerved cigar daily" and worrying about the book on Woodrow Wilson he was writing with William Bullitt. "From Bullitt no direct news. Our book will never see the light of day," he lamented to her.

Freud wrote to his nephew Sam in Manchester that "life in Germany had become impossible." He presumed Sam would be reading about how the Nazis were behaving so "you know how unassured our situation is." But Freud added, "We are determined to stick it out." Freud had become stubborn and stubbornness made him a little blind.

It is striking that Freud kept his views about the Nazis very private. Freud's reticence is clear in a letter he wrote to writer George Sylvester Viereck on Easter Sunday 1933 in response to a letter Viereck had written to the *New York Herald Tribune*. Viereck had befriended Freud during World War I and had been one of those who sent him food parcels. Viereck published an interview with Freud; Einstein also granted him an interview, thinking that he was Jewish. By 1933, however, both men were disillusioned with Viereck, who had become an apologist for the Nazis. Viereck also was a cousin of the Hapsburg Crown Prince, who had become a vocal supporter of the Nazis. The Crown Prince assured the press that no one in Germany suffered injustice on account of their religion. Astutely the Crown Prince offered, in support of this claim, Neville Chamberlain's statement that he was not concerned with the alleged atrocities but would heed official Nazi announcements. At the time Chamberlain was Chancellor of the Exchequer.

Freud knew Viereck wanted him to comment, and Freud told him he would have done so, "and it would have been quite extensive, were I not concerned that you might somehow use it for publicity." Freud told Viereck that he replied on the understanding that the letter would stay private. Viereck had "debased [himself] by siding with those wretched lies in [his] royal cousin's letter," Freud said sharply. But the point was made privately.

7

The Poet and the Analyst

Freud had told his nephew Sam that they intended to stick it out, by which Freud meant continuing to live and work as normal.

One of the most vivid descriptions of Freud at work in his last years comes from notes taken by the American poet, H.D., which she worked up into a small book, *Tribute to Freud*. Hilda Doolittle was an immensely gifted writer who obviously intended to write about her own analysis. Freud was hardly the first great man she met. She met Ezra Pound when she was a student and they became lovers. In 1907 Pound asked her to marry him. She did not accept, but they stayed close and Pound quickly recognized her talent as a poet. In 1919 H.D. started what would be a forty-two-year affair with Annie Ellerman, who called herself Bryher, after one of the Isles of Scilly.

Annie Ellerman was the daughter of an English financier–shipping tycoon, John Ellerman. She helped found the Pool Group, a small film production company, and she published *Film Problems of Soviet Russia,* a critique of Eisenstein and other Russian directors. She also started *Close Up,* probably the first magazine to consider film as an art form. Pool Productions made several experimental films, including *Borderline*, which was made in 1930 and starred Paul Robeson, and his wife, Essie, as well as Doolittle. Bryher astutely compared the pleasures of film production to childhood play. She noted, "I think it is because studios are nurseries on a large scale, with full-size blocks, trains, people, etc., to play with." It is a nice image, Hollywood as a Wendy House.

Bryher first met Freud in 1927 when she did something typically impulsive. She was in Venice. "I saw a flight to Vienna and back, advertised at a moderate price, and smelt adventure." Bryher brought a letter of introduction from the pioneer sexologist Havelock Ellis. When she told Freud she had seen a storm as they flew, "I knew that he wished that he had been with us himself." Freud actually took a plane two years later, the only time he ever flew, though all he did was circle Vienna.

When Doolittle went to see Freud, she had a complicated life and a complicated history in analysis. Her daughter Perdita Schaffner described Doolittle and Bryher as platonic lesbians. Their letters to each other suggest affection and emotional intimacy rather than lust. If they were lovers, it did not stop them from sleeping with men. Doolittle had a number of lovers and Bryher would marry twice. Still the two women were bonded for life.

When Doolittle said she was unhappy in her analysis with Mary Chadwick, an English analyst who was also involved with the Pool Group, Bryher suggested that she go into analysis with Hans Sachs, one of Freud's closest friends. Sachs, however, tended to mix in discussions of film and social chitchat with his interpretations. Doolittle was suspicious of him and wrote to Bryher—they wrote every day when they were apart—that she wondered if Sachs was motivated by "your dollars, my analysis, or my beaux yeaux-es?" Sachs clearly wanted rather more from his patient than he should have; to Freud's horror, Sachs arranged for Doolittle to stay on the same floor of the same hotel as he was. Doolittle then asked Sachs for an introduction to Freud. Sachs could hardly refuse.

In *Tribute to Freud*, Doolittle explains that she went to see Freud because she hoped "to fortify and equip [herself] to face the war when it came" and that meant understanding her neuroses. Her book is not, as she confesses, "a historical sequence." She digresses into the reasons for her own neuroses and seesaws between the two periods when she spent time with Freud—1933–34 and five years later when he came to London. Nevertheless, she gives one of the most intimate accounts of what it was like to be treated by Freud.

Doolitte consulted Freud when there were disturbances in Vienna. The porter at her hotel warned her not to become involved in any political discussions and, indeed, not to go out at all. Doolittle ignored him but she soon discovered that his advice was sensible. Armed men stopped her on the street and demanded to know where she was going. She replied in her "sketchy" German that she was going to the opera and they gave her "almost a guard of honor" to the theater.

Doolittle's "sketchy" German meant that she and Freud spoke in

English. When she arrived, Paula Fichtl, "Freud's little maid, peered through a crack in the door." Doolittle could be a good reporter when she was not on one of her journeys into her own interior. She described the consulting room in detail. The furniture was heavy; small statues and figurines stood on every table and bookcase. She noticed the framed photographs of Havelock Ellis and of Sachs. The honorary diploma from Clark University from 1909 hung on the wall. A bizarre and horrifying engraving of some nightmare, "a *Buried Alive* or some such thing done in Düreresque symbolic detail," caught her eye.

More than most of Freud's patients, Doolittle could detach herself and look. In one of Agatha Christie's books that Freud liked, a sculptor whose lover is killed consoles herself by deciding she will immortalize her dead love. Alabaster, she decides. There is an intriguing divide here between those who see the artist as romantic and those who see him as supremely detached. Doolittle knew that she would turn this experience into material. She started making notes while she was waiting to see Freud for the first time.

Doolittle wrote, "I look around the room. A lover of Greek art." No one had told her that Freud's room was "lined with treasures." A door at right angles, the exit door, led through a rather dark passage to "a little room that suggests a pantry or laboratory." Then there was the hall "beyond it where we hang our coats on pegs that somehow suggest school or college."

Freud eventually appeared and asked Doolittle why she had come. In her account, she often reports what Freud said in sometimes lengthy quotes. No one can be sure that she remembered what he had said perfectly or that she did not invent quotes, but the words she attributes to Freud feel authentic. She gets his tone, one feels. Freud comes across as a little quirky, even crotchety. Doolittle had expected to greet "the Old Man of the sea but no one had told me of the treasures that he had salvaged from the sea depth." She felt he was part and parcel of these treasures "and immensely old, old because he is weighing the soul in the balance."

Freud was struck by how interested she was in her surroundings. "You are the only person who has ever come into this room and looked at the things in the room before looking at me." At this point a chow ran out from under the couch and Doolittle bent down to greet her.

Freud warned her, "Do not touch her—she snaps—she is very difficult with strangers." The chow, Jofie, was not afraid and snuggled her nose into Doolittle's hand. While the dog snuggled and snuffled, Doolittle was thinking to herself, she said. The internal dialogue went: "You call me a stranger, do you?"

Doolittle was determined to show that she was no such thing. The fact that his chow had snuggled into her hand proved that. Freud's dog and his patient were sniffing each other out. In Doolittle's mind, however, a little instant self-analysis was proceeding. She was riffing to herself: "You are a very great man. I am overwhelmed with embarrassment. I am shy and frightened and gauche as an overgrown schoolgirl."

But she was damned if she was going to show it; her stream of challenging consciousness bubbled on: "You are a man. Jofie is a dog. I am a woman. If this dog and this woman take to each other it will prove that beyond your caustic implied criticism there is another region of cause and effect." Doolittle saw that Freud was not jealous because Jofie liked her. Good dog, good sage. His new patient realized Freud's chow was the way to Freud's heart.

When Freud asked Doolittle why she had come to see him, she thought, "What did he expect me to say?"

They were still at the polite stage, however. Doolittle said she felt she would benefit from analysis as her sessions with Mary Chadwick in London had been less than satisfactory. Freud replied in oracle mode, "We never know what is important or unimportant until after. We must be impartial, play fair to ourselves." Doolittle does not report saying anything about Sachs.

The Not Very Freudian Freud

Freud had great respect for artists and their relationship was surprisingly equal. Doolittle soon stopped being the overwhelmed schoolgirl. Freud thought that her play *Ion* was a masterpiece. She was flattered by the fact that he treated her as an intellectual equal. They shared a passion for archaeology, mythology, and Athena, the goddess of wisdom and warfare. Freud had a number of statuettes of Athena and showed Doolittle which was his favorite.

Freud often would say, "But of course you understand," and then offer Doolittle a "rare discovery, some priceless finding." One of his other patients, whom she had nicknamed the Flying Dutchman, had the same kind of relationship. Both of them were, she said, "seekers or students."

Doolittle's mood often changed during her sessions. She could be challenging one moment, nervous, even clumsy, the next. When she dropped the rug that she had wrapped around herself on the floor, she asked Freud to comment on the meaning of that fumble. He did not. She was also embarrassed because the couch was slightly too small for her.

Very early, the poet had the kind of dream patients dream in order to please their analyst. It was a dream of Moses as a baby in a basket. Freud asked her if she saw Miriam, the Pharaoh's daughter, in her dream. Given Freud's fascination with Moses, it could be argued that he wanted Doolittle to dream a dream for him.

Doolittle's description of being in analysis is often quite playful even though she had harrowing issues to deal with. There seem to have been few long silences. She offers the nice image of doing analysis as a "jigsaw" and plays on how she and Freud would play "hide and seek, hunt the slipper, hunt the thimble and patiently and meticulously patch together odds and ends of our picture puzzle." As they tried to complete the jigsaw that was Doolittle, familiar themes emerged. "Freud insisted that I myself wanted to be Moses." There were implications. "Not only did I want to be a boy but I wanted to be a hero." She had better read Otto Rank's book, *The Myth of the Birth of the Hero*, Freud suggested. It would give her perspective.

Fairly early, they seemed to have made considerable progress into Doolittle's problems, which included difficulties with men, something of a fixation on her father, and her relationship with Bryher. One day Freud said, "Today we have struck very deep." Another day Doolittle reports him saying, "I struck oil." "He used the slang of the counting house or of Wall Street," she noted. Freud went on to tell her that the contents of the oil wells, her oil wells, her hidden depths, had only just been sampled. "There is oil but there is enough left for one hundred years or more," Freud said.

Doolittle commented acidly, after a digression on the subject of the prophet Jeremiah, that the profits of the oil went to someone else. "There are astute doctors," she noted, "who will squeeze you dry with their exorbitant fees for prolonged . . . treatments."

One of the many useful insights that Paula Fichtl provides is information about fees. Freud usually charged $25 an hour, which was frankly a fortune. That was £6 an hour at the exchange rate of the time. You could buy a small house in London for £1000. So you could have 160 hours of Freud or a house. An analyst today would have to charge about $4,000 an hour to match that. Sometimes Freud reduced the fees to $15 an hour, equivalent to $2,400 today.

When Doolittle raised the question of fees, however, Freud was utterly unconcerned: "Do not worry about that. That is my concern. I want you to feel at home." In fact, of course, Bryher would have paid Doolittle's fees, but it seems Freud did not want to take more money from Bryher because she had sent money to help the publishing company.

Doolittle was the awed patient who saw that "he knew he was among those who would be counted as immortal" and also that he was very concerned about a "more imminent, a more immediate future."

In one session they discussed time. "When I said to him that time went too quickly he struck a semi comic attitude," Doolittle said.

"Time," Freud said. The word was uttered in his inimitable two-edged manner. Doolittle thought that he managed to pack into that word a "store of contradictory emotions," irony, entreaty, defiance, with a vague and tender pathos. He also had a surprisingly delicate voice.

"Time," Freud repeated. "Time gallops."

She then added a riff on time in Shakespeare. Time gallops with a thief to the gallows. Time and the gallows, images of death, of age, and as the poet Philip Larkin would put it later, "and then only the end of age."

Doolittle had read Freud's *Autobiographical Study* of 1925 where he recorded one of his few positive experiences in the United States. He went for a walk with William James. James stopped and "handed me a bag and asked me to walk on saying he would catch up with me as soon as he had got through an attack of angina pectoris." His courage impressed Freud. "I have always wished I might be as fearless as he was in the face of approaching death," he wrote.

Death was a presence in the room, like a thousand particles of dust, as Freud and Doolittle talked. Among his books there were some plays and one of them was *Alcestis*; she could not recall who had written that, but it did not matter because "the play is going on now—at any rate we are acting it, the old Professor and I. The old professor doubles the part. He is Hercules struggling with Death and he is the beloved, about to die. Moreover he himself in his own character has made the dead live, has summoned a host of dead and dying children from the living tomb."

Freud sensed how attached to him Doolittle was becoming and insisted on one point: "Please, never—I mean never at any time in any circumstance, endeavour to defend me, if and when you hear abusive remarks about my work." If she tried to do that "the anger or the frustration of the assailant will be driven deeper. . . . You will drive the hatred or the fear or the prejudice in deeper." Defending him would do no good for "antagonism once taking hold cannot be rooted out from above the surface and it thrives in a way on heated argument and digs in deeper."

Much of Freud's behavior was not very Freudian. He did not insist Doolittle always lie on the couch. He stood up sometimes rather than sitting unseen behind her. He was worried about how he and his family would cope in the political turmoil. She said, "I am also concerned but I do not openly admit this, about the Professor's attitude to a future life. One day I was deeply distressed when the Professor spoke to me about his grandchildren—what would become of them? He asked me that as if the future of his immediate family were the only future to be considered."

Doolittle, who had no idea of the deaths and suicides in Freud's family, replied that "he knew he was among those who would be counted as immortal" but the Freud she saw was concerned about a "more imminent, a more immediate future."

He "rarely used any of the now rather overworked technical terms invented by himself." She complained about the way "some doctors, psychologists and nerve specialists who form the somewhat formidable body of the International Psychoanalytic Association" use them. Freud was wry. Once she raised a topic and commented: "I suppose you would say it was a matter of ambivalence." Freud did not say. "Or do you say am-bi-valence," Doolittle added. "I don't know whether it's pronounced ambi-valence or am-bi-valence."

Freud's arm shot forward as it often did when he wanted to stress something. Then he said "in his curiously casual ironical manner": "Do you know I myself have always wondered? I often wish that I could find someone to explain these matters to me." The sage takes the Zen-like attitude. With her at least, he could make fun of the pretensions of other analysts.

Freud could keep it simple, too. At one point when Doolittle had revealed some traumatic events that had happened to her, he just said, "Perhaps you are not happy." She found herself unable to explain. "It is not a question of happiness. It is the happiness of the quest," he insisted. Freud told her that he felt she was impatient with him because she felt, sensibly enough, that it was not worth her while to love a man as old as he was.

The Promised Land

The rise of the Nazis made many Jews sympathetic to Zionism, but Freud was initially ambivalent. Both Arnold Zweig and Stefan Zweig (they were not related to each other) tried to make a life in Palestine—and both failed. Arnold was a campaigning Socialist journalist as well as a novelist. He edited the *Judische Rundschau* (*Jewish Overview*) in 1920; seven years later his novel *The Case of Sergeant Grischa* made him famous. He started therapy with Freud that year. He became close to Bertolt Brecht and eventually settled in East Germany. Stefan Zweig was a less political writer. His novels were internationally acclaimed in the 1920s and '30s. He also produced two libretti for Richard Strauss. The Nazis canceled the performance of one of the operas when Strauss insisted on acknowledging that a Jew had written the words. In his letters to both Zweigs, Freud revealed many of his anxieties. His relationship with Stefan Zweig was very much that of two equals, whereas that with Arnold Zweig was less so because the latter had been his patient.

Earlier in 1932, Freud had pointed out to Arnold Zweig that Palestine had produced nothing but religions and "presumptuous attempts to conquer the world of appearances by the inner world of inner feelings." Now that Arnold knew what life was really like there, there was also the problem that one could not be sure of a hot bath. Letters to Freud constantly complained about how primitive their life had become. On January 21, 1934, Arnold wrote from Tel Aviv: "At one moment the central heating did not function, at another the oil stove smelt. We are not prepared to give up our standard of living and this country is not yet prepared to satisfy it. . . . I don't care anymore about 'the land of my fathers.' I don't have any more Zionistic illusions either. I view the necessity of living here among Jews without enthusiasm, without any false hopes and even without the desire to scoff."

Seven days later, Freud replied: "I have long waited eagerly for your letter. . . . I am eager to read it, now that I know you are cured of your unhappy love for your so-called Fatherland. Such a passion is not for the likes of us." Quite what he meant by the last sentence is not clear.

On January 9, 1934, Max Eitingon officially gave to the Berlin Institute all of the modern furniture he had previously loaned to it. He then took a train to the French Riviera, the first leg of his journey to Palestine. He stayed a few days in the expensive resort of Cap Ferrat, took another train, this time to Marseilles, and then a ship for Haifa. Soon after he got to the Promised Land, he founded the Palestinian Psycho-Analytical Society. He was disappointed that no Arabs or Orthodox Jews were interested. Eitingon saw just four patients in his first year and never saw more than twenty patients a year. Virtually all of them were Jews from Central Europe. The rather sad letters he wrote to Freud about life in Palestine—almost no cafés, almost no cultural life—would not encourage anyone to leave Vienna for the Promised Land, even if the Nazis were baying across the border.

The Nazis might have been banned in Austria, but that did not stop their plotting. One of the best descriptions of their activities can be found in Stefan Zweig's short story "The Royal Game." Zweig is reckoned by many to be one of the greatest twentieth-century writers. The story centers around a chess game, one of whose players is Dr. B., who lives in Vienna. Given that Zweig and Freud were in constant correspondence and that Zweig lived in London after 1938 when Freud was there, it seems likely that Zweig based Dr. B. partly, at least, on Freud. Dr. B. described how the Nazis had started to position themselves to take power. "The Nazis had begun long before they re-armed their military forces to organize another army—just as dangerous and well trained—in all the neighbouring countries, the legion of the underprivileged, the downtrodden and the maladjusted. In every office, in every business, they established their so-called cells in every government department up to the private offices of Dollfuss."

The Nazi cells did not remain in hiding for long. On February 12, 1934, a gang searched the Hotel Schiff in Linz, which was owned by the Social Democratic Party. Shooting started; the police and the regular Federal Army became involved. Fighting spread to Vienna. Members of the Socialist *Schutzbund* (safety group) barricaded themselves in housing estates, including one member named after Karl Marx. The Socialists only had small arms but Dollfuss ordered the army to use artillery.

Many buildings were destroyed before the Socialists surrendered to the army on February 13. Several hundred people died and more than a thousand were wounded. The police made over fifteen hundred arrests and executed nine Socialist leaders. On February 19, 1934, Freud wrote to Marie Bonaparte, "If the Nazis come here and bring with them the same lawlessness as in Germany then of course one must leave." The next day he wrote to his son Ernst: "Thanks to the guiding principle of all journalistic reportage —of making as much noise as possible—it is probably not easy to learn from the papers what is really happening in a city where shooting is going on. What affected us most was that we were without electric light." But the matches worked at least, Freud joked. The victors were bound to make "every error that can be committed in such a situation."

After these disturbances, Dollfuss established a quasi dictatorship, but he was also a devout Catholic and had no intention of attacking the Church the way the Nazis did in Germany. There has been much controversy on how the Catholic Church resisted or failed to resist Hitler. In Germany, however, the Nazis were becoming less and less restrained. They passed edict after edict, restriction after restriction, and committed violence after violence against Jews. Kosher slaughter was banned; Jews were banned from the army even if they had served with distinction in the First World War. Jews were banned from the civil service. New laws were going to outlaw sex between Jews and non-Jews. At least German Jews were not being forcibly sterilized yet.

Seven months after he took power, Hitler forced through a "Law for the Prevention of Hereditarily Diseased Offspring." Anyone who suffered from schizophrenia, epilepsy, "imbecility," and chronic alcoholism would be sterilized. The Interior Ministry set up special Hereditary Health Courts to examine inmates of nursing homes, asylums, prisons, and homes for the elderly to decide who should be sterilized. About 360,000 disabled and mentally ill people were sterilized.

Most German doctors blithely forgot the Hippocratic Oath, which insists that the first duty of the doctor is to do no harm.

Hitler passionately hated those whom he thought "unworthy of life." His doctor, Dr. Karl Brandt, and the head of the Reich Chancellery, Hans Lammers, said Hitler had told them that sterlization was just the first step. Killing the incurably ill made more sense, but public opinion would not accept this in peacetime. "Such a problem could be more smoothly and easily carried out in war," Hitler judged, and he intended "in the event of a war radically to solve the problem of the mental asylums." He had, of course, been in one himself at the end of World War I.

"The future is uncertain," Freud wrote to his son Martin. It would be either Austrian fascism or the "swastika." Native fascism may be just about tolerable—he did not believe that Austrian Nazis would be as brutal as their German counterparts. The alternative, going to live in a foreign country, would not be pleasant, Freud added.

Daily Life at the Freuds' House

Life in a new country would be unpleasant because it would mean change, and Freud was an old man who had his routines. Paula Fichtl described the routines in detail. She was the first person to be up because she had to switch on the boiler for hot water. Freud would wake up at seven in the morning. You could set a clock by him. Freud and his wife shared a big wooden brown double bed. Almost the first thing Freud would do was to take a bath. Once the maid went into the bathroom to find "the Professor who was utterly naked" while his wife was toweling him dry. She was using a rough towel because Freud got itchy and liked to have his back scratched. Fichtl ran out flustered, but not just because she had trespassed. She also noticed that Herr Professor had a large member, she said daringly in her memoirs.

The double bed and the toweling make it clear that if Ernest Jones was right and the "passionate side of the marriage faded after Freud turned forty," the couple were still physically affectionate even in their seventies.

After Freud bathed, he and his wife had breakfast in the dining room. Then the barber would come to shave and trim Freud's beard. The Professor hated the smell of the aftershave; Fichtl noted he left it to her to pay the barber his regular one schilling. Because Freud smoked so heavily, his suits were flecked with tobacco and the smell made Fichtl slightly sick; her job was to keep his clothes looking impeccable. She sometimes hung his suits out to dry in the window at Berggasse. Freud had many fine suits and took some care choosing which one to wear every day. His socks were a problem because he had long, sharp toenails; his socks were full of holes and needed constant darning.

After breakfast, Freud would go to his study to write or to see patients. The room was impeccable. Fichtl dusted his study, his statues, and the analytic couch every morning. The dog sat at his feet. Fichtl then offers a shocking detail: Freud kept two urine bottles by his desk and was clearly in the habit of peeing into them. This is very strange because there was perfectly good plumbing in the apartment about sixteen feet away. Fichtl had to empty the bottles and clean them. This was not her only personal hygiene task. Martha Freud had explained to her when she started the job that Fichtl would sometimes find flecks of blood and fecal matter on the bedsheets, on the Professor's side. She had to make sure the sheets were clean. The rest of the bed linen, however, was changed every two weeks.

Lunch was always at 1:00 p.m. Freud liked vegetable soup because the prosthesis made it hard to chew. Often he did not finish his lunch and gave some of it to the dog, which sat by the table. Sometimes Freud had a short nap after lunch, snoozing on the analytic couch. He sometimes hummed to the dog.

Often Freud would work very late into the night. Fichtl always laid out his pajamas for him. He liked to read both in the study and in bed. His taste was eclectic. He loved Dickens, Thackeray, and detective novels including those of Arthur Conan Doyle, Dorothy Sayers, and Agatha Christie. He knew who the murderer was, or should be, most of the time, and he got extremely annoyed if he did not guess correctly. He was a fast reader and very rarely needed more than an evening to finish a book. If he was in the middle of one, he used a matchstick to mark his place.

Fichtl got on well with the Professor, who obviously was not standoffish and chatted to her at times during the day. Once she broke a statue of an angel and offered to pay to have it fixed. Freud would have none of it. When the angel came back restored, he joked that the angel was "now presentable again." At Christmas, Freud gave Fichtl gold coins, which she treasured and often did not spend. She noticed, as the 1930s progressed, that the Freuds were more worried about money. At the start of the decade, a tailor used to come every other month to measure Freud for a new suit. But that stopped around 1934.

Paula Fichtl loved Freud's wife, Martha, but she had problems with Martha's sister Minna, who became jealous of "the little maid" performing many quite personal tasks for Freud. Minna felt she had been partially replaced as the third woman in Freud's home. The home was, Fichtl said, "quiet but not happy." Freud talked about his work more to his sister-in-law than to his wife. Sometimes when she answered the phone, an instrument Freud loathed, Minna gave the impression that she was his wife.

The political situation worried Freud. On February 20, 1934, he wrote to his son Ernst: "Our attitude to the two political possibilities for Austria's future can only be summed up in Mercutio's line in Romeo and Juliet: 'a plague on both your houses.'" Freud did not send the letter at once. The next day, martial law in Vienna was repealed. Freud added a sentence to the letter: "Our government and our Cardinal expect a great deal from God's assistance." Despite his lack of belief in God, Freud was quite capable of invoking the Almighty. In a letter to Arnold Zweig, Freud spoke of the power of the Nazis and concluded, "God has much to put right there."

The choices were few. On February 25, 1934, Freud told Arnold Zweig: "You are quite right in your expectation that we intend to stick it out here resignedly. For where should I go in my state of dependence and physical helplessness? And everywhere abroad is so inhospitable. Only if there really were a satrap of Hitler's ruling in Vienna I would no doubt have to go, no matter where."

More Analytical Battles

At the start of 1934, Ernest Jones became president of the International Psychoanalytic Association. He believed it was vital to keep politics out of psychoanalysis so that it would survive in Germany. If the German Psychoanalytic Society were expelled from the International Psychoanalytic Association, it would provoke a huge crisis. Preventing expulsion would not be easy, however, Ernest Jones told Felix Boehm, because of the "storm of indignation and opposition" among some members, especially among the "exiles from Germany."

Ernest Jones consoled Carl Müller-Braunschweig: "You will know that I myself regard these emotions and ultra-Jewish attitudes very unsympathetically and it is plain to me that you and your colleagues are being made a dumping ground for much emotion and resentment which belongs elsewhere and has been displaced in your direction."

Brenda Maddox, Ernest Jones's biographer, is forced to defend one of Jones's letters in which he said that one Jewish analyst, Isidor Sadger, should be sent to a "concentration camp." (Sadger had written a memoir about Freud. The first version included many anecdotes about the early days of psychoanalysis and was quite critical in places. The Viennese Society put pressure on Sadger to rewrite the book which he duly did.) In 1934 when Jones attacked Sadger, Maddox is at pains to point out that concentration camps did not mean what they came to mean later. Perhaps, but they were still brutal places of arbitrary detention.

That same month, Ernest Jones warned Felix Boehm that Boehm might be attacked at the forthcoming international psychoanalytic congress because he had tried to negotiate with the Nazi Ministry of Culture. Jones insisted: "My only concern is for the good of psychoanalysis itself, and I shall defend the view, which I confidently hold, that your actions have been actuated only by the same motive."

The good of psychoanalysis could be compromised by Wilhelm Reich and his radical ideas. Felix Boehm, Carl Müller-Braunschweig, and Ernest Jones knew that there would be no hope of reaching any compromise with the Nazis if Reich were still a member of the German Psychoanalytic Society. But many analysts saw Reich as much a victim as a viper. Worse, no one had bothered to tell Reich he had been expelled from the international association. Edith Jacobson was supposed to inform him but she chose not to. So Reich traveled from Norway to attend the Lucerne congress on August 26, 1934, expecting to take part. When he got there, Müller-Braunschweig told him that he had been expelled.

Max Eitingon arrived for the congress from Palestine—he had only a few patients he was treating—and persuaded Ernest Jones that it would only be right to have a special arrangement for those analysts who had been forced out of Germany or had fled. They should be allowed to have individual membership in the International Psychoanalytic Association if they were now in a country with no national association. Jones was persuaded to set up an emigration office to keep track of where analysts were settling.

Freud was kept in touch with all the developments. Anna Freud and Jones were writing to each other. Soon after the congress ended, Anna Freud and Jones were both alarmed by the arrest of Edith Jacobson in Berlin. She was accused of treating patients who were Communists and of harboring at least one subversive in her house. Jones came to the city intending to help her, but Boehm told him that one of her patients had been killed (the patient's identity was never discovered) and that if Jones tried to intervene on her behalf, psychoanalysis would suffer. Jones promptly returned to Britain.

The success of the Nazis affected the ways the analysts behaved toward each other. Otto Fenichel saw that Felix Boehm had started to identify with the dictatorial style of the Nazis. Fenichel wrote: "I told him that he was already infected with the modern Fuhrer principle." Boehm often said that he was "the Fuhrer of psychoanalysis," but Fenichel enjoyed bursting his balloon by pointing out that the Führer of the couches was "a leader who in many respects trembled with more anxiety than many other leaders."

Freud's correspondence shows that many anxious friends, patients and former patients relied on him for advice on how to cope with the political uncertainties. For example on April 23, 1934, Arnold Zweig wrote: "Dear Father Freud, I am taking up my analysis again. I just cannot shake off the whole Hitler business. My affect has shifted to someone who looked after our affairs for us in 1933 under difficulties. But this affect of mine is an obsession. I don't live in the present, but am absent."

As a Gentile, Carl Jung could take a much more assertive line with the Nazis. In June 1934, he wrote to Matthias Goering that he felt he had to protect psychotherapy from psychiatrists "who had always made it their business to suppress psychotherapy." If German psychotherapy lost its independence and had to defer to psychiatry, he would resign. The letter is very telling; the status of therapy is the only issue Jung raised with the Nazis over which he threatened to resign.

In the summer of 1934, Freud left Vienna as usual for his holidays in Grinzing, but he did not enjoy a peaceful summer. No one did. On July 25, 1934, a group of Nazis stormed the chancellery in Vienna and killed Dollfuss. Many Viennese thought Hitler would invade at once, but Mussolini sent troops to the border to warn the Germans against crossing into Austria. The Western allies, however, hardly protested the murder.

Kurt von Schuschnigg succeeded Dollfuss. The new chancellor was just thirty-six years old and had only been in Parliament for seven years but had already been minister of education and minister of justice. Schusschnigg tried to keep his options open. He talked to Austria's neighbors about creating an anti-German alliance, he talked to Otto von Habsburg about restoring the Habsburg dynasty; he talked to Franz von Papen, the German envoy to Vienna, about closer links with Berlin and the Nazis. These positions were contradictory, of course, but von Schuschnigg wanted to explore every way of preserving Austria's independence.

The political uncertainty meant that Freud had fewer patients than before and so he had time to return to a subject he had never stopped thinking about: Moses. He wrote to Arnold Zweig in September 1934: "In a time of relative freedom and at a loss to know what to do with my surplus leisure [I had written something and] it has taken such a hold of me that everything else has been left undone." Freud admitted that circumstances compelled him, when it came to Moses, "to keep the completed essay secret."

On November 6, 1934, Freud wrote to Arnold Zweig again: "I have written to Eitingon that you are right in your view that it would be a risk to get my Moses published." Freud believed the Catholic Church had to be appeased because it had the power to protect psychoanalysis, but that would require some political deftness in light of an influential monk who hated all his work. "It is said that the politics of our country are made by a Father Schmidt," Freud wrote. Schmidt was a monk at the monastery of St. Gabriel near Mödling and had published papers on the religious beliefs of primitive peoples.

Schmidt had made "no secret of his horror of psychoanalysis" and in particular of the totem and taboo theory. This theory was a grim Neanderthal fairy tale which Freud devised to explain the origins of religion. Jehovah was a projection born out of insecurity. First, lusting for their mothers, some strapping Neanderthal sons murdered their father. Then overwhelmed by remorse they turned their dead father into an object of veneration—a totem—and worshipped him. Neanderthal man and woman also needed to believe in a power that would protect them in the face of the power of nature.

Father Schmidt, however, had proved to his own and to the Vatican's satisfaction, at least, that many primitive tribes had some sense that there was just one God. Schmidt complained that it was absurd to suggest, as Freud did in *Totem and Taboo*, that primitive savages behaved like "modern sex-ridden neurotics." The monk argued that savages were much more civilized.

Father Schmidt was not some lowly monk—he had the ear of the pope. An analyst, Edoardo Weiss, who had direct access to Mussolini, found that the *Italian Journal of Psychoanalysis* was forced to stop publishing and "the ban is said to come straight from the Vatican. And Father Schmidt is said to be responsible."

Father Schmidt could not stop Freud from publishing his book on Moses, but the publication would "be bound to create a sensation and it would not escape the attention of the inimical priest." Freud did not care if he were the only one who was hurt, but he suspected other analysts would suffer. He had no right to "deprive all our members in Vienna of their livelihood." It was not "quite the proper occasion for martyrdom." Freud was honest enough, however, to admit that he also had his doubts about his Moses and that "this historical novel won't stand up to my own criticism." His concerns about the work and how it would be received made him postpone any plans to publish it.

Five weeks later, on December 12, 1934, Freud admitted that his decision depressed him. "Don't say any more about the Moses book," he wrote to Arnold Zweig. He was making no progress, and he had a new worry. "My memory of recent events is no longer reliable." Freud blamed the treatment he had received for the cancer that had been diagnosed eleven years earlier. The radium treatment had shattered him. "I react to this diabolical stuff with the most frightful pain." In French he added that he often thought the game was no longer worth the candle. "Resolutions" and willpower did not help in the face of unrelenting pain.

But Moses would not let Freud rest. On March 14, 1935, Freud wrote to Arnold Zweig that he had read a new book by the German scholar Elias Auerbach, but it was disappointing. Auerbach provided no support for Freud's heretical ideas. The book did not argue that Moses was an Egyptian prince or a "fusion" of that prince and a Midianite priest. Instead of being relieved that the new book had not stolen his thunder, Freud had hoped Auerbach would provide some basis for his own ideas, making his work more historical and less of a fiction.

Electrocoagulation

On March 23, 1935, Freud had to have another surgical procedure. Hans Pichler performed an electrocoagulation to clot tissue at the back of Freud's mouth; it involved applying a high-frequency electrical current locally with a needle to stop bleeding. It was cutting-edge medicine; it was easier to bear than the radium and also succeeded in lessening the pain. That was a blessing as Freud prepared for his seventy-ninth birthday.

Arnold Zweig was one of many friends to send him his best wishes. Despite his own problems, Freud was still very aware of other people's difficulties. He worried about the state of Arnold Zweig's eyes and wondered if the optician he had recommended had helped.

Freud was resilient, but realistic. On May 2, 1935, he wrote to Stefan Zweig and admitted that his hope of enjoying spring on Mount Carmel was a mere fantasy. Now as ever "supported by my faithful Anna Antigone I could not embark on a further journey." He was referring to his daughter Anna. Freud went on to complain: "Since I can no longer smoke, I no longer want to write," but he was restless because "Moses won't let go my imagination."

Freud remained very alert to archaeological developments. He learned of an excavation at the desert site in Egypt, Tell el-Amarna, which mentioned a mysterious Prince Thothmes about whom nothing was known. "If I were a millionaire in pounds I would finance the continued excavations. This Thothmes could be my Moses and I would be able to boast I had guessed right."

By his birthday on May 6, Freud was still in pain. He complained to Lou Andreas-Salomé, one of the first women analysts, who also had a flamboyant romantic career. She wrote one of the first psycho-analytic books on female sexuality, *Die Erotik*, as well as books on Ibsen, Nietzsche, and Rainer Marie Rilke; Nietzsche and Rilke had both been her lovers. Freud now told her "what an amount of good nature and good humour it takes to endure the gruesome business of growing old." She should not expect "anything intelligent" from him because coping with his own poor health took time and energy. He quoted Mephistopheles in Goethe's Faust: "In the end we depend / On the creatures we made." Again he praised Anna. "It was very wise to have made her." Even his farewell "your old Freud" was mournful. The creatures Freud "made" have turned out to be an astonishingly successful galaxy of grandchildren and great-grandchildren.

The pressure of events made Freud more willing to confide in friends and risk the authority he always worried about compromising. On June 13, he admitted to Arnold Zweig that he told Arnold many things he had withheld from other people. Freud disliked having so much free time due to having so few patients. He also noticed that "as far as my own productivity goes it is like what happened in analysis." He had repressed working on Moses because of his doubts but "nothing could take its place. The field of vision remains empty." He was always tinkering with the text, however, and looked forward to reading his manuscript to Arnold if he came to Vienna. Freud also told Arnold that he had worries about money.

There was some good news, too. Freud had just been made an honorary member of the British Royal Society of Medicine and that would make "a good impression on the world." The image of psychoanalysis could do with a boost. Dictators and devious divines like Father Schmidt might respect it more and persecute it less. "Analysis can flourish no better under Fascism than under Communism or National Socialism," Freud said.

Freud came to a pessimistic conclusion. Arnold Zweig had been writing *Education Before Verdun,* his novel named after the longest battle ever fought. An estimated 700,000 men died or were wounded in the ten months from February 21 until December 19, 1916, fighting over the city and perhaps six miles of land. Freud discussed the novel with his daughter and told Arnold Zweig how much he admired his book and the lessons he drew from it. "Today one says to oneself: if I had drawn the right conclusions about Verdun then I should have known that I could not live among these people. We all thought it was the war and not the people but other nations went through the war as well and nevertheless behaved differently. We did not want to believe it at the time but it was true what the other nations said about the Boches."—"Boche" being French slang for Germans.

Just as Freud was being honored by the Royal Society of Medicine, Carl Jung chose to make his presence felt. There has been much controversy about his behavior and he has been accused of being a secret Nazi, a committed Nazi, and an anti-Semite. Jung always denied that he had any political interests, but he was either unforgivably naïve or he exploited the situation. He accepted the editorship of a leading psychoanalytic journal and became president of the German General Medical Society for Psychotherapy. He claimed later he was not motivated by revenge against Freud but by a desire to protect psychotherapy. Some of Jung's biographers, including Deirdre Bair, maintain that he was politically innocent, but that seems a shade unquestioning especially in the light of his writings on the German psyche.

Without telling Ernest Jones, Felix Boehm and Carl Müller-Braunschweig arranged meetings with Jungians, though Jung himself stayed away. They talked about setting up a new institute, whose director would be Matthias Goering. Goering knew that it would be extremely useful to have Jung on his side, and Goering alternately flattered and pressured him. Jung did not resist these blandishments.

From then on, Felix Boehm collaborated fully with the Nazis. He advocated harsher racial laws and expelled Jews from the German Psychoanalytic Association in December 1935. Ernest Jones became suspicious of Boehm and thought he was now "pure black," in other words, a total Nazi supporter. To Anna Freud, Jones carped that Boehm was a weak and inadequate leader: "He has neither the personality required to manage a group nor a sufficiently quick grasp of the essentials of the strategic situation."

Ernest Jones also criticized Carl Müller-Braunschweig: he "is busy coquetting with the idea of combining a philosophy of Psycho-Analysis with a quasi-theological conception of National-Socialistic ideology. . . . No doubt he will proceed further along these lines, and he is definitely anti-Semitic, which Boehm is certainly not."

But Ernest Jones was himself a little duplicitous at times. In November and December 1935, he sent telegrams urging Jewish analysts to resign from the International Psychoanalytic Association, as ever, for the good of the cause. Jones did not say that the Nazis were keen to keep the German group in the International Psychoanalytic Association because 1936 would see the Olympics held in Berlin. There was some pressure to boycott the games in America, but that did not gather very much momentum. The Nazis wanted the event to go smoothly and compromised on some of their "principles." For example, the signs that stopped Jews from going on buses were removed in Berlin. Such signs were also removed from a number of tourist attractions. The American team did not run two Jewish sprinters in the 4 x 100-meter relay, but the black sprinter Jesse Owens (who won four gold medals) claimed that he suffered more racial prejudice in America than in Berlin. He wrote that it was not Hitler who had snubbed him but Roosevelt.

The psychoanalysts failed to make use of this moment when the Nazis did not want to outrage international public opinion. Ernest Jones did not go into great detail about the way Goering's institute took over the German Psychoanalytic Association, perhaps because by the time Jones wrote the Freud biography in 1953, he questioned how he himself had behaved.

Otto Fenichel was especially critical, as usual. He noticed how his colleagues had changed. The "Aryan" members of the Germany Psychoanalytic Association "are avoiding any contact—both the slightest professional contact as well as personal contact—with their non-Aryan colleagues: an almost incredible example of the devil, who will grab your whole hand when you stretch out your little finger," Fenichel wrote.

The non-Jewish analysts might seem surprisingly easy to influence, but they were hardly the only ones. Hitler had some surprising admirers even among liberals. In 1936, David Lloyd George, the British foreign minister at the time of the Treaty of Versailles, argued that Germany was benign, even a marvel of social progress. The Communists would triumph if Hitler were to be overthrown. Lloyd George told the House of Commons: "Do not let us be in a hurry to condemn Germany. We should be welcoming Germany as our friend." He wrote an article in the *Daily Express* where he called Hitler "the George Washington of Germany." He said, "The idea of a Germany intimidating Europe with a threat that its irresistible army might march across frontiers forms no part in the new vision" and "the Germans have definitely made up their minds never to quarrel with us again."

The führer had many other admirers in England, including Sir Oswald Mosley, who founded the British Fascist movement, his wife Unity Mitford, and her sister Diana. There were six Mitford sisters, all stylish socialites. Hitler's highest-ranking British admirer was the Prince of Wales, who became Edward VIII before he abdicated in 1936. Churchill in the mid-1930s was seen as a volatile spent force in the political wilderness who exaggerated the Nazi threat. He held no government post between 1926 and 1938. In America Hitler also enjoyed considerable support. Henry Ford and William Randolph Hearst, for example, praised him.

Like most Jews, Freud worried about where he could seek refuge. He warned Arnold Zweig in a letter dated February 21, 1936, not to be tempted by the United States, even though life in Palestine made Zweig feel "isolated" and "ill at ease." Tel Aviv might not have a good café life, culture, or even constant hot water, but "at any rate you have your personal safety and your human rights." The United States would be, "I would say from all my impressions, far more unbearable." Arnold Zweig would have to give up "not an article of clothing but your own skin," by which Freud meant that he would have to stop speaking German. Then the letter became strangely optimistic. Freud believed that "the prospect of having access to Germany in a few years really does exist." The country would have changed but "one will be able to participate in the clearing-up process."

The Analysts' Final Compromise

In February 1936, the German Ministry of Culture told Felix Boehm that psychoanalysis would be allowed to continue only if the Berlin Psychoanalytic Institute came under Goering's leadership as part of a new body that would forge a "New German Psychotherapy." The Nazis were in a position to extract painful concessions. Anna Freud was prepared to discuss with Boehm the question of the German Psychoanalytic Association joining the new Goering Institute. She wrote to Ernest Jones on March 10, 1936: "I can understand why he wishes to make this attempt. If it fails, analysis has lost nothing. . . . If he *saves* a little workgroup for the future then all to the good." She would never have written that if her father had disagreed.

The Nazis demanded many compromises for their very partial support. Felix Boehm had to let Matthias Goering take over the German assets of the International Psychoanalytic Publishing House. He also arranged for the library of the Berlin Psychoanalytic Institute to be confiscated. The new Nazified German Institute for Psychological Research and Psychotherapy began with a good deal of property, much of which belonged to Jewish analysts.

On July 19, Matthias Goering, Felix Boehm, and Carl Müller-Braunschweig met Ernest Jones and A. A. Brill, who had done much to introduce psychoanalysis to the United States. Both sides had anxieties. The plotters were well aware of Freud's presence and power. Bizarrely, some Nazis had a grudging respect for psychoanalysis and even a little respect for him. The analysts were still doctors and doctors had high status in German society. Goering went so far as to promise Jones and Brill that psychoanalysis would remain an independent faculty within his new institute. Jones believed him, too.

"I found Goering a fairly amiable and amenable person, but it turned out later that he was not in a position to fulfill the promises he made to me about the degree of freedom that was to be allowed the psychoanalytical group. No doubt in the meantime the Jewish origin of psychoanalysis had been fully explained to him," Ernest Jones wrote. This was a bizarre claim. Matthias Goering had known Freud's work for over twenty years and the Nazis had been attacking analysis for over fifteen years. After that meeting Jones and Goering exchanged letters, but the Nazi had the sense not to end these letters with his customary "Heil Hitler."

The new institute began work on May 26, 1936, and soon became known as the Goering Institute. Matthias Goering did nothing to discourage that. In his inaugural lecture in October, he told his audience the new German psychotherapy would flourish but on a non-Freudian, pro-Nazi, and anti-Semitic basis. Students who wanted to train as analysts would have to read that penetrating work of psychology, *Mein Kampf*. Carl Jung did not object to these arrangements. According to Ellen Bartens, who worked at the institute as a secretary, "Freud's name was never mentioned, and his books were kept in a locked bookcase." Freudian terms were renamed; the Oedipus complex, for example, became the "family complex." The words might be different but the concepts were much the same.

Freud could have issued a strong statement condemning the new institute, but he did not do so. It might have made a difference. Even Felix Boehm did not want to be excommunicated by Freud and went to Vienna to assure him of his loyalty. He had not really sinned, but

Freud said to him: "Different peoples, with different destinies, have developed a capacity, varying in strength, of holding on to their convictions, even if they have to be abandoned on the outside. Our Jewish people have had the misfortune, or fortune, of accumulating a host of experiences of this kind. . . . Other peoples are less capable of resisting, and when they give in on the outside, they eventually give in on the inside too. It will all depend on what you hold on to inside." We only know of this conversation now because Fenichel recorded them in his *Rundbriefe* or round-robins. No one outside of Freud's closest associates knew at the time that he had said this.

After Felix Boehm left 19 Berggasse, Freud said he did not believe psychoanalysis would survive in Germany. "They are a submissive people," he said, according to one of Fenichel's *Rundbriefe* of November 30, 1936. Freud had made the same judgment when discussing Arnold Zweig's *Education Before Verdun*.

In September, Carl Jung exchanged letters with A. A. Roback, a Polish-born psychologist and student of Yiddish culture. Jung said, "Concerning my so-called Nazi affiliation there has been quite an unnecessary noise about it." He claimed he was defending analysts and the "Jewish science" and that he had stepped in to defend Jewish analysts.

Matthias Goering made good use of his family connections. In 1937 he established close links with the Health Department of the Reich Interior Ministry as well as contacts with Hitler Youth, the League of German Girls, the SS Lebensborn, and the Reich Criminal Police Office. The flourishing institute set up local branches in Munich, Stuttgart, Düsseldorf, Wuppertal, and Frankfurt am Main. Goering remained suspicious of Felix Boehm, however, because he assumed Boehm had been closer to Freud than Matthias was. Matthias banned him from teaching.

The institute even had a bit of an admirer in Hitler because Hitler had been appalled when he learned how many German doctors were Jewish. The worst statistics from a Nazi point of view concerned pediatricians: 72 percent were Jewish. On June 14, 1937, Hitler explained to Martin Bormann how important it was to move against Jewish doctors "since the duty of the physician is or should be one of racial leadership. It was important to wean the Aryans away from their dependency on Jewish doctors." It has been estimated that as late as 1937, 75 percent of German Jewish doctors had not even tried to leave.

The institute turned out to have a surprisingly important role in the Third Reich. Goering persuaded many of the Nazi leadership that it could serve the needs of the German people by developing a "Nazified" psychotherapy. Neurotic Nazis would become more efficient. This was just what Carl Müller-Braunschweig had suggested in 1933.

Goering was rewarded for his efforts. When the second conference of the German General Medical Society for Psychotherapy—as the German Psychoanalytic Association had been renamed—took place in Düsseldorf in 1938, Hitler sent a telegram thanking the society for its "vow of fidelity and for the announcement of the establishment of a German Institute for Psychological Research and Psychotherapy." He wished it "great success in [its] work."

There is no way of knowing if Freud learned of Hitler's congratulatory telegram but, if he did, he would have enjoyed the irony. The Nazis who loathed psychoanalysis were supporting an institute that publicly condemned Freud but privately kept on using many of his ideas and techniques. Geoffrey Cocks claims that although Jews were formally excluded, a tiny number somehow kept working at the institute until the end of the war. Cocks also draws attention to the fact that Harald Schultz-Hencke, whose wife was Jewish, did not merely survive but thrived. Schultz-Hencke became the chief psychiatrist to the German army.

During the war, Goering's institute would play a role that shows again how ambivalent the Nazis were toward therapy. Psychoanalysis might be a "dirty" Jewish science but the Third Reich was more than willing to use its insights, for example, to help Luftwaffe pilots. Some Jewish analysts were also astonishingly unrealistic. A prime example was Georg Groddeck, who had written about the id. Groddeck imagined quite seriously that if he could only get to meet Hitler and persuade him to agree to analysis by a Jew, the reasons for his anti-Semitic paranoia would soon become clear. The führer could be healed. Groddeck's close friend, the analyst Karen Horney, spent hours trying to explain to him why this was not a practical proposal and would almost certainly end with Groddeck being murdered. Horney left for Chicago soon after she had advised her friend.

Freud and Zionism

As the decade progressed, it would seem that Freud became more Jewish than ever. A memoir by Joseph Wortis, one of Freud's patients,

shows how loyal Freud was to Jews. Wortis had been reading about
Einstein and told Freud that, though Einstein seemed likeable, "I
confess I am not easily in sympathy with his or your Jewish nationalism." Wortis wondered, "How far ought I to let my allegiance to
Jews bring me?"

"That is not a problem for Jews," Freud replied, "because the
Gentiles make it unnecessary to decide; as long as Jews are not admitted into Gentile circles they have no choice but to band together." He
added that "ruthless egotism is much more common among Gentiles
while family and intellectual life are on a higher plane among Jews."

Rather amazed, Wortis replied, "You seem to think that the Jews
are a superior people."

"I think nowadays they are," Freud said. To emphasize the point,
Freud asked Wortis to consider the high number who had won Nobel
Prizes. Freud also now became more interested in Zionism—and sym-
pathetic to those who believed in it.

Freud was struck by the fact that Max Eitingon and Stefan Zweig remained in Palestine. Albert Einstein and Chaim Weizmann persuaded
Freud to become a trustee of the Hebrew University in Jerusalem.
Palestine was no longer just a place of religious delusions. Freud even
wrote to Stefan Zweig a little mystically about the Land of Israel "and
we hail from there. Our forebears lived there for perhaps a whole
millennium and it is impossible to say what heritage from this land we
have taken over into our blood and nerves."

Freud also wrote very warmly of Montague David Eder, an
English analyst who wrote a book *War-Shock* and then moved to
Palestine, where he worked with Weizmann. Eder was elected to the
Zionist Executive in Palestine and served from 1921 to 1927. When
he died in 1936, Freud confided to British psychoanalyst Barbara
Low that Eder represented "a rare blend of courage and an absolute
love of truth, together with tolerance and a great capacity to love."
Eder remained a firm Zionist to the day he died. The real change in
Freud's Jewish identity was that he had some sympathy for Zionism.
It would be quite wrong to suggest he became a Zionist, but it did not
seem deluded for Jews to want to build something in a land to which
they had a claim.

Marthe Robert, the author of *From Oedipus to Moses* claims that in his writings on Moses, Freud was making a final attempt to deal with his relationship with his father and suggests that Freud began to fear he was becoming more and more like "the old man." We have seen that Freud identified with Goethe. Freud noted that "even the great Goethe, who in his years of storm and stress had undoubtedly looked down on his unbending and pedantic father, developed traits that formed part of his father's personality." Freud had not identified with his father when he was a little boy, Robert argues, because Jacob was not strong enough. Now as an old man, Freud might finally do what little boys did to resolve their Oedipus complex, identify with his father. His book on Moses was central to that process, she argues.

By the end of 1935 Freud had a draft of his Moses book, a draft he was too frightened to publish. He had never expected to find himself in such a quandary as he neared his eightieth birthday.

8
Freud's Eightieth Birthday

Freud wrote three pessimistic letters at the end of 1935 and in January 1936. "It goes so overall bad in the world, why should psychoanalysis have it any easier?" he wrote to Oskar Pfister, a Swiss Protestant clergyman, at the end of November 1935. A month later Freud complained to Hilda Doolittle that Vienna was gloomy and that "it reminds me of those bygone days when I was still able to move around and visit the sunshine and beauty of southern nature myself." She had given him a plant that was related to the tobacco plant, which "used to do so much for me in former times but now can do little."

Early in 1936, Freud wrote to the dramatist and poet Richard Beer-Hofmann, "Life has gone by in the endless tension of demanding work and now that I have more leisure time, there's not much I feel like doing anymore." Freud could not even face contributing to a Festschrift for the seventieth birthday of his old friend Romain Rolland who had won the Nobel Prize for Literature in 1915. Rolland is best known now for his ten-volume novel *Jean-Christophe*, but he was influential in the theatre, too, both as a theorist and as a playwright. His ideas for a "people's theater" anticipated some of Brecht's. Freud and Rolland had been corresponding for fifteen years, but Freud told Victor Wittkowski, who was organizing the Festschrift, "I would like to give but have nothing to give."

Some of Freud's loyal followers had no intention of letting him wallow in misery as his birthday neared. A. A. Roback, one of Freud's devotees, wanted to publish a testimonial to mark Freud's eightieth birthday. Roback invited many luminaries to contribute, including George Bernard Shaw, H. G. Wells, President Masaryk of Czechoslovakia, the psychiatrist Adolf Meyer (who had worked with the behaviorist John B. Watson, a man Freud thought daft for denying the existence of consciousness), as well as the psychologist William McDougall, who is best remembered for his work on instincts. Most of these luminaries did not send encouraging replies, but worst of all, Freud himself "frowned upon the project." Ernest Jones rebuked Roback, who replied, "I was not aware that anyone could possibly object to a Festschrift in his honor."

Freud had a sensible reason for doing so, however; he told A. A. Roback the possible contributors included many people who had no connection with psychoanalysis, some who knew nothing about it and others who were its "declared enemies." He hoped no one would contribute. Roback's idea of bringing out a volume for the fiftieth anniversary of the creation of psychoanalysis was also a fantasy. "I don't know what ignorant journalist is responsible for this fairy tale," Freud barbed. Analysis was born between 1895 and 1900. By 1945 or 1950, when it would be fifty years old, Freud was sure he would be dead. He then seems to have remembered that it was rather rude to scold and said he regretted that "a meritorious man" like Roback should find himself involved with such a project.

Freud did not feel like celebrating and was more honest to a man he respected more than A. A. Roback. He told Romain Rolland that his days of glory were so long past. He recalled he had had "passionate desire to travel and see the world" when he was a boy. Seeing the world was also escaping the poverty that he had grown up in, as well as the limitations of his family. Freud was always aware of natural beauty. "When one first sees the sea, dips the toe in the ocean, looks at the sights in foreign cities, fulfilling what had long seemed unattainable things of desire one feels oneself like a hero who has performed feats of improbable greatness." His days of greatness were behind him now, he told Rolland.

On February 20, 1936, Freud's physician Max Schur was concerned by the state of Freud's jaw and noted, "It doesn't look good." Hans Pichler was worried that the operation he performed three weeks later "was probably enough to destroy the whole mucous membrane, but at the edge" there were still problems. Two weeks later Freud started to suffer migraines, which were unusual for him. He also started to lose things. All that did not put him in a happy frame of mind for turning eighty. "Everyone will expect something from me and I shall not be capable of doing it," he told Marie Bonaparte. Then, as if to prove the point, he addressed his letter to the wrong street. It was sent to rue Yvon Adolphe rather than to the correct rue Adolphe Yvon.

Freud had canceled one birthday party when he turned fifty. "We only made a fuss about celebrating landmarks such as our sixtieth, seventieth, and eightieth birthdays as a way of fooling ourselves about the fact that none of us can avoid death." So he was not in the mood and made sure there was no party. Paula Fichtl had to receive many flower bouquets and other presents.

Einstein sent congratulations, which pleased Freud especially because Einstein said that he was coming to see the truth of analytic ideas. Freud replied that he had known that Einstein only admired him "out of politeness" and had been convinced by few of his theories. He was very happy that Einstein seemed more positive toward analysis now. Einstein was much younger and Freud hoped that by the time Einstein reached the age of eighty, he would have become a disciple. Deftly, Freud then poked fun at his own wish, quoting Goethe, who had written of "the lofty bliss" of anticipation. It was a charming letter. The press even produced a caricature of Freud and Einstein. Ludwig Binswanger, a Swiss psychiatrist, wrote to Freud, "As is well known one can put up with any amount of praise."

On May 6, 1936, Freud turned eighty. The minister of education sent congratulations but the government ordered newspapers not to report the minister's kind words in case they upset the Nazis. Freud told Arnold Zweig that he had received "not many numerous" presents of antiques but that he was especially pleased with the signet ring Zweig sent him. Like a wise but disappointed child, Freud added that for all the birthday celebrations, "I am the same as before."

Three great novelists paid tribute. One was Selma Lagerlöf, the first woman to win the Nobel Prize for Literature. Stefan Zweig produced a glowing tribute in the *Sunday Times*, while Thomas Mann gave a lecture two days later at the Vienna Academy of Medicine. In fact, Mann first delivered "Freud and the Future" in Freud's home in Bergasse, a preview that Freud rather enjoyed because the future would be glowing. One day his work would be seen as the foundation "of a new anthropology and of a new structure, to which many stones are being brought up today, which shall be the future dwelling of a wiser and freer humanity," Mann said. The science of the unconscious was more than a therapeutic method. "Call this, if you choose, a poet's utopia." Mann knew that Freud believed the future "would probably judge the significance of psychoanalysis as a science of the unconscious to be much greater than its value as a treatment. But even as a science of the unconscious psychoanalysis is still a treatment, a super individual treatment, a treatment of great style." Freud was touched and called Mann a noble *goy*; he had doubted such a creature existed, he said to Stefan Zweig.

Freud received so many congratulations that he had a card printed saying, "My sincere thanks for your kind remembrance on the observance of my eightieth birthday. Your Freud," it was signed. To Hilda Doolittle, he added that he hoped she would forgive him "this barbaric reaction to such loving expressions of friendship." He then went into dog lover mode. Jofie came into his bedroom to show him her affection in her own fashion, something she had never done before or since. Freud, the soppy dog lover, asked, "How does a little animal know when a birthday comes around."

On May 18, Freud thanked Stefan Zweig for his tribute and said he and Mann's speech "almost reconciled me to growing old." Almost but not quite, as he found it hard to accept "the wretchedness and helplessness of old age." He had been "exceptionally happy" with his wife and his children, especially with Anna. But death would come in the end. He "could not spare his loved ones the pain of separation."

Arnold Zweig now wanted to write a biography, but again Freud was having none of it. "I am too fond of you to permit such a thing. Anyone who writes a biography must engage in lies, concealments, hypocrisy, flattery and even hiding his own lack of understanding, for biographical truth does not exist and, if it did, we could not use it." He was "not the most interesting person in your wax museum" and quoted his beloved Hamlet. Was the prince "not right when he asks who would escape whipping were he used after his desert?"

Arnold Zweig accepted Freud's verdict and never asked again. The Hamlet quote led to a discussion of Shakespeare. Zweig gently poked fun at Freud's belief that Edward de Vere, the 17th Earl of Oxford, had written all of Shakespeare's plays. (This theory has now become the subject of a feature film, *Anonymous*, which has advertised itself as the oldest conspiracy theory.) Freud had been convinced by a book written by an author with the telling name of Thomas Looney. Then, in a letter on June 17, Freud had fun at the expense of the old adversary. He thought it was to their credit, he told Zweig, that "our archenemy" Father Schmidt had received a decoration from the Austrian government for "his pious lies" in the field of ethnology.

Freud sniped that he imagined this was a consolation for the fact that Schmidt had to deal with the trauma that Freud had survived to the age of eighty. Freud's father and his half brother Emanuel had only lived to the age of eighty years and six months, Freud told Zweig. Death was very much on his mind.

The Cancer Returns

Early in July 1936, Freud's cancer returned. The electrocoagulation Hans Pichler had performed had only given temporary relief. Freud wrote to Marie Bonaparte in December that he kept brooding on whether he would reach the age his father and brother had reached, let alone that of his mother. On December 12, Pichler performed another operation using "short-wave treatments with a portable machine." This was a considerable innovation, Max Schur noted with some admiration.

Freud now faced a crisis that related to the early days of analysis. Wilhelm Fliess whose laws of periodicity had so entranced him in the 1890s died in 1928. Fliess's widow, Ida, knew that her husband and Freud had corresponded at great length. In 1931 she asked Freud to find her husband's letters. Freud had destroyed them, in fact, but pretended otherwise to a woman who in private he called "the witch." He made excuse after excuse and tried to palm her off by saying he could not find them. His apartment had so many nooks and crannies that it could take forever to unearth them. Finally he had to confess, not the truth, which was that he had taken the dramatic step of destroying the letters, but that they had been mysteriously lost. Ida now asked him to buy back his own letters and demanded 12,000 schillings. Freud did not have the money but he wanted the letters badly; they could damage his reputation, as he had discussed various mistakes, even tragedies of the 1890s. One was the death of Ernst Fleischl, Freud's teacher whom he had tried to wean off morphine with cocaine; a second calamity was the botched treatment of Emma Eckstein. Fliess had operated on her nose, cauterized it with cocaine, and forgotten to remove a long piece of surgical gauze, an error that nearly led to Eckstein bleeding to death. The letters also make it obvious that Freud did not stop using cocaine until around 1900. Attitudes to cocaine had changed radically since then. The 1912 Hague International Opium Convention saw twelve countries including the United States, Britain, and France agree to make the use of cocaine, opium, and hashish illegal unless prescribed by a doctor. It would delight the Nazis to be able to depict Freud as a drug addict. When it was clear Freud could not pay, Ida Fliess sold the letters to a dealer and also wrote to Marie Bonaparte.

Freud's failure to cure Marie Bonaparte's frigidity—and even his advice that it would be unwise to commit incest with her son—had not made her less loyal to him. She had started to translate his works into French and to take on patients herself. Her methods were even more unorthodox than those of her mentor. Chauffeurs were sent in Bentleys and Rolls-Royces to bring her patients to her house in Saint-Cloud, where they were often analyzed in the garden, with the therapist crocheting while she listened. When she traveled to Athens or Saint-Tropez, she encouraged her patients to come with her and put them up in her villa.

Marie Bonaparte bought the letters, but that was not the end of the matter. Freud wanted them destroyed but the Princess refused. They were of great historical importance, she said. Freud was very annoyed but he had to defer to her. They made a bargain, however. She promised not to read the letters and seems to have kept that promise. They were not published until 1984, twenty-two years after she died.

Disagreements about the letters did not damage their friendship, as became clear in an extraordinary episode. At the end of 1936, Freud congratulated Marie Bonaparte on the book she had just finished writing. It was "moving and genuine" and revealed the "analyst's thirst for truth and knowledge," Freud told her.

The book was not about female sexuality, but about her dog. *Topsy* is a touching and, at times, frankly loopy memoir that tells how the Princess's chow suffered from cancer and how Marie Bonaparte faced the possibility of her pet's death. Freud recognized that the book was an odd love story, but he agreed to translate it into German. He even asked the princess whether Topsy realized she was being translated. The memoirs of Topsy would eventually appear in French, German, and English.

Some of the chapter headings sound like parodies—"Topsy and Shakespeare," "On the Frontiers of Your Species," and "Implorations to the God of the Rays." I am not going to suggest that Freud identified with the dog, but there is little doubt that what made the memoir touching for him was not just that he loved dogs himself but that Topsy had cancer, as he did himself. The book started: "Somewhere in Paris here is a huge house where steel apparatus of a fiendish appearance glitters in the dim light of armour plated rooms. They produce mysterious rays which sometimes heal poor human suffering from the most horrible diseases."

Marie Bonaparte asked why she had not interceded for Topsy with the deity "who reigns over these realms" and knew the answer. Dogs were not supposed to receive the most advanced radiotherapy. She would later bring the doctor who treated Topsy to London to examine Freud. Topsy might be a dog, but "life, august life, dwells in her humble body."

After Topsy was X-rayed, her besotted owner had to wait to see if the rays worked their magic. Did they destroy "the death-dealing cells" or did the cancer survive so that these necrotic cells "grafted themselves on her breathing lungs?" Freud knew those issues all too well. He told the Princess she had managed to explain something he had experienced—why it was possible to love an animal like Topsy or his own dog, Jofie, with extraordinary intensity. In a 1936 letter to Stefan Zweig, Freud had discussed the sensitivities of his dog; now he told him that his "beloved dog Jofie is a stickler for accuracy." The dog did not like being called Zofie, as Zweig had called her. Her real name was Jofie, "Jo as in Jew," Freud added.

Marie Bonaparte told Freud that when she and Topsy were cocooned in the garden of her villa in Saint-Cloud, they were completely happy, "a kind of unique self-absorbed couple." In his response, Freud even quoted an aria from *Don Giovanni* and the line "a bond of friendship unites us both." Their mutual dog admiration society knew few limits. "Topsy knew nothing of the complication of human quarrels and only knew how to love me," the Princess said. Topsy offered "respite from human ambiguity. You either hate, as you hate cats, frankly, totally without limit or you love bouncing with joy when I return."

The book was illustrated with frankly sentimental pictures of Topsy. Freud even made sure the book was published in German by Allert de Lange, who published many of his own books. Freud devoted time to this when he was quite ill and finding that pain made him "grumpy." This time the postoperative recovery was especially long.

Hitler as Wotan

While Freud was translating *Topsy*, Carl Jung published his most serious essay on the Nazis. *Wotan* is a curiously ambivalent work, and parts are often quoted out of context by both those who accuse Jung and those who defend him. He described Germany as "infected" by "one man who is obviously 'possessed'" and as "rolling towards perdition."

Those who remembered 1914, Jung began, "find ourselves living in a world of events which would have been inconceivable before the war." Intelligent people believed war between civilized nations would become "a fable, an absurdity" in our "rational, internationally organized world." Instead the world had conjured up "a veritable witches' Sabbath." Jung did not blame native human aggression, as Freud had done in *Why War*, but the decay of religion. Christianity was a projection of the God-image in the unconscious and, while it ruled, we were God-fearing and Church-controlled. But as we had become free from superstition, "the archetypes" had "come loose from their moorings. The result was widespread alienation; more precisely, modern man has put himself at the mercy of the psychic "underworld."

Bertolt Brecht compared Hitler to a gangster in *The Resistible Rise of Arturo Ui*, but Carl Jung was more romantic. The führer should be likened to the old god of storm and frenzy, Wotan. Jung wrote: "There is no question but that Hitler belongs in the category of the truly mystic medicine man. As somebody commented about him at the last Nuremberg party congress, since the time of Mohammed nothing like it has been seen in this world. This markedly mystic characteristic of Hitler's is what makes him do things which seem to us illogical, inexplicable, curious and unreasonable. . . . So you see, Hitler is a medicine man, a form of a spiritual vessel, a demi-deity or, even better, a myth."

While there were many Christians in prewar Germany, "the god of the Germans is Wotan and not the Christian God." Carl Jung added—and here he was in agreement with Freud—that gods have always personified psychic forces. Wotan appealed to a specifically German characteristic, which Jung defined as *Ergriffenheit*—a state of being seized or possessed. It is a state that requires both an *Ergrif-*

fener (one who is seized) and an *Ergreiffer* (one who seizes). Wotan is an *Ergreiffer* of men and, Jung added, "unless one wishes to deify Hitler—which has indeed actually happened—he is really the only explanation." Even *Punch*, the satirical British magazine, agreed. Jung added: "It was soon after Hitler seized power, if I am not mistaken, that a cartoon appeared in *Punch* of a raving berserker tearing himself free from his bonds."

Hitler was Wotan's mouthpiece. The image could have prompted Carl Jung to comment about some of the orgies of Nazi violence, but he said nothing about the Nazis burning the books or the attacks against Jews but recorded that "the Hitler movement literally brought the whole of Germany to its feet, from five-year-olds to veterans, and produced a spectacle of a nation migrating from one place to another." The power of Wotan was not merely destructive; he also was a "superlative magician and artist in illusion who is versed in all secrets of an occult nature."

Carl Jung condemned Wotan-cum-Hitler at only one point where he suggested: "Hitler is an illusion. I venture the heretical suggestion that the unfathomable depths of Wotan's character explain more of National Socialism than all three reasonable factors put together." Both Jung and Wilhelm Reich, utterly different men and theorists, realized that the appeal of the Nazis had so much to do with the unconscious energies they harnessed.

Carl Jung went on to say that "one man, who is obviously 'possessed,' has infected a whole nation to such an extent that everything is set in motion and has started rolling on its course toward perdition." Germans now had "an opportunity, perhaps unique in history, to look into their own hearts and to learn what those perils of the soul were from which Christianity tried to rescue mankind," but he was not optimistic because "Germany is a land of spiritual catastrophes." He predicted, "National Socialism would not be the last word." Wotan's reawakening would unleash other forces. Jung ended that "the Obstruction will not last forever; it is rather a *reculer pour mieux sauter*, and the water will overleap the obstacle. Then, at last, we shall know what Wotan is saying when he 'murmurs with Mímir's head.'" Mímir was a figure in Norse mythology who was famous for his knowledge and wisdom but was beheaded during the Æsir-Vanir War. Afterward, the god Odin carried Mímir's head, which murmured its secret knowledge and counsels to him.

Carl Jung's ambivalence to the Nazis aroused controversy in the United States. Harvard proposed to give him an honorary doctorate, but there were protests from Jewish analysts. These protests did not succeed any more than protests against the Berlin Olympics had. Those who campaigned against Jung were told their protests were motivated by scientific jealousy. Jung was delighted he did not have to cancel his trip.

The analysts certainly could have done with Mímir's counsel.

The Imperfections of Analysts

On February 2, 1937, Freud learned of the death of his old friend Lou Andreas-Salomé. The Gestapo ransacked her house and destroyed many of her books, those written by Jews. Freud had been close to her, but their once quite intense friendship had become less important to him. He took her death as another reminder that he himself had not long to live. He had some consolations, especially his grandchildren. Grandson Clement Freud recalled that his father took him to Vienna where he had pillow fights with Paula Fichtl and sat dutifully at meals. Once he was taken for a walk by his grandfather, "me holding one hand, the leash of his Alsatian dog in the other. On that walk we came across a man having an epileptic fit. The man's hat had fallen from his head and, as he twitched and salivated, people placed money into the hat as a token of sympathy. We walked away, grandfather, the dog and I. Why did you not give him any money, I asked. Grandfather looked at me and said: 'He did not do it well enough.'" Freud had not lost his wit.

Freud had also been working on an old problem. As early as 1900, he had written to Wilhelm Fliess about a Herr E., a patient who was making good progress but had problems with transference. Herr E. had what seemed to be a simple choice to make: he could get better or he could persist in being ill. Freud tried to end the analysis but there were resistances; the patient did not want to let go of the process and, of course, of the precious sessions themselves. The sheer length of analysis had led to much criticism; it was not supposed to be a lifelong procedure. Freud now published the paper "Analysis Terminable and Interminable," which confronted the issue, and he did so in combative style. The origins lay in a quarrel with Otto Rank, who had once been close to Freud.

Otto Rank claimed he could finish an analysis in four months. This act of defiance led to another question, Freud said: "Is there such a thing as a natural end to an analysis?" Analysis should only end if the patient has been cured of symptoms, inhibitions, and anxieties, Freud insisted. That was only possible if enough repressed material had been made conscious and if enough resistances had been overcome. Otherwise the symptoms could return.

If the main problem was some underlying trauma, it should be possible to work toward a "definitively terminated" analysis. Freud had cured one patient, the Rat Man, of his obsessional neuroses in just over a year. But if it was not just a trauma, concluding the analysis would be trickier. Negative factors that would make it harder to end an analysis included: if a patient had very powerful instincts, if he was very aggressive, and if he was rigid in his attitudes.

The paper shows Freud's rather depressed mood in 1937. At the very end, he refers to a paper written ten years earlier by Sandor Ferenczi that said that analysis "is not an endless process." If the analyst had enough skill and patience, it should be possible to bring an analysis to a "natural end." A good analyst should have learned from mistakes and also would have "got the better" of the weak points in his, or her, own personality. The imperfection of analysts was the trouble as "in their own personalities (they) have not invariably come up to the standard of the psychical normality to which they wish to educate their patients."

"Normal" was not an adjective that applied to that many analysts, Freud thought. Carl Jung was repressed and deceitful; Alfred Adler had left the Vienna group because he could not bear deferring to Freud; Otto Gross was a cocaine addict who organized a free love commune and died penniless on the street; Victor Tausk committed suicide after Freud told his analyst to stop treating him; Ernest Jones had endless difficulties with women; Wilhelm Reich had even more difficulties with women and thought sexual energy rained down from outer space in the form of orgone dust. No wonder Freud complained to Swiss psychiatrist Ludwig Binswanger, "What a gang." But Freud had nearly always complained in private. In public, he had insisted that no one expected doctors to be utterly healthy. A surgeon who had breathing problems could still operate on diseased lungs. Analysts had acquired "a particular art" and they should be allowed "to be human beings like anyone else."

Freud offered the analyst sympathy "in the very exacting demands" of his work. He compared the job to two other "impossible professions (which) are teaching and government." Part of the problem was that training analyses were too short. They had to be concluded quickly so that the fledgling analyst could start work on patients.

The imperfections of analysts were not the only reasons some analyses lasted too long, but Freud said little of a more empirical issue. Every analyst was supposed to judge when the cure had been achieved. There were no objective criteria. Freud had never allowed any study to be made of how successful analysis was, which might have led to some agreement as to when the treatment could be stopped. Nicholas Rand and Maria Torok argue this was the deeply buried legacy of Uncle Josef and his forgeries. If one produced something very definite, whether it was a well set out theory or a banknote, it could be judged—true or false, real or fake. That was an absolute Freud wanted to avoid, they claimed.

Just after the paper on interminable analysis was published, Freud wrote to Marie Bonaparte that when he died, he hoped "you will quickly console yourself and let me live in your friendly memory—the only form of limited immortality I recognise." He had not lost his black sense of humor, however, as he described an American ad which he considered "the boldest and most successful" example of American publicity he had ever seen. It was for a cemetery. *"Why live if you can be buried for ten dollars?"*

The political anxieties continued. In March 1937, Freud wrote to Ernest Jones that there was probably no way of preventing the Nazis from invading Austria. "My only hope is that I shall not live to see it. It is a similar situation to 1681 when the Turks were besieging Vienna. . . . If our town falls, the Prussian barbarians will flood over Europe."

One of Anna Freud's oldest and closest friends tried to persuade the Freuds to flee while they still could. Anny Rosenberg Katan had splashed Anna with water when both girls were seven; the memory of the incident apparently made Anna hesitate about analyzing her old friend when Katan asked her to do so in the 1920s. By 1934, Katan was married, divorced, remarried, and realistic. She and her husband left for Holland. She wrote a nicely WASPish account of her conversations with the Freuds:

I tried to warn them before I left Vienna. . . . Freud's humorous fantasy was that the Austrians were so disorderly that they would also be disorderly in applying Hitler's ideas, views and laws. I told him that the disorderliness of the Austrians would play no role because the Germans would follow. I could not persuade him. Freud and Anna really tried to prove that nothing would happen. It shows what a great role denial can play even in personalities like Professor Freud and Anna.

After a gap of five years, the correspondence with the Manchester Freuds suddenly started again. Polly Hartwig wrote to tell Freud that his nephew Sam was ill. Freud thanked her and said that he was sorry that he had not been a "Furstlicher" uncle—*furstlicher* means "nobler"—but life was so full and England was far away. The last time Freud had seen Polly was when she was two years old. He had evidently not done so when he visited Emanuel around 1908. He was not even sure of Polly's address, so he hoped the letter would reach her somehow.

Freud's son Ernst and his family were in London, Freud wrote to Sam, "in a flying visit." In a peculiarly modern turn of phrase, Freud added that they "may turn up at yours."

Despite all these problems, in August 1937, Freud finished what he called "Moses II" and put most of it aside, though he did publish some fragments in *Imago*. He wanted to produce a final version but he found it hard to concentrate and he was afraid. "I am so little used to concealing my ideas and taking into account various foreign considerations (i.e. political ones) that I do not seem to get over the conflict."

As 1937 ended, Freud got several offers to publish a book on the psychoanalysis of the Bible. He rejected them all because he was determined to finish his Moses. Now the barbarians were at the gates.

9
World History in a Teacup: The *Anschluss*

In *Mein Kampf*, Hitler wrote: "Reunion [of Austria to Germany, the Anschluss] must be regarded as the supreme task of our lives, and one to be achieved by any means possible. People of one blood should belong to one Reich." Hitler's dream was more personal; he longed to return in triumph to the country he had left as a total failure.

On November 17, 1937, a group of Austrian politicians visited Hermann Goering. He asked Count Peter Reverta, the director of security along the Upper Austrian Border, "Do you really think that, if the Fuhrer wanted to force the Anschluss, Austria would be able to defend herself?" Austria was not making any defensive preparations, Reverta started to say, but Goering interrupted, "I may as well tell you that this union will be carried out no matter what happens, for the Fuhrer is determined at all costs to settle the question."

Goering specialized in bombast, but there were no specific plans to invade. Hitler wrote a document in June 1937. This file, called Operation Otto because of Otto von Habsburg, assumed that the emperor would be delighted to be set back on his throne by Nazi forces. But Otto resisted the temptation. So Hitler had to improvise and create some pretext for an invasion. It did not have to be too convincing, since Britain and France did not want a new war.

By November 1937, Nazi leaders were hinting at the exact time when they would order troops across the border, knowing that neither Britain nor France would lift a finger to stop them. Stanley Baldwin, the British prime minister, had said he "knew little of Europe and disliked what he knew." His successor, Neville Chamberlain, felt he had a special mission "to come to friendly terms with the dictators of Italy and Germany."

On December 20, 1937, Freud wrote to Stefan Zweig: "The government here is different but the people are the same as their brethren in the Reich. Our throat is being squeezed ever more tightly although for the time being we are not choked completely." Some Nazi "rules" amazed Freud, particularly the one that banned German Jews giving their children German names. In return, Freud suggested, Jews should ban Germans from using Jewish names like Joseph. "One cannot avoid occasionally thinking of Meister Anton's closing words in one of Friedrich Hebbel's dramas: 'I no longer understand this world.'"

Freud had already told Stefan Zweig ruefully that he felt his work was behind him and that no one could know how the future would judge it. "I am not so certain myself," he said and then admitted in a letter of October 17: "I have surely not discovered more than a small fragment of truth. The immediate future looks grim for psychoanalysis as well. In any case I am not likely to experience anything enjoyable during the weeks and months I may still have to live."

Freud's doctor, Max Schur, noted that 1938 started badly in terms of his patient's health. Freud had an ulcer, and Hans Pichler had to operate inside the oral nasal cavity. There were clear signs that the cancer had become more threatening. Freud took the news stoically, as he had done two years earlier.

Despite the bombast of November 1937, Hitler hesitated to invade Austria, but Schuschnigg played his hand poorly. For six weeks he delayed meeting the führer so that when he did finally visit him in Berchtesgaden in January, it looked as if he had been forced to do so. Hitler refused to let the Austrian chancellor smoke and he yelled constantly at him. Schuschnigg had, in fact, prepared a list of concessions before going to Berchtesgaden. For example, he would relax the anti-Nazi laws and allow Austrian Nazis to take part in student and athletic associations. The concessions merely whetted Hitler's appetite. Schuschnigg was forced to do more than let Nazi athletes compete and had to offer the Austrian Nazi leader a seat in his cabinet. Schuschnigg admitted later that he did not dare contradict Hitler when they were face-to-face.

"I was sure of one thing. Never again war against Germany," Schuschnigg wrote in his memoirs. But he still had some pride. "I am neither capable nor desirous of playing the puppet's role. I carry the political responsibility. . . . I cannot be expected to look on while the country is being wrecked by violence. I am in the fortunate position of being able to call up the whole world as a witness of who is right and who is seeking for peace. I am absolutely resolved to do this at the time I think necessary."

Carl Jung missed these developments because he had been invited to give the Terry Lectures, "Psychology and Religion," at Yale University and then set off for India in December 1937. While Hitler cum Wotan threatened storm, frenzy, and blood, Jung enjoyed the subcontinent. He became passionately interested in Hindu philosophy, but then became desperately ill and had to be admitted to a Calcutta hospital. Not for the first time, his problems were psychological; Jung collapsed into a delirious state. He was frank in admitting that his break with Freud in 1913 had led to a temporary schizophrenic episode, but he never seems to have written much about his collapse in India. If it was triggered by the criticisms of his "Nazi affiliations," he never said so.

Wilhelm Reich was in a different kind of trouble. He left Denmark for Norway, where he started work on the physiology of sex, devising experiments that predated those of William Masters and Virginia Johnson. Reich monitored the mechanics of bodies when couples made love. It should be remembered that Scandinavia in those days was far more Puritan than permissive. The Norwegian authorities were outraged. Wisely Reich left Norway on one of the last ships to sail for the United States before the Nazis installed the Quisling regime.

In February 1938, writing to Max Eitingon, Freud praised the "brave and in some way honest government" of Schuschnigg, which was trying to find some way of holding out against the Nazis. There was a solution, but the Austrian chancellor knew it risked provoking Hitler. On March 9, Schuschnigg finally announced that he would hold a plebiscite four days later on whether to unite with Germany. Organizing a national election in four days was, of course, desperate as well as bizarre.

The announcement triggered panic in Berlin; even after five years in power, Hitler did not feel in complete control. A trial was about to start that might reveal how the Gestapo had plotted against a German World War I hero, General Frisch. Hitler was terrified that when news of this plot got out, there would be action to remove him as chancellor. He needed to distract attention; he ranted and raged, and rage made him decisive.

Seventeen hours after Schuschnigg announced a plebiscite, which would allow Austrians to decide whether they wanted to join the Reich, the German border was closed. Trains were stopped. German troops moved to the Austrian frontier. At 9:30 a.m. German and Austrian representatives met for two hours. A defiant Schuschnigg refused to accept new Nazi demands, but the Austrian president, Dr. Wilhelm Miklas, panicked. He insisted his chancellor resign. Schuschnigg had no option. The plebiscite was called off. Hitler had been right. After that, no one paid much attention to the trial involving the heroic General Frisch anymore.

Jews in Vienna were terrified. The large number of secret Nazis and Nazi sympathizers were jubilant. But they were sure many Jews would try to escape and hide their assets before they took over. In "The Royal Game," Stefan Zweig's character Dr. B., the doctor who seems to have been an odd mix of a younger Freud and his son Martin, explains:

> I was able to burn the most important documents the moment I heard Schuschnigg's resignation speech. The rest of the papers along with the essential certificates for the securities held abroad . . . I sent literally at the last minute just before those fellows [by which Dr. B. meant the SS] smashed my door in—to my uncle hiding them in a laundry basket carried by my elderly and reliable housekeeper. . . . They suspected—and in fact rightly so—that of the money which had passed through our hands substantial amounts were still hidden and out of their reach. People like me from whom important information might be extracted were not bundled into concentration camps but were reserved for special treatment.

Martin Freud behaved in an almost identical manner, which is why it seems likely that Zweig wrote "The Royal Game" after talking to Martin, Martin's sister, and their father. Freud himself had a tense conversation with Paula Fichtl and told her that the next day the Nazis would be coming. "That is bad," he said. The next morning Paula served breakfast as usual. Freud fed some of his softly boiled egg to Jofie. We owe to Fichtl the nice detail that the telephone Freud hated was in the dining room. It would become a lifeline to the outside world in the next eleven weeks.

On March 12, 1938, German troops marched across the border and met no opposition. A young American who was living in Vienna,

George Clare, watched trucks packed with screaming men drive into the city, each vehicle draped with a huge swastika flag. The men shouted "Ein Volk, Ein Reich, Ein Führer"—"one people, one land, one leader." Clare was shocked by the "full fury of their hate. It is a sound one can never forget." Squadron after squadron of Luftwaffe bombers flew over the city. *The Times* called Vienna a "City of Frenzy and Fear."

Paula Fichtl still wanted to go shopping, however. Freud warned her to be careful and he was right. When she walked down the street, neighbors who knew she worked for a Jewish family screamed, "You should be ashamed of working for Jews." She ran back into the apartment.

Freud listened to the radio, which gave an hour-by-hour commentary. There was no resistance. "I was able to listen first to our challenge and then to our surrender, to the rejoicing and then the counter rejoicing," he wrote to Arnold Zweig.

German troops were astonished by the warmth with which they were welcomed. Freud had assured Ernest Jones that the Austrians would not be as barbaric as the Germans, but now he wrote to Arnold Zweig, "The people in their worship of anti-Semitism are entirely at one with their brothers in the Reich." Freud and a writer for the official SS paper *Das Schwarze Korps* (*The Black Corps*) agreed. The paper noted, "The Viennese have managed to do overnight what we have failed to achieve in the slow moving ponderous north to this day. In Austria a boycott of the Jews does not have to be organized—the people themselves have initiated it."

Respectable men and women went into Jewish-owned toy shops and sweet shops, allowed their children to take what they wanted, and swaggered out without paying. Jews were grabbed and forced to their knees in the street; they were made to rub out slogans in favor of the plebiscite with acid. Sometimes the Austrians made them do that without gloves so the acid burned their hands. "At last the Jews are working," people yelled. Within a month 90 percent of Austrians wore the swastika. Many Jews fled to the border and some did manage to get out to Italy and Switzerland.

Hitler came to Vienna on March 14 and addressed cheering crowds in the Heldenplatz. Twenty-five years after he had left Vienna with no money and no prospects, Hitler returned as the conquering hero who united the *Volk*. Wotan had risen to power indeed.

Freud had to cope with the Anschluss in terrible physical pain. Three weeks earlier he had had an operation, according to Max Schur. Freud wrote to Zweig on March 21, 1938: "[I had] to cancel my work for twelve days and I lay with pain and hot water bottles on the couch that is meant for others." Freud seems to have found it hard to believe what was happening. Until I had read Anny Rosenberg Katan, I hesitated to suggest Freud was in a state of denial, but she described precisely that in him and in Anna Freud. But if so, he was hardly the only "great" Jew to suffer from that during the 1930s.

On March 1, 1938, the Austrian head of the banking family, Baron Louis Rothschild returned to Vienna after a skiing holiday. Ten days later a telegram warned him that a German invasion was imminent, but Rothschild ignored the warning. Finally, as German troops came over the border, Rothschild had himself driven to the airport. As he tried to get on his plane, he was recognized by an SS man. His passport was seized. Rothschild went back to his mansion with his valet. In the evening, men with swastika armbands surrounded the Rothschild palace.

The butler, who seems to have been an Austrian version of P. G. Wodehouse's Jeeves, informed "the gentlemen of the SS" that it was not convenient for the baron to be arrested. The Nazis had no way of dealing with this fusillade of etiquette and went away. But snobbery could not outface guns forever. The SS came back on Sunday with more men. The butler managed to stall them again. The baron was at lunch and if they wanted to arrest him, they would have to wait until he had finished his meal. Watched by six SS men, the baron proceeded to act as if nothing out of the ordinary were happening. He finished his lunch with dried fruit, as usual, smoked his after-dinner cigarette, as usual, took his heart medicine, as usual, and then kindly agreed to be arrested. The Nazis marched him off, one would like to imagine, in golden handcuffs.

When it became clear that the baron was not coming back home, the valet packed a small bag and took it to police headquarters at the Hotel Metropole. He was sent away. The baron himself showed poise, too. When he was asked the next day what his palace was worth, he replied, "What is Vienna cathedral worth?"

"Insolence," the Nazi interrogator replied.

For all his wealth, Rothschild was sent to a room in the cellar where the Nazis thought it a nice joke to keep him locked up with the general secretary of the Austrian Communist Party. Within days they would be joined by another prisoner, the ex-chancellor, Karl von Schuschnigg himself.

The day after the Nazis marched into Vienna, Martin Freud went to his office at 7 Berggasse, which was also the office of the publishing company Freud had helped start in 1919. Martin wrote later: "I knew I must destroy documents of great importance. I had in the course of my normal duties as a lawyer invested money of my clients in reputable and stable currency abroad, this having been perfectly legal under lenient Austrian laws, but I knew it would be a crime in the eyes of the dollar-hungry Nazis." He had to protect his clients, "including my father," by destroying any evidence of these transactions.

As he was pulling out files, Martin Freud was interrupted by a nervous client who demanded to have all his documents immediately. Even with the Nazis threatening, it was important to remember one's manners. "Natural Austrian courtesy made this man stay and chat," he wrote. By the time he finally left, Martin Freud had not destroyed any documents. As he was about to begin doing so, a gang strutted into his office. Even the radio that was now controlled by the Nazis warned that gangs were roaming the streets, taking advantage of "the new situation," and looting.

A haggard-looking man took out a pistol and pressed it against Martin Freud's head. "Why not shoot him and be finished with him?" he shouted. Martin Freud was terrified, but then he saw that someone was watching from across the road. When he realized who this neighbor was, he knew he would get no help from him. The man was a Nazi sympathizer.

The gang took their time, knowing they had no reason to be worried that the police would stop them. They opened the safe and took all the foreign monies. After some hours they got bored and the atmosphere got a little less tense. Their hostage asked if he might have a cup of tea. The gang put this to the vote and decided that he could as long as he washed the cup and saucer. Amazingly, Martin Freud rejected these conditions.

Ernest Jones then walked into the office. The gang did not allow him to speak to their hostage. Jones, with his usual instinct for survival, told them he was British, not a Jew, and managed to persuade them to let him leave. He walked down the stairs and decided that the most sensible step was to get a Nazi of some seniority to deal with the situation. Jones also went to tell Anna Freud what was going on.

The gang drifted away one by one, until only one of them was left. Martin Freud started to bribe him—he must have had some money left on him—saying he had to go to the toilet because the stress had brought on diarrhea. At every trip he took some of the files and flushed the documents away.

But the toilet was under observation. The Nazi sympathizer, watching from across the street, realized something funny was going on and called the Gestapo. So for the first—but not the last—time, a Nazi came to the help of the Freuds.

Within minutes a young blond district commissioner arrived. He sent his men to find the rest of the gang. This officer "radiated an authority which had an immediate effect on the rabble which had been tormenting me for so long," Martin Freud noted. The commissioner was even polite and allowed Martin's sister, Anna, to join him. She had been waiting outside.

The commissioner told his men that this matter did not merit a formal report. He then gave Martin Freud a *Passierschein*, a pass that would allow him and his sister to see him the next day. Martin Freud does not say what happened when they went, but it seems likely that the district commissioner realized documents had been destroyed and he could have arrested Freud. But he did not. This was not the only time Freud's son found himself at some risk after the Nazi takeover.

Anna and Martin Freud went back to their parents' apartment to find there had also been an incident there. Paula Fichtl described it. A number of Gestapo men turned up. Martha Freud was calm. She told them that in her house they did not let guests stand up while they waited so would they please sit down. She then graciously told the Gestapo that they had some cash in the house.

"Help yourselves, gentlemen," Martha Freud said.

The cash came to the not small sum of 6,000 schillings. Freud then walked into the room looking worried, but said nothing. The "gentlemen of the SS" took the money and, bizarrely, provided a formal receipt.

As the Nazis took the 6,000 schillings, Freud said to his wife, "Dear me, I have never taken so much for a single visit."

Even more frightening, the Gestapo men took the passports of the entire family, just as Baron Rothschild's passport had been confiscated. The Freud family now had no official papers in a city where anyone could be stopped at any time and asked to prove who they were. Those who could not produce papers were often arrested.

Freud had powerful friends he could telephone, and he did so. One was his former patient William Bullitt, who was now the American ambassador in Paris. Bullitt went to see the German ambassador in Paris, Graf von Welczeck, and let him know the world would be outraged if Freud were ill treated. Welczeck knew Freud's reputation and did not need much persuading. He promised to make the point to Berlin, but the ambassador was not much liked by the Nazis and had little influence. If Goering and even Hitler were interested in developing a Nazi psychotherapy, other Nazis hated anything that smacked of psychoanalysis. Goebbels and Himmler wanted all psychoanalysts jailed.

Like many buildings, the block at 19 Berggasse was draped with a swastika flag. The Gestapo, well aware that Freud lived there, set up an observation post outside the main entrance. But the Freuds were able to call on a number of well-connected people in the building to help protect them. Dorothy Burlingham, Anna Freud's "devoted friend," had an apartment two floors above them.

Burlingham had installed an internal telephone between her apartment and that of the Freuds. If the Gestapo came again, Paula Fichtl was supposed to steal away and quietly call Burlingham on the house phone and Burlingham would then get help. She rang the American consul, John C. Wiley, who came and met Freud. Bullitt also told Wiley to visit the apartment frequently so that the watching Gestapo would know they themselves were being watched. An official American embassy car, with the Stars and Stripes on show, was usually parked outside.

Bullitt and Burlingham were not the only support Freud could draw on. Marie Bonaparte talked to friends at various embassies in Vienna. Diplomats were asked to inform the descendant of Napoleon of any threat to the Professor's safety. "The Princess is of inestimable value to us," Freud told Arnold Zweig.

From the windows of his apartment, Freud could see that the street outside was full of Nazi soldiers and sympathizers. Jews were being stopped, humiliated, and beaten up. It had an immediate effect on Freud. Paula Fichtl saw that her master was no longer able to write, but he could not let his patients down. They continued to come and he continued to treat them.

On March 13, the Vienna Psychoanalytic Society met. Freud reached into his knowledge of Jewish history for the apt anecdote to boost their morale. "After the destruction of the Temple in Jerusalem by Titus, Rabbi Jochanan ben Zakkai asked for permission to open a school at Jabneh for the study of the Torah," he said and added, "We are going to do the same. We are after all accustomed by our history and tradition, and some of us by our personal experience, to being persecuted."

The society voted to dissolve itself and recommended that all of its members flee. They would reconvene wherever Freud went to live, but he still hoped he would not have to leave Vienna. Anna Freud took the precaution of getting Hans Pichler, her father's surgeon, to issue a certificate saying Freud was very ill. The fact that Pichler was "a prominent Nazi" made that especially useful.

Sauerwald, Trustee of Freud's Assets

The board of the psychoanalytic publishing company met the next day at 7 Berggasse with the Nazis present. The sheer speed of these developments suggests that Austrian Nazis had long planned to target Freud and, under the new regime, they had a man on the inside, Anton Sauerwald. He was now thirty-five years old. His employee, Emil Rothleitner, had climbed in the ranks of the Nazi Party. By 1938 Rothleitner was a senior person in the running of the party in the Ninth District, which included the Berggasse. He was in a position to recommend who should be appointed to the new roles the new situation required.

The moment they took over, the Nazis decided to set up the same system of control they had set up in Germany. Every Jewish business would have a Nazi appointed to run it. Sauerwald never explained whether he specifically asked to be appointed as Freud's commissar or whether this was a decision made for him. Geoffrey Cocks suggests that the reason he was appointed was that Sauerwald was also a doctor, but there is no evidence that Sauerwald was a doctor of anything other than chemistry. It seems much more likely that Rothleitner recommended his boss for the job because, as an educated man, Sauerwald was less likely to be intimidated by Freud than most others. Later, Sauerwald claimed that a lawyer, Dr. Mann, appointed him as trustee.

Sauerwald had the confidence to be very hostile at that first meeting. He shouted at the two non-Jewish analysts, Richard Sterba and Ernest Hartmann, and asked why they had become mixed up with "Jewish pigs." He told them that "since the circumstances had changed," as the Nazis liked to put it, he now controlled the publishing company. He demanded to see all the records of the business. The directors had no option but to comply.

Freud's friends abroad were desperately worried. Arnold Zweig wrote on March 16 to ask how he was. He and Max Eitingon wanted to know if the Princess and Ernest Jones were in Vienna. They were worried. "Without you we are like a flock without a shepherd, like children without a father, to put it in Biblical terms." Zweig added, "The Berggasse dominates all our thoughts." Freud said he had been recovering from his illness when "these events occurred, world history in a teacup."

To make sure they could squeeze the last assets out of the Jews, the Nazis sent one of their "Jewish specialists" to Vienna, Adolf Eichmann. Sauerwald would have been very conscious of his presence; the Vienna police now reported directly to Berlin. Sauerwald was told to do the same, and it would complicate matters.

In 1937, Eichmann had traveled to Palestine with Herbert Hagen, who had become a senior officer of the SS when he was only twenty-three years old. Their orders were to see whether Jews could be sent to Palestine, which was then under the British mandate. The two men landed in Haifa and hoped to meet Jewish leaders like David Ben-Gurion. The last thing the British wanted, however, was to have more Jews come to Palestine because that would provoke further tensions with the indigenous Arabs.

Eichmann and Hagen were only given transit visas and had to take the train from Haifa to Cairo. (In those days there were regular trips from Beirut to Cairo via Tel Aviv.) In Cairo they met Feival Polkes, an agent of the Haganah, the Jewish resistance, who was understandably wary but more than ready to negotiate helping Jews emigrate from Germany. Eichmann and Hagen realized, however, that the British would never allow hundreds of thousands of Jews into Palestine, so a plan that could have saved many lives was not even considered.

In Vienna, Eichmann was often in the Hotel Metropole where Rothschild was being held as the Nazis tried to work out just how large a ransom they could extract for him. Berlin sent economists and accountants to Vienna to estimate the wealth of the Jews. This was not the first "terror" to spawn a terrifying, but at times ludicrous, bureaucracy. A secret Vienna instruction, for example, told the police how to handle Jews of good standing. Healthy men should be arrested. Their property could be destroyed without interference from the local police. But that had to be done carefully. If officers had to use fire to destroy property, they should take care not to start "a general conflagration."

According to Paula Fichtl, if the Gestapo came to 19 Berggasse again, they would have to swarm past a film star–like apparition on the stairs leading up to the apartment. Princess Marie Bonaparte had arrived and she took up sentry duty, ready to repel the Nazis with style. She wore full regalia—a blue mink stole wrapped around her shoulders—and was enveloped in "clouds of Stephanotis," a fashionable perfume of the time. White leather gloves and a brown crocodile handbag completed her outfit. Fichtl brought her tea and chocolate regularly, a kindness the Princess did not forget.

To be able to enlist the help of the president of the United States as well as that of a descendant of Napoleon was not given to many Jews. William Bullitt knew Roosevelt well. There would have been no problem in getting a visa to go to the United States. President Roosevelt would probably have signed one personally for Freud and every member of his family. Roosevelt was also persuaded to telegram Hitler to say it was unthinkable that Freud would be harmed. Hitler does not seem to have replied.

Going to America was never an option for Freud, though. He called the country a "gigantic mistake" that had only one redeeming feature—and that was "tobacco (which) . . . is the only excuse I know for Columbus' misdeed." He might have told Max Eastman that he did not hate the country but he had bad memories of his visit to Clark University. Carl Jung had been temperamental, there were not enough toilets, and the food was too rich. According to Clement Freud, Freud had to ask Jung to walk very close to him while he urinated down his trouser leg. On the subject of America, Freud was not rational. England was the only option, but the British authorities did not want to let many refugees in.

Some well-meaning friends had no idea what life was now like for Jews. Six days after the Nazis marched into Vienna, Ludwig Binswanger wrote from Zurich, "You would be welcome here at any time as soon as you feel the need for a change of air." Binswanger imagined Jews could just hop on a train to Switzerland; he had no sense of the paperwork Jews needed to leave Vienna.

The Nazis wanted to know about everything Jews owned. Freud's assets were valued at just over 125,000 reichsmarks. He would have to pay a "flight tax" of 25 percent. The valuation was based on his books, artwork, furniture, and other goods, as well as cash. Freud did not have 31,250 reichsmarks in money in Vienna. If he did not pay the flight tax, however, he and his family would not be allowed to leave. He did not dare draw on any accounts abroad. Martin Freud was right to say the "dollar-hungry" Nazis would make it a crime for Jews to have sent money out of Austria. Evidence of the now illegal bank accounts would allow the Nazis to make life hellish for Freud. Some Nazis wanted to put the old Jew on trial. Freud and his whole family were suddenly "in a very dangerous situation," Anna Freud wrote, but she knew two friends would help pay the expenses, Marie Bonaparte and William Bullitt. Bullitt, however, was concerned that it might cost him more than $10,000 to help get the Freud family out of Vienna and wrote to the American consul, John C. Wiley, to instruct him not to get into a situation where more cash might be demanded of him. Ten thousand dollars was, of course, a huge sum. It would buy at least one house in London.

The tension got to Paula Fichtl. The next time the Gestapo arrived, she tried to stop them from getting into the flat by pushing all of her 120 pounds against the door. "Shameless hussy," a Gestapo man yelled as they swept past her. Freud told her his fate did not matter much because "I am almost dead." The Nazis behaved like perfect gangsters. Fichtl overheard one say, "Nothing will happen to the Professor if he does what we want." Though she does not name him it seems very likely that the man who said that was Anton Sauerwald. His career at Vienna University had left him with a certain respect for intellectuals. In the next few months, the student who had liked "Professor Herzig" often referred to Freud as "Herr Professor."

10

The Worst Day of Freud's Life

As a trustee, Sauerwald's task was to find Jews guilty of something so that more pressure could be put on them to hand over more money. The Nazis protested against the Swiss banking laws in 1933; they believed, not entirely wrongly, that any sensible Jews who had any money had opened secret bank accounts all over Europe.

In the light of the Holocaust it is easy to forget that Nazi policy was initially more modest; its aim was to terrorize Jews, rob them of their assets, and expel them from Europe. The Nazis only decided at the Wannsee Conference in 1942 to devise the "future final solution of the Jewish question." Fifteen senior Nazis were present. Reinhard Heydrich, who had been appointed as the chief executor of the "final solution to the Jewish question," presented a plan. The Jewish population of Europe and French North Africa would be deported to eastern Europe and used as slave labor on road-building projects, in the course of which they would eventually die. Any survivors would be killed once the projects were completed. Eichmann was at Wannsee, as well as two officials who worked under the Aryan theorist Alfred Rosenberg and a career civil servant, Martin Luther. Luther seems to have been the only one who did not destroy his copy of the minutes of the conference, which were written up by Eichmann personally. The chief American prosecutor at Nuremberg, Robert Kempner, searched Luther's papers and found these minutes. They were of huge significance, as they were the blueprint for the Holocaust.

Nothing in Sauerwald's history up to 1938 suggests he had any sympathy for Jews, but he knew how to work and pay attention to details. Sauerwald examined the records of the Freud family and of the publishing company; he read the letters people had sent them, including those where Freud's nephew Sam thanked his uncle for money received. It did not take Sauerwald long to realize that "Herr Professor" had been sending money out of the country for years. Martin Freud had not succeeded in destroying every record. Sauerwald also discovered that Freud's publishing company owed money to its suppliers. Jews were not allowed to leave Austria until they, and any businesses they owned, had paid all their debts. Freud would need to find considerable sums of money to settle the publishing company's debts as well as the flight tax for himself and his family.

Sauerwald had to deal with three organizations in Berlin who had very definite views on what should happen to Freud's publishing company. The Gestapo, the Ministry of Health, and the Presspolizei demanded an immediate liquidation of all its assets. Sauerwald did not try to argue with them but went to see two of the non-Jewish analysts, August Aichhorn and Ernest Hartmann. He wanted them to become joint liquidators of the publishing company with him. Both men refused.

Sauerwald's behavior remains puzzling. He had been abusive at the first meetings of the board of the publishing company, but he then became far less hostile. No one could understand why. After the war Sauerwald explained what his first impressions of Freud were. It was clear to him that Freud was in an "emotionally fragile condition," a very sick old man. Sauerwald insisted that he tried to be "sympathetic to his condition," and with perhaps a trace of vanity, that he behaved to him like a good doctor would. "I tried to find the necessary calming words for him and his family," Sauerwald claimed. "I decided I would make sure he did not suffer any more shocks."

We do not have to rely exclusively on what Sauerwald said, which was probably tailored to show him in a good light. Anna Freud, Freud's lawyer, Dr. Alfred Indra, and Marie Bonaparte supported his version of events. So did Max Schur. During one of the Gestapo's many visits to 19 Berggasse, Martin Freud saw an SS man push Sauerwald aside as Sauerwald was politely knocking at Freud's door to ask if he could come in.

"We do not knock at doors," the SS man shouted.

"What can you expect of Prussians," Sauerwald said, but not to the SS man. He said that later to Max Schur. Prussians had no decent manners. Schur kept a note of this unexpected exchange.

After the war, Sauerwald emphasized his own decency. He felt it would have been inhuman to treat an old man with no respect.

But there may have been a more academic reason for Sauerwald becoming less hostile. He had always been quite conscientious and he was now responsible for the publishing business. The first thing it was sensible to do was to read the books it had published, which included *Beyond the Pleasure Principle*, *The Ego and the Id*, and *Civilization and Its Discontents*.

The books had an extraordinary impact on Sauerwald, an impact Sauerwald knew he must not let his Nazi superiors suspect. Freud loved Arthur Conan Doyle, who had made Sherlock Holmes say that when you have eliminated the impossible, the improbable must explain what happened. It was improbable that Sauerwald would help Freud. It is improbable that the only reason Sauerwald's attitude changed was reading Freud. It is probable that Sauerwald decided Freud was worth helping for, at least, two reasons. He was a world figure and he was a friend of Sauerwald's old professor, Josef Herzig. But it was also clear that Freud had money abroad, and many influential friends. There is a note appended to the court proceedings after the war that Sauerwald had estimated the worth of Freud at between 2 and 3 million schillings, a considerable fortune. In *Why War*, Freud had noted how mixed people's motives were in times of crisis—greed, idealism, fear, and humanity all combined. Sauerwald tried to suggest that he had acted just out of humanity. If that were so, he would have been a saint, and he does not seem to have been that.

Oskar Schindler's motives for helping Jews were also mixed. He needed good workers for his factories and could see no sense in killing Jews; it was only gradually that he became outraged by the Nazis. Even those whom he had helped admitted he was a flawed hero.

Some psychologists who have studied how individuals respond in dictatorships say there is a growing pattern of rebellion, of crossing the line. Some individuals start with small transgressions. After having studied Freud's books, Sauerwald did not disclose to his superiors that Freud had many secret bank accounts abroad. Instead, he took the evidence back to his own apartment where he had a Panzerkassette, a locked box for important documents. Taking documents home was not specifically against orders and he could explain to his superiors that he had brought the documents back to study. He was looking at the line but he had not crossed it yet.

Father and Daughter

On Tuesday, March 22, the Gestapo marched into 19 Berggasse again. Ernest Jones had left Vienna on the same day and so was in no position to help. The Gestapo men said they had come to arrest Anna Freud. They were confronted not just by the family, but by Princess Marie Bonaparte. Her husband was worried about what the Nazis might do to her and had made her promise to stay at the Greek embassy. She ignored him, as she often did, and spent her time at 19 Berggasse—and not just on the stairs in her mink.

When the SS men said they were arresting Anna, the Princess tried to insist that she should also be arrested. She told Martin Freud that the idea of marching a princess into their cells terrified the Nazis. He had returned to the apartment too late to see this confrontation, but he was just in time to rush to the window and see his sister being bundled into an open car by four heavily armed SS men. She appeared quite calm.

Inside 19 Berggasse, the remaining SS men ransacked everything. One burly man pulled on the handles of a cupboard and finally yanked it open. He found himself looking at piles of beautifully laundered linen tied together with colored ribbons, not gold or secret bank documents. He had opened Martha Freud's laundry cupboard. He started to pull the contents out, only to be met with splendid disdain. "Without showing the slightest fear mother joined the fellow and in highly indignant tones told him precisely what she thought about his shocking behavior," Martin Freud wrote. The SS man looked terrified at her outburst and so Freud's wife saved her linen—and her dignity.

When he heard that Anna Freud had been taken away, Max Schur came at once. He knew her father would be distraught and he was right. Freud was terrified he would never see her again. The usually calm therapist showed all his feelings, raw. He paced up and down and smoked one cigar after another.

When the Nazis arrested her, Anna Freud was forty-two years old. Photos taken when she was just a few years younger show her as an intense, attractive, and very Jewish woman; she liked to wear a beret, which gave her a gamine look. She was the only one of Freud's children who had made a success of her career. She was recognized as a brilliant child therapist. She had managed this both because of her relationship with her father, and despite it. They loved, respected, and depended on each other. Freud had some reasons to feel guilty toward her. He knew, even if he did not say it, that she had never married at least in part because of her devotion to him.

When she was eighteen years old, Anna went to England to improve her English. Freud had asked Ernest Jones to look after her, but Jones did rather more; he began to court her. Freud was not happy about that for both good and bad reasons. Jones had lost two hospital jobs because of complaints women patients had made about his behavior. The "Welsh wizard" had had a number of mistresses and was not likely to make an ideal husband, but Freud would probably not have been happy if his beloved Shakespeare himself wooed his daughter. He told Jones that she was "still far away from sexual longings." Freud was usually alive to irony, but he was too close to his daughter to see any irony in that. The pioneer who had argued children were sexual was protesting that his eighteen-year-old daughter had no sexual feelings. Father and daughter had agreed "that she should not consider marriage or the preliminaries before she gets two or three years older," he told Jones, and added that he did not expect her to "break the treaty."

For once Jones did not meekly accept what Freud said. He shot back that Anna "will surely be a remarkable woman later on, provided that her sexual repression does not injure her. She is of course tremendously bound to you." She stayed cool toward Jones, though whether this was because she did not find him attractive or because of her relationship with her father, we do not know.

When Anna Freud was twenty-three years old, her father started analyzing her. Today that would be thought totally unethical. The usual defense is that in those early days, the rules were less fixed. If so, one wonders why the fact Freud was analyzing his daughter was "a jealously kept secret." Paul Roazen, the distinguished historian of analysis, states father and daughter agreed she needed help because she suffered from depression, insomnia, and daydreams linked to masturbation. She expressed some of these conflicts in many poems and stories she wrote, but none were published in her lifetime. Small extracts were quoted in her authorized biography. For four years, the daughter lay on her father's couch like any other patient. He always saw her at 10:00 p.m., just before he went to bed.

Freud did not hide how much he depended on his youngest daughter. In a letter to Lou Andreas-Salomé written in 1922, he had said: "I have felt sorry for her for quite some time now, because she is still living at home with us old folks &, but yet, on the other hand, if she really had left us, I would have felt diminished, like what is happening to me now, for example, almost as if I had to give up smoking." We have seen that Freud compared the pleasure Anna gave him to smoking a good cigar.

Father and daughter do not seem to have agreed on how successful the analysis was. In a letter to Lou also in 1922, Anna Freud said: "With me, everything became so problematic because of two basic faults: from a discontent or insatiability with myself that makes me look for affection from others, and then from actually sticking with the others once I have found them. [The first] is just what you and *Papa* cannot understand."

Freud believed, however, that he had understood his daughter perfectly. In 1935 the Italian analyst Eduardo Weiss asked Freud whether or not he should analyze his own son; Freud said that his analysis of his daughter "had gone well." Paul Roazen suggests there were unspoken conflicts and that "Anna may have been more afraid of her father than either of them knew." Her father's motives may have been "the very best, but medically and humanly the situation was bizarre."

A basic part of analysis is usually for patients to work through their problems with their parents through their relationship with the analyst. The analyst represents the parent so the child can work through his or her childhood issues again. But how could that happen if the analyst is one of the patient's parents?

Freud would have been "invading the privacy of her soul"; he added new transference emotions to their relationship, without the possibility of ever really dissolving them. Taking his daughter into analysis undoubtedly gratified an Oedipal tie on his part, Roazen judged. The psychoanalytic movement might benefit as she became an analyst, but for her, "the analysis helped to limit the possibilities for personal gratification, although she had a role in her father's life as well as her eventual leadership of the movement, which constituted a rich exchange." Then Roazen softened; after all, he was talking about the father of psychoanalysis. "Perhaps only by normal standards was her relationship to such a father a tragic one."

One sign of that "Oedipal tie" was that, even in her late twenties, Anna Freud could become jealous of both her mother and her aunt Minna. They fought over who should accompany him on trips as well as sometimes over who should fit his prosthesis. Aunt Minna was, in turn, jealous of the fact that Freud shared his thinking with his daughter more than with anyone else.

Anna Freud became director of the Vienna Psychoanalytical Training Institute and in 1937 she started a nursery school for poor children. The money came mainly from Dorothy Burlingham and Edith Jackson. The nursery was experimental. Children were allowed to choose their own food and organize their own play. Though some of their parents had been reduced to begging, Burlingham and Anna Freud were very struck "by the fact that they brought the children to us, not because we fed and clothed them and kept them for the length of the day, but because 'they learned so much,' i.e. they learned to move freely, to eat independently, to speak, to express their preferences. To our own surprise the parents valued this beyond everything." As soon as the Nazis took over, the nursery school had to be closed down.

On March 22, Anna Freud did not go unprepared to meet the Gestapo. She was frightened that she would be tortured and thus persuaded Max Schur to give her two tablets of Veronal to swallow as a last resort. But she had a plan. She felt that it was dangerous to be kept waiting too long in the corridors of the Hotel Metropole. People could vanish into the cellar without anyone noticing. Martin Freud added mysteriously that "through the influence of some friends," his sister was allowed to leave the corridor and taken to a room where other Jews were being questioned. No one objected.

In "The Royal Game," Stefan Zweig described the interrogations at the Hotel Metropole. Reading his text, it is hard to believe his descriptions are not based on real experiences that had been recounted to him. Zweig's "fictional" Dr. B. certainly hated waiting.

"I had to wait in the ante room of the chief interrogator" Dr. B. lamented. "You always had to wait before every session. Making you wait was also part of the technique." The aim was to produce tension that would reduce "your will to resist," so the Nazis "made you wait pointlessly, pointlessly waiting, one hour, two hours before the interrogation to exhaust your body and break down your spirit.

"Then at last the interrogation begins," Dr. B. continued. "They sent for you and you were taken along a corridor or two. You didn't know where you were going. You waited somewhere and you didn't know where you were. Then abruptly you were standing in front of a table with a few people in uniform sitting at it. On the table was a pile of papers, documents whose contents you knew nothing about. Then the questions started, genuine and fake, straightforward and crafty, superficial questions and catch questions."

In the apartment at Berggasse, Max Schur did not manage to calm his patient. Freud continued to pace up and down, lighting one cigar after another, smoking, smoking, and smoking. Paula Fichtl and Dorothy Burlingham both wrote that it was obviously the worst day of his life.

In the Hotel Metropole, Anna Freud had to wait and wait. When it was finally her turn to be questioned, the Gestapo men put a clever question to ruffle her. She was asked what it meant to be a member of an international organization. The Gestapo told her they had information about a conspiracy of Jewish ex-soldiers who were about to terrorize Vienna. It was too dangerous to laugh at the idea. She explained the only international organization she belonged to was the International Psychoanalytic Association. Analysts might be a "gang," as her father had said to Ludwig Binswanger, but they had not yet resorted to bombing each other with anything more than words and emotional threats. The International Psychoanalytic Association did not have guns hidden under the analytic couches. But it was hard for her to stay calm. Like Dr. B., Anna Freud had a secret, the secret her brother had protected when he flushed documents about his father's secret bank accounts down the toilet at 7 Berggasse.

Dr. B. described the anxieties being questioned provoked well: "Gradually I could feel how my nerves were beginning to break up and . . . recognising the dangers I braced myself to my nerve ends. The same thought came flickering in and out. What do they know?" And when they found out, how would they use the information?

Anna Freud thought she had one advantage, however, as she faced her interrogators. Carl Müller-Braunschweig might now be working for Matthias Goering at the institute, but he was still devoted to her father. There are two accounts of what happened next. According to one, Anna Freud produced a "letter of homage"

Müller-Braunschweig had written to her about her father. She wanted to let the Gestapo know they had friends in high places, but this only angered the Nazis. It was again a matter of etiquette, which could be so treacherous. The letter began very correctly with "*Sehr geehrtes gnaediges Fraulein*," a gracious form of address Jews were now not entitled to. The second version of this story suggests Anna Freud did not show the Gestapo this letter, but that it had been intercepted by them.

The Gestapo was very interested in the attitude of non-Jewish therapists toward Freud. Matthias Goering was in an excellent position to ask the Gestapo to keep track of the letters written by analysts so that he would know who was loyal to him and the Nazi cause, and who still hankered after the old master. Goering had his moments of paranoia, which was why he had banned Felix Boehm from teaching and would take revenge on Carl Müller-Braunschweig. The latter claimed he paid a heavy price for writing his letter. He was accused of being a Jew lover and never allowed to publish and teach again at the institute.

The interrogators did not put Freud's daughter in the prison cells that had been set up in the basement. She was allowed to leave the Hotel Metropole by the end of the evening.

Freud was relieved beyond words when she finally returned home safely late on March 22. Max Schur said that for once Freud showed his true feelings. The frail old man wept. He had been terrified he would never again see his Antigone, as he called Anna.

Her arrest was the turning point. After years of hesitation, Freud knew he had no choice, even if he did not have long to live. In the next few days, he prepared a list for the British consul in Vienna of those he wanted to accompany him to England. Schur reproduced the list in full.

Sigmund Freud—aged 82
Martha Freud—aged 77
Minna Bernays, sister-in-law—aged 73
Anna Freud, daughter—aged 42
Martin Freud, son—aged 48
Esti Freud, wife of Martin—aged 41
Walter Freud, son of Martin—aged 16
Sophie Freud, daughter of Martin—aged 14?

Enkel Ernst Halberstadt, grandson—aged 24

Mathilde, daughter—aged 50

R. Hollitscher, husband of Mathilde—aged 62

Max Schur, Freud's personal doctor—aged 39

Schur's wife, Helen—aged 26

Schur's two small children

Paula Fichtl—housekeeper, aged 36

Mitzi, the other maid to the Freud household—aged around 30

At first Ernest Jones claimed that Freud leaving Vienna and his fellow analysts would be like a soldier deserting the army. Then the Welsh wizard waxed lyrical. He reminded Freud of events on the Titanic. The captain went down with the ship, a heroic but useless sacrifice. The second in command was more sensible, made sure the passengers got in the lifeboats, and then accompanied them to help them survive. Jones perhaps overstated his own part in persuading Freud that he had to do everything possible to leave, but he did work hard over the next three months to make the escape possible.

As soon as he got back to London, Ernest Jones went to see his cousin Wilfred Trotter, a well-known doctor. Trotter gave him a letter of introduction to Sir William Bragg, the president of the Royal Society, which had been set up in 1662 to promote scientific research. Isaac Newton was one of its founders. The most famous physicist in the world, Einstein, might have condemned the Nazis, but Bragg still asked Jones, *"Do you really think the Germans are so unkind to the Jews?"*

Ernest Jones could assure him of their "unkindness." Jews were being beaten up in the streets by mobs, he told Bragg. At his best, Jones was a terrier and he did not leave the offices of the Royal Society until he got a letter from Bragg inviting Freud to Britain. Jones then walked across St. James Park to the Home Office to see a man with whom he had an unlikely bond, the Home secretary, Sir Samuel Hoare. The two men had gone figure skating together and before he wrote his biography of Freud, Jones's most successful book was *The Elements of Figure Skating.*

Samuel Hoare had had to resign as foreign secretary after Mussolini invaded Ethiopia and he felt he had to be careful because there was a lot of opposition to letting too many Jews come to Britain. Ernest Jones again insisted. He finally got Hoare to issue an entry visa for all the Freud family as well as for Fichtl and the maid, Mitzi. It was Jones's finest hour. It is hard to believe that he could not have persuaded Hoare to also issue visas for Freud's four sisters who were living in Vienna. But they were not on the list.

It was no good having Freud be allowed into England if he could not get out of Vienna. The uncertainties depressed him. On April 17 Paula Fichtl reported something that had never happened before; Freud lost his hearing. He had never before had any such problems but he was, Sauerwald noted, very anxious.

Then Anna Freud had a conversation with her father when they seemed to have no chance of escape.

"Wouldn't it be better if we all killed ourselves?" she asked her beloved papa.

Freud was adamant. "Why? Because they would like us to?" Freud replied. He had no intention of giving them the pleasure.

Anna Freud only allowed Max Schur to report this dialogue in *Living and Dying* thirty-four years later. Her reticence makes sense if one remembers how many of Freud's relatives had killed themselves.

On April 13 Ernest Jones wrote a letter to the *Times* in which he assured the world that Freud "was not a dying man who has been denied his liberty." Freud was in good health for his age and was still at work. Jones added that Freud was free. There was no point in aggravating the Nazis.

The rhythm in their thirty-year-long correspondence had been clear; the junior man, Jones, wrote more letters to Freud than Freud wrote to him. Now that changed; Freud suddenly was writing more and it was he who was making the requests. For example, on April 23, he asked Jones to arrange an entry visa to Britain for a dermatologist, Maxim Steiner, one of the first members of the Viennese Psychoanalytic Society. Freud had also consulted him as a doctor.

In March and April 1938, the suicide rate among Jews soared. Rumors had it that five hundred Jews had killed themselves "since the circumstances changed," as the Nazis liked to put it. Even Berlin was embarrassed by such figures. Toward the end of April official statistics were issued saying that only ninety-six Jews had, in fact, killed themselves. Ironically just at this moment, Dorothy Burlingham's husband, Robert, whom Freud had treated, committed suicide.

Writing could sometimes distract Freud from the uncertainties. "I also work for an hour a day at my Moses which torments me like a ghost not put to rest. I wonder if I shall ever complete the third part despite all the outer and inner difficulties," Freud told Ernest Jones. Freud needed to work more than ever. On May 12, Freud wrote to his son Ernst: "Two prospects keep me going in these grim times—to rejoin you all and to die in freedom." But it would take a lot of negotiations before he could die in freedom and it was vital not to upset Sauerwald. Sauerwald had abused Ernest Hartmann and Richard Sterba for working with Jews. Nothing before his encounter with the Freuds suggests Sauerwald would take risks for Jews.

Vienna was a small place, and Anton Sauerwald had been a student at the university. Anna Freud and Dr. Alfred Indra now asked discreetly what people knew about him. The answers they received were alarming. Sauerwald was not merely a well-qualified chemist, but he had been a member of the Nazi Party for years and had almost certainly made bombs during the disturbances of 1933 and 1934. Their fate was in the hands of not only a sincere Nazi but also a terrorist.

11
Anton Sauerwald

On May 5, Anton Sauerwald summoned another meeting of the Vienna Psychoanalytic Society and the publishing company. Ernest Jones returned from London, as did Marie Bonaparte from Paris. Despite having written his letter of homage, Carl Müller-Braunschweig was not frozen out and he attended as well as Professor Goering, Sauerwald's name for Matthias Goering. The meeting took place at 7 Berggasse, so Freud did not go himself.

Anton Sauerwald was brisk. The financial situation of the publishing house was not good and it was "passiv"; its assets were no more than 30,000 reichsmarks and it owed far more than that. Its debts would have to be settled before Freud could leave Vienna.

The meeting then considered how to move the business to London. Seven weeks after the Anschluss, Sauerwald was at least disposed to try to be helpful. He had to clear the matter with Berlin, however. There was a more clinical problem. Freud and his colleagues had been treating a number of patients who were not Jewish. They were now forbidden to continue practicing, so there were a number of Aryans who needed therapy. The meeting tried to find new therapists for these patients, but there were not enough non-Jewish therapists left in Vienna. The meeting agreed it was not possible to refer these to ordinary psychiatrists.

The same day Anton Sauerwald signed the exit visa for Minna Bernays, something dear to Freud's heart. She had been recuperating in a sanatorium for a few months and was too ill to travel on her own, so Dorothy Burlingham came back to take her to London.

The next day, May 6, was Freud's eighty-second birthday. He had now lived longer than his father and his brother. There were no celebrations but there was another meeting at Freud's apartment, which Anton Sauerwald himself attended. In the presence of their lawyer,

Dr. Alfred Indra, Freud and his daughter both signed a *Gedenkpro-tokoll*, which translates as a "deed of intention." It promised the Freuds would pay all the taxes the Nazis demanded.

Anton Sauerwald was in a strange position. He knew that Freud had money abroad but not much in Vienna. The Gestapo had not returned the 6,000 schillings they had taken. Freud had had to pay the exit tax for his sister-in-law. What Sauerwald did not know, however, was that when the Gestapo searched the apartment, they had not found some gold belonging to Freud. He gave that to Marie Bonaparte, who took it to the Greek embassy. Was this failure a miracle or the result of some aristocratic bribery? I have not been able to establish that, but it is known that the gold was smuggled out in a diplomatic pouch. It was worth $4,824 at the then rate of exchange. Since its price was $38 an ounce, Freud's gold weighed about 130 ounces (more than eight pounds). This is not a small amount to have managed to conceal and smuggle out.

Martin Freud was the next person to leave, but he never mentions having to pay an exit tax and he wrote about the event a little mysteriously. "Finally I was ordered out of Vienna, a measure which could have possibly been inspired by friends who did not think my temperament sufficiently equable to be trusted." Under pressure, he might have betrayed secrets.

What Martin Freud was unwilling to admit is that he had been making provocative remarks about the Nazis that could have ended with his being sent to the kazzette, a form of internment. This is clear from an affidavit Dr. Alfred Indra swore to after the war. Dr. Indra went on to give a remarkable piece of information. The person who helped keep Freud's son out of trouble usually was Anton Sauerwald. Sauerwald intervened on a number of occasions when Martin was in danger of being arrested.

The story Martin Freud tells about his escape also does not seem totally frank, a suspicion confirmed by a letter Anna Freud wrote years later to her cousin Harry:

> About Sauerwald I do not know what Martin ever told you about him.
>
> I suppose you know that Martin, who was quite beside himself at that time, had kept some very incriminating papers about our affairs in Switzerland in his desk. They were found there but Sauerwald kept them

safely locked up until we were gone. Martin will never forgive the position that he was suddenly powerless while Sauerwald had all the power. But he did not misuse his power and very few people are able to withstand such a temptation.

Martin Freud wrote that he managed to get out thanks to his cook. The vice president of the Vienna police was a friend of hers and so Martin was able to leave and, also, to buy back documents that had been seized. It seems likely Freud's son bribed the vice president of the Vienna police to make his escape, at the very least, easier. It was best to have both a proper visa and the help of a police chief.

It would be dangerous to be found on the train with very much money on him, so Martin Freud took the risk of sending some banknotes by post to Paris and kept only a quantity of coins. He did not want to waste these, though, so he went to the restaurant car and ordered a whole roast chicken. He asked the dining car attendant to keep the chicken in the train fridge until they got to Paris. The man became suspicious; there must be something bizarre about a Jew who wanted a chicken kept on ice. Martin Freud claims the attendant threatened to report him for breach of regulations so he took the chicken to his compartment where he "devoured it without pleasure." He reached Paris safely and rather full.

On May 24, Freud's daughter Mathilde left Vienna with her husband and reached London with rather fewer complications. But Anton Sauerwald would still not sign an exit visa for Freud, his wife, and his daughter Anna. One reason was that there were still difficulties with the liquidation of the publishing company. A few days after the May 5 meeting, a certain Dr. Ehrlich stormed in from Germany. He said that Berlin did not want the publishing company to transfer its operations to London. Sauerwald discussed the problem privately with Marie Bonaparte and they came to an arrangement. She agreed to buy the business and pay all its debts. But Sauerwald again had to clear this with Berlin. Fearing he might not get approval, he appealed to Matthias Goering, who appealed to his cousin Hermann Goering for help. It says something about the weird politics of the Reich that even though Hermann Goering, Hitler's deputy, intervened, Berlin would still not allow Freud's publishing company to be sold to Napoleon's great-grandniece.

Anton Sauerwald was in a quandary. Three organizations in Berlin were demanding reports, and the records of Freud's secret bank accounts were in his locked box at home. Sauerwald began to feel that he was taking a risk in hiding documents about Freud's banking operations. Research suggests that in dictatorships, dissidents often start with small transgressions that set them on the path. Sauerwald went much further now. He began to disobey direct orders from Berlin. The first actual disobedience was modest. He checked which books did not belong to the publishing company but to foreigners. The regime had no right to seize those; many of the foreigners were not even Jews. Sauerwald packed these books and returned them to their original owners.

It was the next step Anton Sauerwald took that completely crossed the line and put him at great risk. He did not want to destroy the books Freud's company had published. They were the root documents of psychoanalysis. Sauerwald got in touch with the director of the Austrian National Library, who also knew the Gestapo wanted all the stock of books destroyed because they were "Jewish filth." Sauerwald persuaded the director, Dr. Paul Heigl, to work with him. In the dead of night, Sauerwald and Marie Bonaparte packed the books up and transported them to the Austrian National Library. Dr. Heigl made sure that only reliable helpers were on hand to take them in and lock them away. The books were still there when the war ended.

Anton Sauerwald had now crossed the line. It is a pity that the People's Court did not commission a psychological assessment of him. He had abandoned a promising research career. He had walked out of his job at a time of great economic uncertainty. He had persuaded his parents to put up the money for his chemical laboratory, which he claimed was a completely reputable business, but, in fact, the business made bombs. He fooled the Vienna police into hiring him as a forensic expert to investigate crimes he helped commit.

After the war, Anton Sauerwald made much of the fact that in 1937 he acquired a pistol and a rifle for hunting. He would not have been allowed to get the necessary permits if the authorities believed he was a threat to public order or an illegal Nazi. All scientific activities were strictly controlled by the authorities, he said. His lab was respectable, Sauerwald insisted over and over again.

Max Schur said no one could understand why Anton Sauerwald had saved the Freuds and thought that Sauerwald read Freud's books, which changed his attitude. Schur eventually gave a more rounded explanation. Freud's brother Alexander met with Sauerwald and asked him very directly what his motives had been. It is impossible to be sure whether the speech Schur said Sauerwald then made is accurate word for word, but he reports it as follows. Sauerwald told Alexander Freud:

> The führer of course knows best and realizes that the Vaterland is in a state of siege. The Jews, due to their internationalist leanings and their tendency toward individualistic behavior, cannot form a reliable element of the population. Thus they have to be eliminated. This might be deplorable but the end justifies the means. This does not mean, however, that an individual should not be permitted to alleviate individual hardship in selected cases.

What is odd is that Schur dates this speech to 1939, two years before the Wannsee Conference. In public by then, not even Hitler had suggested that Jews should be "eliminated" the way the mentally ill should be. Eichmann, who was sent to take charge of Vienna, made it clear that Nazi policy was to rob rich Jews and expel poor ones. It is hard to believe that Sauerwald would have spoken of "elimination" so early. But the rest of the explanation attributed to him by Schur makes sense. Schur went on to argue that Freud's trustee "gradually developed some guilt feelings and tried to come to terms with his conscience whenever circumstances permitted."

As he wondered whether or not to sign the papers for Freud's exit visa, Anton Sauerwald got a new order from Berlin. The Freuds were to be moved out of their apartment and the premises used to house a new "Race Institute"; it would study why the Aryan race was superior. That was an unnecessary insult. It tilted the balance, it would seem. Sauerwald finally signed the papers that said there was no impediment to Freud leaving. But that was far from the only paperwork Freud needed to get out.

Last-Minute Panic, Last-Minute Packing

It was a huge wrench for Freud to leave Vienna. He had books, he had an art collection, he had medical records, he had letters. He complained about the amount of work involved in packing, doing accounts, and giving final presents. He wrote to his son Ernst on May

12 that he feared he would lose most of his art collection, apart from two small pieces Marie Bonaparte had already taken to Paris and a few others she had bought in Athens for him and also taken to France. How much of his collection could travel with him from Vienna was "very uncertain. The whole thing reminds me of a man trying to rescue a birdcage from a burning house."

The next day Freud wrote to Ernest Jones that he had no wish to celebrate his birthday on the sixth and that he was sitting in his study "with nothing whatever to do and generally useless." He was finding it hard to write because he knew his letters were being opened by a censor. Once, Freud reminded Jones, he had traced back "the so-called physiological feeblemindedness of women" to the fact that women were forbidden to think about sex. Women had come to dislike thinking as a result and he now compared his lot to theirs. "Imagine how such a censorship must affect me who have always been in the habit of expressing freely what I believe."

Despite the censorship, one can follow the many twists and turns of the next month because once Minna Bernays reached London, she and Freud exchanged letters that show how his moods changed as he tried to master his anxieties. He was an old man in fear for his life. On May 14, Freud wrote that they were now in possession of the French and English passes they needed. But an obsessional bureaucracy ruled and these passes were valid for only fourteen days. Anna Freud also had to go every day to the police to try to negotiate the final bureaucratic hurdles. Sauerwald often accompanied her on these visits.

Even leading Nazis felt there was too much bureaucracy. A memo sent to the Security Head Office II 1 12 in Berlin with the approval of Eichmann complains that "there were more and more instances in Vienna where Jews, eager to emigrate, had to stand in line for days and weeks to arrange the necessary paperwork for their emigration. Over that time there were many failures because of lack of organization and unqualified officials. This damages our interest in forcing the Jews to emigrate from Austria."

The memo then noted:

One of the problems with the emigration of Jews from Vienna is created by the activity of lawyers. Because of the complicated system, obtaining the necessary paperwork for a passport can take up to two or three months. For example, a certificate confirming that one does not have a criminal record may take 6–8 weeks to obtain. Rich Jews therefore employ Aryan lawyers to get the papers.

These lawyers manage to obtain favourable treatment by the authorities. They or their workers will come to an office with 20–30 applications and take up a great deal of the clerk's time, while poor Jews are standing in the street in a line that hardly moves for days. This has caused only problems. First, it has enabled the rich Jews to leave the country without problem, while the poor Jews stayed behind—this is contrary to our interest. Furthermore, it is already being said abroad that obtaining a passport in Vienna costs RM 1,000. The lawyers take enormous sums for each passport, and the rich Jews pay willingly. Since obtaining a passport by the Central Office for Emigration takes only up to 8 days (we get the certificate from the police within 48 hours), lawyers have already approached some of the government and party offices.

They have lost good business since the creation of the Central Office.

Furthermore, the Central Office has not arranged separate hours for these lawyers—a fact which increases their bitterness. The aim of the Central Office for Emigration is to force the poor Jews to emigrate and to make the rich ones pay.

Anna Freud had to cope with the bureaucracy. One of the new Nazi rules was that Jews who had permission to leave Vienna had to report to the police every day. Anna had to comply once Anton Sauerwald had signed her exit visa. When she first told her father she had to do this, he replied, "You have of course refused to obey so humiliating an order." Martin Freud said this showed his father's "defiant spirit," but given the way Anny Rosenberg Katan viewed Freud, it seems another instance of denial. Anna Freud, at least, was well aware of the risks run by anyone who refused to obey a Gestapo order. Defiance was a luxury Jews could not afford, even if they were world famous.

Freud still did not have a paper called *Der Steuer*, which was a certificate that all taxes due had been paid. "Everything depends on this," he wrote to his sister-in-law in London because "without that we are not certain to get across the border. We await this paper with anxiety." It was not the only paper he discovered he would need. The

Nazis had a genius for obstructive bureaucracy. To leave, Jews also needed a *bedenklichkeitserklaerung*. This document confirmed that the police had no reasons for detaining a Jew: that the Jew had completed the necessary formalities, had left no debts to Aryans, and had paid the exit tax.

Freud was worried about the logistics of the trip. He fussed to his sister-in-law that he needed one night in a decent bed between the two nights he would spend in sleeping cars. He fretted he would have to take the night train across the Channel. His daughter had to cope with too much but "she looked after everything."

If the Gestapo were brutal, that was not true of Anton Sauerwald, Freud told his sister-in-law. Sauerwald had promised that within a week the fate of the antique collection would be clear. Freud ended by saying that Minna and Dorothy Burlingham should "be joyful that you are outside." He hoped they would meet in Paris again.

Freud was not sure what to do about those of his personal books that had not been removed to the National Library. He chose those he wanted to take with him to London and sold some to a Jewish bookseller called Sonnenfeld who had a shop on the Berggasse. But Sonnenfeld was himself arrested a few days later and robbed of the collection. Other books went to a more substantial dealer. Within weeks, they were offered for sale for 1,850 marks as "a special collection on neurology and psychiatry of a Viennese scientist." The scientist was not named but some people knew who he was.

A sharp New York librarian, Dr. Jacob Shatzky, heard the collection was for sale and bought it for the New York State Psychiatric Institute where a special Freud library was established in 1939. He had been tipped off that the scientist was Freud. The ease with which this sale was achieved suggests that Anton Sauerwald helped and, perhaps, received some money for that piece of inside information. Hans Lobner gave a meticulous account of the items that were in the library. The collection contained some rarities including *Artine* by the French poet René Char with an original engraving by Salvador Dalí, a man who had been inspired by Freud. Dalí first read Freud in a Spanish translation. Char had sent the book as a present and offered it "with deep admiration and the greatest respect." Char later became a hero of the French resistance.

When he wrote to Minna Bernays a few days later, Freud could not help saying, "You have so often wanted to come to England and now you are there." He had cleared his writing desk, but they were still not allowed to leave and Anna still had to strive with "much intelligence and good humor to work us free." But money was still a big problem, even though the exit taxes had been paid. "We don't know with what means we shall pay our bills," he confessed to his sister-in-law. "Hopefully we shall sort out the money problems for the tickets." Twice he had gone out into Vienna to bid farewell to some of his favorite places. This was a risk because he might be recognized as a Jew. Neighbors had mistaken one elderly man for Freud and beaten him up. As a result Freud did not manage to take his leave of all his old haunts. He did get out two more times but never managed to get "to the garden of our childhood," by which he meant the Prater.

We are lucky to have a detailed visual record of the apartment at 19 Berggasse as it was that April. One of the analysts who had refused to help liquidate the publishing company, August Aichhorn, had written a minor classic, *Wayward Youth*, on young criminals. He was very fat, rather eccentric—he always wore black—and had something of a crush on Anna Freud. He often had coffee at the Café Museum with a young Jewish photographer, Edmund Engelman.

A few weeks after the Anschluss, August Aichhorn told Edmund Engelman that "a museum can be created once the storm is over." But a museum had to have exhibits. Engelman agreed to take photographs of the apartment. He would have to do so without using a flash because 19 Berggasse was being watched by the Gestapo. The Gestapo wanted to make sure that the family did not smuggle any of their valuables out, especially after the suspicions Martin Freud's behavior had aroused.

Edmund Engelman recalled that on his first visit to the apartment, "I was amazed by the unbelievable number of fine artistic objects." The photographs give a beautiful record of Freud's home. Some tables are laden with ten or more statuettes, many of which Hilda Doolittle had described. The photographs included one of a chair Anna Freud had had specially designed for her father so that he could sit comfortably while writing. Behind Freud's analytic chair in the consulting room were four original paintings by Wilhelm Busch—an ass who is looking at a painter who is working, a fish spitting at a fly, a rhinoceros looking at a black man, and a chicken struggling to spit out a fly.

After Edmund Engelman had spent some days in the apartment, Freud walked in on him. "We stared at each other," Engelman wrote.

The young photographer said that he felt "flustered and embarrassed" in the presence of the great man who August Aichhorn had insisted he must not stress. Freud "looked concerned" but stayed calm and "matter of fact." Aichhorn explained who Engelman was and, very luckily, he had some of his photographs with him. He presented these to Freud, explaining they were souvenirs that he had been meaning to give him.

Freud looked at August Aichhorn and Edmund Engelman and then broke into a smile. He was very pleased and thanked the young man. This record of his apartment would mean a great deal to him when he was in London. Engelman then asked Freud if he would allow him to take photographs of Freud himself. Freud agreed and so we have pictures of him, his daughter, and his wife just before they left Vienna.

Edmund Engelman gave the photographs to August Aichhorn to keep because, as a Jew himself, he felt it was imperative that he should leave the city quickly. He heard a few days later that the Gestapo was looking for him. He managed to get away to France, from which he sailed to Bolivia. He felt it was much too dangerous to try to carry the negatives with him.

Since the Nazis had taken over, Freud stayed in his apartment nearly all the time, a prisoner in his own home. Hans Pichler came to see him quite often. Max Schur visited every day. Freud's physical condition was not bad and there were no new lesions, but "the crust formations were bothersome and needed constant attention," Schur said. He was referring to crusts high up in the nasal cavity.

In his next letter to Minna Bernays, written on May 23, Freud complained that it was raining and his study was darker than usual. But he had one piece of good news. He had arranged, with the help of "unser Kommissar," the trustee Anton Sauerwald, for some of his antiquities to be sold for 30,000 reichsmarks. That "would nearly secure the border fees," Freud wrote. But he was not telling his sister-in-law the whole truth. Marie Bonaparte knew that Freud was short of money and paid all the exit taxes for all of the family. Alfred Indra, Freud's lawyer, explained that the Princess had sent him the necessary funds, which he handed over to the tax authorities.

Money was still a major problem because not all of the family was leaving. Freud and his brother Alexander wanted to leave as much as they could for their four sisters who were staying behind.

Freud had to contemplate selling more of his books, part of the stock he wanted to ship to London. The idea did not please him but he had to do it. To his sister-in-law, Freud quoted Lord Byron, who had had to sell his library and said, "I won't be plucked of my feathers."

On May 26, Freud continued to Minna Bernays, "The situation has stayed the same. Once a day we speak with London, twice a day with Paris." He had been telephoned by an English journalist who wanted to confirm the rumor that Freud was coming to London. Freud was careful with him. In the midst of all of his anxieties, some routines persisted. Freud had started playing Tarok in the 1890s and once a week he had had Tarok parties in his house—the women were, of course, excluded. Paula Fichtl served coffee and dry cakes. Anxiety about leaving was no reason not to continue playing Tarok, so he had a Tarokpartie with August Aichhorn and other friends.

Again Freud complained of the "ghastly weather," which meant that he could not go out. Marie Bonaparte had decided to "visit us once more in Vienna and to accompany us over the border," he had written in an earlier letter, but now, it seemed, the Princess had to stay in France for a wedding. Freud was bitterly disappointed.

Two days later, Freud's first sentence in his letter to his sister-in-law again reveals his anxiety. "From Headquarters there was no news 'naturally.' The way they treat us," he added, "showed no urgency at all."

Still, Freud was now more hopeful but he was frightened of being too hopeful. It could yet go wrong so easily. He was also careful in his letters, because the letters might be being intercepted by the Gestapo. Stefan Zweig thought so because, he wrote to Freud only after he had left Vienna, "your handwriting revealed what your words had to conceal."

In his analysis of Hitler for the OSS, American psychiatrist Walter Langer pointed out that the führer was often awed by royalty and awkward with them. The Nazis were made anxious by having to deal with people who previously would have been seen as their social betters. Freud's friends now used these social insecurities. Anna Freud had spent weeks being charming to Anton Sauerwald. Princess Marie Bonaparte and Dorothy Burlingham were also utterly sweet to him. The deal that the Princess and Sauerwald discussed would allow Freud to take his library, sculpture collection, and much furniture, including the famous couch, to London. Sauerwald said that he supervised the packing of one thousand pieces of art, as well as of a very large number of books. That was not all. The man who accused the Jews of not being a reliable element of the population had to help pack a large quantity of their clothes and bed linens.

Though all the taxes had been paid and all the documents agreed, Freud was still afraid to believe he would be able to leave. On June 1, he took a walk to Tuerkenschanz Park in the Eighteenth District. The effort "showed me once again how little I can trust myself to do." Martha had to stop all the time because she got so tired.

In the evening Freud started a letter to Minna but he did not have the energy to finish it, though not because he was too tired. He felt too anxious in case there was some unexpected hitch, some new bureaucratic obstacle, some new demand for money, papers, or permits. They were also in danger of running out of suitcases. Twenty suitcases had already been packed.

The next day Freud started the letter to his sister-in-law again, and this time he did finish it. He wrote, "Today I can see more clearly and try again." He felt more certain now that they would leave, but his mood was still somber. "I was not prepared for how dark it was on my dining table. I tried to use the electrical light but then shadows fell across my hand." So Freud preferred to write half in the dark. He was still oppressed by all the details that had to be finalized, and by the failure of "Headquarters" to move more quickly. "We still have xyz formalities" to get through, he wrote.

Freud talked again of "unser Kommissar" and "die Anwalt," the lawyer. Both were very friendly and "we believe we will be able to travel tomorrow." Anna went to Thomas Cook to buy tickets and to get whatever foreign currency they could extract from the bank. The queues were long. In addition they were not yet able to make sleeping car reservations. In this frenzy of last-minute activity, one tiny detail is striking. One of Freud's sisters brought a small amount of foreign change she had kept from a trip abroad. Her brother would need every sou when he got out, she thought.

"You cannot imagine what the small things are," Freud added, and Anna had to deal with them all. The Berggasse tenants included couples Freud had known for years and people still tried to observe the decencies. The Freuds wanted to say a proper good-bye to their neighbors, and even to leave them some small gifts, which they did.

Freud hoped that his physician would travel with him, but Max

Schur suddenly came down with acute appendicitis. "I was desperate and tried to wait for a few hours but eventually had to be operated on," Schur said. Five days after the operation, Schur tried to get up to visit Freud, but he collapsed on the way to 19 Berggasse.

Anna came to tell Max Schur that they couldn't wait for him; the situation was getting too dangerous. Her father was too frail to travel without a physician, so they had to find a last-minute replacement. A friend of hers, Dr. Josephine Stross, agreed to travel with Freud as his doctor. Anton Sauerwald claimed that it had not been easy to arrange this. He must have worked bureaucratic wonders to get Dr. Stross an exit visa so quickly; Ernest Jones must have performed equal miracles to get her entry visas to France and Britain in such a short time.

Hans Pichler came on June 2 to give his famous patient a final check. The examination revealed no suspicious areas. He and Freud imagined they would never see each other again.

Stress and Leaving

There was a final bureaucratic hitch, as Freud had dreaded. The Gestapo wanted a reference, as they did not want to be accused of brutality against a famous man. They asked Freud to confirm he had been treated properly. They did not see, or pretended not to see, the irony of his reply. "I most warmly recommend the Gestapo to everybody," he wrote.

The news that the Freuds were leaving even reached Palestine. Max Eitingon in Jerusalem phoned Arnold Zweig in Tel Aviv, who wrote at once to Freud. "Although I still cannot quite believe that everything will go according to plan I want to think that after all the frightful things that have happened this little favour of fortune will at last come off." Athena had to smile on them, he said. There is no evidence that Carl Jung offered Freud any help in arranging his escape.

The best account of the day they left comes from Paula Fichtl, who noted small ordinary details. She took the precaution of sewing some gold coins into the lining of her coat. Breakfast was served as usual. Freud had a soft-boiled egg and Anna suggested he sip a vermouth, one of his favorite drinks. No one talked much.

At midday, the maid ordered two taxis to take them and the twenty suitcases to the Westbahnhof. As she was about to leave the apartment she loved for the last time, she saw some dust on the sofa and whisked it off. New tenants would be coming and she did not want anyone to complain it had been left dirty. The taxis came at two o'clock. Freud kept the chow, Lun, on his lap as they drove to the station. (Jofie, his previous dog had died; Freud was distraught and eventually his family bought him Lun to whom he also became very attached.)

Freud, his wife, his daughter, Josephine Stross, Paula Fichtl, and the maid Mitzi were to join the Orient Express coming from Istanbul. So many others had left, or died, Freud observed, that they only needed two compartments. The last word Freud wrote in Vienna is now in the collection in the University of Manchester Library. He scribbled a postcard to his nephew Sam saying they were leaving and that he hoped finally to meet his nephew after a gap of thirty years.

They had reservations in the new steel S-class sleeping cars, which were painted blue with gold lining and lettering. The restaurant car had the same livery. At 3:25 p.m. the train pulled out of the Westbahnhof. The first stop was Salzburg where Paula Fichtl's relatives lived. All her family came to the station to say good-bye to her and one of her brothers gave her a bouquet of edelweiss, Austria's national flower. The train crossed into Germany and stopped in Munich. From Munich it traveled close to Dachau. The group was not alone, however. Freud did not know that on Bullitt's orders, the American consulate in Vienna had sent a man to watch over Freud and his family. Bullitt's "agent" was under instructions to intervene if there were any problems.

At 2:45 a.m. on June 4, the Orient Express reached the border between Germany and France. All Jews who were getting out feared trouble at the last minute. As Wilhelm Reich had observed, the Nazis created fear brilliantly. Freud and his wife were very tired so their daughter had to handle the officials. The Nazis looked at the passports and the exit visas in complete silence and then walked out of the compartment. After they had marched down the corridor to the next carriage, the conductor came to see the Freuds. "I wish I could come with you," Paula Fichtl remembered the conductor saying.

As they crossed the Rhine, they were all relieved. Freud wrote in his diary, "After the Rhine Bridge we were free." Anna brought out her father's favorite vermouth and they toasted their escape.

Stefan Zweig wrote to Freud, "But whatever may have been lost, whatever must be built anew, the main thing is you are out and you look back on the smoking ruins like people fleeing from Sodom."

In Vienna, Max Schur, who had been too sick to travel because of his ruptured appendix, said he felt "lonely and abandoned as never before." Anton Sauerwald had a problem, too. He had agreed to get one thousand items out of Vienna. To do that would take squaring the Gestapo and dealing with customs and the police, a formidable task.

The moment Freud crossed the border, the change in him was remarkable. He shook off the stress of the previous three months and was ready to concentrate on work. The productivity of the last fifteen months of his life would turn out to be remarkable.

12
Freedom

On the morning of June 4, six passengers got off the Orient Express at the Gare de l'Est. William Bullitt, Marie Bonaparte, Ernest Jones, and Martin Freud were there to meet them. Freud and his party were settled in the Bonaparte Bentley and the Bonaparte Rolls, and the Princess took them to her house in Saint-Cloud. They would sit in the garden where Topsy had scrapped with the chow mongrel.

The pictures that show Freud lying down on a chaise longue wearing a cap suggest it was just a day of rest. It was not though. First the Princess offered them a fine lunch to celebrate. Paula Fichtl was amazed to be asked to sit at the table with all the other guests. She had never been waited on before.

Freud's first task was to discuss an unfinished book project he had started long ago with William Bullitt. Bullitt had been a member of the American delegation to the Paris Peace Conference and was sent by President Woodrow Wilson on a secret mission to Russia. Bullitt wanted America to recognize Lenin's Bolshevik government, but his advice was rejected and he resigned. When the United States did finally agree to send its first ambassador to Moscow in 1933, Roosevelt chose Bullitt. Bullitt thought he would never find time to work on the book project again. Freud, for his part, was annoyed by Bullitt's tendency to secretiveness. Both men, however, were now set on finishing the book since Hitler's rise to power made their thesis supremely relevant.

The collaboration was not easy. Bullitt was often very aggressive and was far less deferential to Freud than most of his patients and ex-patients. Freud inserted a number of passages to which Bullitt objected. They now set about discussing how they could resolve their disagreements.

The book is neither pure biography nor pure psychoanalysis but rather a long *J'Accuse*. Freud and Bullitt find President Wilson guilty as a man, as a politician, as a university president, as a writer, and even as a patient because he irritated his doctor.

Freud hardly went into the inquiry without prejudice; back in 1926, he had told Max Eastman, "You should not have gone into the war at all" and "your Woodrow Wilson was the silliest fool of the century if not of all centuries."

It took Bullitt and Freud seven years to achieve a first draft because Freud insisted they find out as much as possible about Woodrow Wilson's childhood and his private life. Bullitt knew many of the late president's friends and wrote to them all. Few were reticent. The book does not acknowledge, however, that Freud's nephew Edward Bernays had also known Wilson well. Freud and Bullitt had access to many intimate details; the book was history written by formidably privileged insiders.

Woodrow Wilson was a man in the grip of powerful unconscious forces, Freud and Bullitt claimed. Wilson would not have agreed to the French and British demands at Versailles if he had been analyzed. Because he had never been on the couch, the wily monsters Lloyd George and Clemenceau ran rings around him.

Woodrow Wilson's father was a Presbyterian minister who had high ambitions for his son, even when Woodrow was only four months old and, presumably, in diapers. "That baby is dignified enough to be Moderator of the General Assembly," his father wrote proudly. Wilson's father was physically very affectionate. He liked to chase his son in the garden, catch him, and give him a great hug. Even as adults, the two men kissed emotionally whenever they met.

The relationship was inevitably unequal; the son was the passive one and that passivity would come to haunt him. Freud and Bullitt had no doubt that Wilson's love for his father went too far: "He not only expresses his love and admiration for his father but also removes his father by incorporating his father in himself as if by an act of cannibalism. Thenceforth he is himself the great admired father." American presidents have been accused of many things, but only Wilson has been accused of cannibalism, I think.

Woodrow Wilson only rebelled against his father once. He did not go into the ministry but into academia. After a minor breakdown, he taught politics at Princeton and published a book on George Washington. In 1895 Wilson's father came to live with him. The result: Woodrow Wilson broke down completely. The reasons were as purely Oedipal as you could get, Freud and Bullitt said. Wilson could not allow himself to express any hostility to his father, but in his unexplored unconscious, he was a boy with an unresolved Oedipal complex who wanted to "annihilate the Reverend Joseph Ruggles Wilson."

Woodrow Wilson became the president of Princeton in June 1902. Three months later, his father died. "After his father's death his [Woodrow's] addiction to speech making, which was already excessive, grew to fantastic proportions." One of the pleasures of the book is its bitchy tone. They wrote with biting irony. "The Reverend Joseph Ruggles Wilson, who incidentally is not to be recommended as a model for fathers, had made his son love him so deeply and submissively that the flood of passivity he had aroused could be satisfied by no other man or activity."

The turning point came when Woodrow Wilson met Colonel George Harvey, who admired Wilson's speeches and decided he could be nominated to run for president of the United States. It then all happened very quickly. Woodrow Wilson was elected governor of New Jersey and two years later, in 1912, elected president. "Thenceforth there was a somewhat unusual amount of deity in the character of Woodrow Wilson," sniped Bullitt and Freud. The president was now inclined to see himself as God's instrument on earth. Freud had more sympathy with patients who thought rats were gnawing at their buttocks.

Freud and Bullitt wrote—and the voice is pure Freud—that they could not escape the conclusion "that a man who is capable of taking the illusions of religion so literally and is so sure of a special personal intimacy with the Almighty is unfitted for relations with children of men."

When the First World War broke out, Woodrow Wilson proclaimed the neutrality of the United States. His adviser, Colonel Edward M. House, wrote on November 10, 1915, that the president must use all his skills and the resources of America "in behalf of some plan by which the peace of the world may be maintained." House went on to say, "This is the part I think that you are destined to play in this world tragedy and it is the noblest part that has ever come to a son of man."

Freud and Bullitt commented, "Woodrow Wilson, who in his un-conscious was God and Christ, could not resist such words." He longed to be the bringer of peace on earth, not just because that was a noble ideal, but because his masculine side identified with God and his feminine side identified with Christ.

Ten months before the war ended, Woodrow Wilson set out four-teen basic points for a just peace, but his failure to deal with his inner conflicts with his father crippled him. The world was paying the price, according to Freud and Bullitt.

When the president came to Paris in March 1919, huge crowds lined the avenues to cheer him. He was seen as a savior but he did not know how to turn this to his political advantage. He wilted when faced by Clemenceau and Lloyd George. When he was confronted by strong men, "the deep underlying femininity of his nature began to control him and he discovered he did not want to fight them with force. He wanted to preach sermons to them."

Clemenceau and Lloyd George sensed the president's vulnerabil-ity. On March 27 Clemenceau demanded a thirty-year occupation of the Rhineland and an annexation of the Saar. When the president said this had never been part of the war aims, Clemenceau exploded. "You are pro German. You are seeking to destroy France." Woodrow Wil-son then sulked that perhaps Clemenceau wanted him to go home.

"I do not wish you to go home but I intend to do so myself." With that Clemenceau put on his hat and walked out. Deeply offended, the president went for a long drive in the Bois de Boulogne and missed lunch. When he got back, he stood up and made an appeal. His speech even impressed Clemenceau who shook the pres-ident's hand.

"You are a good man, Mr. President, and you are a great man."

Clemenceau might flatter but he did not change his position. Woodrow Wilson told his aides the problem was that Clemenceau had "a feminine mind." In fact, nothing "less feminine than Clemenceau's refusal to be swept off his feet by Wilson's oratory could be imagined," Freud and Bullitt judged. It was a textbook case of projection. Woodrow Wilson, the man with the feminine mind, claimed Clemenceau was too feminine, but nothing more feminine could be imagined than Wilson's refusal to use "the masculine weapons in his hands." Instead he merely repeated his peace plan. Not surprisingly, this failure of nerve triggered another "nervous" collapse.

On April 9, Woodrow Wilson compromised on the Saar and "never again did he threaten to fight for the peace he had set out to give the world." Freud then invoked his beloved Shakespeare and complained that Lloyd George, the "Welsh Shylock," was "unwilling to abandon one molecule of the British pound of flesh."

The Treaty of Versailles was delivered to the Germans on May 7. The German president called it a document "dictated by hate" and reminded Woodrow Wilson that it broke many promises he had made to him. The U.S. president was so disturbed he was even rude to Poincaré, the French president, and refused to sit down to dinner with him. Freud and Bullitt bitched that Woodrow Wilson was also jealous because Poincaré was himself an excellent public speaker.

Divorced from reality by his psychological weaknesses, Woodrow Wilson referred to the Treaty of Versailles as a "99% insurance against war." Few predictions have been so wrong.

The writing of the psychobiography has verve, wit, and urgency. Agreeing on the final text gave Freud great pleasure, as did everything else during his brief stay in Paris. He told Marie Bonaparte that her home "had restored our dignity and morale. After having been wrapped in love for 12 hours, we left proud and rich under the protection of Athena." She had given him a little antique statue of the goddess with the following note:

Athena
Peace and Reason
Greets those who have fled
From the mad inferno.

It was an inferno whose causes Freud and Bullitt had now explained.

At the end of the day, the Princess's magnificent vehicles drove them to the Gare du Nord, which appropriately has imitation Greek figures on its front entrance. This time there was no reason to be anxious about crossing the frontier. Ernest Jones had obtained documents from Samuel Hoare so that Freud and his family would be treated as if they belonged to a diplomatic mission.

As he crossed the Channel, Freud dreamed that he was landing not at Dover (where the train landed), but at Pevensey, where William the Conqueror had landed in 1066. This was hardly the dream of a dispossessed or depressed man but more of a conquistador.

Freud was now an old man in a hurry. He had two more books to finish, *Moses and Monotheism* and *An Outline of Psychoanalysis*. Four years earlier Freud had written, "I do not only think but I know [his italics] *that I shall let myself be deterred by this second obstacle, by external danger, from publishing the last portion of my study on Moses.*" In Britain, he would be free of those external dangers and finally be able to write what he believed. He would also have the chance to see his nephew Sam at last.

Life in Hampstead

When Freud arrived at Victoria Station, it was what we would now call a media event. Newsreels recorded him getting off the train; the papers put it on their front pages. *The British Medical Journal* noted that doctors would feel proud that their country had offered him asylum.

One immediate problem was Freud's dog, Lun. Even the ever-energetic Ernest Jones could not manage to circumvent quarantine regulations designed to stop rabies from coming into Britain. Lun was taken to what Fichtl called "the animal asylum" in South Kensington. Freud missed his chow dreadfully.

Freud now realized that in letters to his colleagues, he had said so little of his fears of the last eleven weeks. He wrote to Max Eitingon: "It is hardly an accident that I have remained so matter of fact up to now. The emotional climate of these days is hard to grasp, almost indescribable. The feeling of triumph on being liberated is too strongly mixed with sorrow for in spite of everything I greatly loved the prison from which I have been released."

Freud worried about "how long will a fatigued heart be able to accomplish any work." He very much wanted to see his sister-in-law Minna but had not managed to do that yet.

Freud had other reasons for being depressed. The *New York Times* reported Freud saying, "All my money and property in Vienna is gone." He was not being totally truthful, but the *New York Times* did not get to see his bank records. An account card shows that three accounts were still active. One of Freud's accounts in Holland was closed—the guilder-denominated account—on June 30, 1938; his other two accounts that we have records of were closed on July 31 and September 19, 1938. There were more accounts because his letters to his nephew Sam in the 1920s show money being sent by Freud from at least five banks. Anna Freud also admitted later that there were Swiss accounts.

Stefan Zweig, who had given up on Palestine and moved to central London, wrote to Freud on June 6 from his Hallam Street address. Zweig did not want to disturb Freud yet, but they must meet once Freud had recovered "from your bitter journey." Zweig gave Freud his ex-directory number, Langham 3993.

On June 8, Freud wrote to Marie Bonaparte that they had been flooded with flowers. There had been three autograph collectors and a woman painter who wanted him to sit for a portrait. He also received a letter from a woman whose mother had been diagnosed as incurable, but surely the great therapist could heal her. There was also a letter from "an enterprising delicatessen"—presumably a Jewish one. The next day, Freud's nephew Sam came down from Manchester, so the two men finally did meet. Sadly there is no record of what they said to each other.

Freud received "a rambling four-page telegram from Cleveland, Ohio" inviting Freud to make his home there. He told Marie Bonaparte that he would write back saying it was not possible, since they had already unpacked. He could hardly bear to pack twenty suitcases again. Finally he thanked her for the cigars she sent, which had been stripped of nicotine and were rather tasteless. Freud did not like these unmanly cigars. "He soon found some tasty ones," Max Schur noted.

News of Freud's triumphant arrival had repercussions in Vienna. The Gestapo made inquiries at the hospital where Max Schur had been operated on; they wanted to satisfy themselves that he had had appendicitis and did not have some sinister reason for not leaving Vienna. On June 8 Schur's wife, Helen, was summoned to the exit tax office to satisfy them about some new detail. If she could not provide the information they requested, they would revoke her permission to leave. Luckily she succeeded.

Max Schur finally left Vienna with his family on June 10, 1938, and reached London five days later. Freud, he found, had had some cardiac problems during the trip and had an irritable bladder, but otherwise was in rather good health. Schur did not seem to realize that escaping Vienna was better than the best medicine for Freud. He was free and free to work. The liberation meant he could consider another potential triumph, the Nobel Prize again, with some detachment. This time Einstein would not be arguing against Freud getting the award.

Chaim Weizmann came to visit on June 17 and told Freud a resolution had been passed at London's Institute of Sociology welcoming him. H. G. Wells visited two days later. Three secretaries of the Royal Society came on June 23 so that Freud could sign its charter of Fellows. He had been made a "foreign" Fellow of the Society. New Fellows were supposed to sign the charter at the Royal Society's offices but Freud pleaded infirmity. He did not admit, however, that a few days earlier he had been well enough to visit Lun at the "animal asylum."

Rome had been Freud's obsession and he had only written briefly about London, but he had drawn a poetic comparison between memorials and the mind: "If you walk through London you will find before one of the greatest railway stations of the city a richly decorated Gothic pillar—'Charing Cross.'" Charing was, Ernest Jones told Freud, derived from the French chere reine or beloved Queen. The Gothic pillar commemorated Eleanor of Aquitaine the wife of the 12th century king Henry II. Henry had Gothic crosses erected along the route her coffin took to Westminster. Charing Cross was of the places where such a cross was built. The Monument is another memorial, a tall pillar that was built after the Great Fire of London in 1666 in honor of those who had died in the conflagration. "These monuments are memory symbols like the hysterical symptoms." In his diary Freud likened some Londoners to his patients claiming that "hystericals and all neurotics behave like these two unpractical Londoners, not only in that they remember the painful experiences of the distant past, but because they are still strongly affected by them. They cannot escape from the past and neglect present reality in its favor."

But Freud *had* escaped, if not his past, at least the city of his past. He was delighted he had met "with the friendliest reception in lovely, free magnanimous England." He could not allow himself to relax entirely as, every day, there was "distressing news from Vienna and the continuous appeals for help which serve only to remind one of one's helplessness." But the joy of liberation meant, "I am once more able to speak and write—I had almost said 'and think'—as I wish or I must," he told Stefan Zweig. He sat down every day at his writing desk to finish *Moses* at last.

On July 12 Freud recorded a two-minute speech for the BBC. It is the best recording of his voice we have—and sounds disconcertingly squeaky. Freud explained he had started his career as a neurologist, briefly outlined the nature of analysis, and thanked England for the wonderful welcome it had afforded his family and him.

Freud had not totally escaped the Nazis, in fact, because they continued to "bleed" him, as he put it. On July 18, the Nazi foreign currency office ordered Freud to turn over a Swiss account denominated in Dutch guilders. He complied because he was afraid his four sisters in Vienna would suffer if he did not. This Swiss account was finally closed on July 31, so the Nazis got yet more money out of him, which was transferred to them by the lawyer, Dr. Alfred Indra. But there was still some money left in at least one account that he had managed to keep secret with Anton Sauerwald's help, as well as the gold smuggled out through the Greek embassy. There had to be some funds as Freud arranged to buy the house at 20 Maresfield Gardens for £6,000, though it took a few months for the sale to be completed. He did not borrow the money from Marie Bonaparte. Sauerwald's estimate that Freud was worth over two million schillings was a good one. Local real estate agents who have some sense of the history of London property prices believe Freud paid far too much for his new house. Even more remarkably, Freud managed to get a mortgage from Barclays Bank, some achievement for a man of eighty-two in those financially conservative days.

Freud received so many letters that the post office said they knew where to deliver one that was addressed only "Freud—London." This matters because Carl Jung claimed after the war that he had sent a telegram congratulating Freud on his escape. In her biography, Deirdre Bair states that no sign of that telegram has ever been found.

Freud also received "with a frequency surprising to a foreigner," many letters which fretted about the state of his soul and enjoined him to convert. These "good people" wanted to make him a Christian before it was too late. They stood no chance. Freud would die as he had lived—a true atheist though rather tribal in his Jewishness.

Marie Bonaparte came to London for three days on June 23. Freud asked for her help in getting his four sisters out of Vienna and she promised she would try. But even with her connections, she could not get permission from the French authorities to allow the sisters to come to Paris. The evidence suggests that the Princess only really tried hard for Rosa who, she suggested, should be awarded Greek citizen-ship. Celia Bertin, Marie Bonaparte's biographer, says very little about Marie Bonaparte's attempts. Yet there were powerful allies she could have enlisted. Bullitt was now the American ambassador in Paris and could have asked the French government for a personal favor. Ernest Jones had not lost his contacts in Whitehall. Yet the sisters remained in Nazi Vienna as the plight of Jews there got worse.

On June 24, Arnold Zweig wrote that he was delighted Freud's name was being considered again by the Nobel Committee. Freud refused to get too excited, saying analysis had "several good enemies" among the grandees who decided who would receive the award. "So though the money would be very welcome after the way the Nazis bled me in Vienna and since neither my son nor my son-in-law is a rich man, Anna and I have agreed that one is not bound to have everything." Freud ended with some irony that he and his inseparable daughter had decided that he would renounce the Prize and she would renounce the journey to Stockholm to collect it.

Surrealist Surprise

Freud received many visitors, perhaps the most interesting being Salvador Dalí, who first read Freud's *The Interpretation of Dreams* in a Spanish translation in 1925. Dalí's *The Tragic Myth of Millet's Angelus* is written rather like a Freudian case history. In 1956, the artist was asked if he had ever undergone psychoanalysis and replied that he had met Freud two years before Freud died. "My first period is influenced by Freud completely," Dalí said, but he had never needed psychoanalysis "because I am not crazy. You see my kind of craziness is a craziness of precision and clarity, to the contrary of a psychopathological's craziness."

Some people doubt the meeting ever took place. Dalí himself was to blame. In his autobiography, he said he tried to visit Freud three times and found the great man out of town each time. But there were two reliable witnesses. Stefan Zweig took him and a would-be ana-lyst, Edward James, to see Freud on July 19, 1938. The three of them were together when Dalí drew his famous sketch of Freud, one of his most evocative and moving likenesses.

Freud wrote to Stefan Zweig the next day, thanking him for bringing the visitors, and said, "I had been inclined till then to take the surrealists who seem to have chosen me as their patron saint as absolutely mad—95% mad let's say as if we were discussing alcohol." But the young Spaniard with his "fanatical eyes and his undoubted technical mastery" would make an interesting subject for an analytic study. This letter completely contradicts some accounts that claim the meeting was not a success and that Dalí seems to have bored Freud.

Freud did not stay long in the rented house at 39 Elsworthy Road. In late August he and his family moved into the Esplanade Hotel in Warrington Crescent in Maida Vale. The hotel is now called the Colonnade and has a Freud suite. There is a telling photograph of Freud outside the Esplanades at the bottom of some ten steps. He must then have been well enough to walk up them. The hotel was run by an Austrian couple and Freud would stay there till September.

Medical Vanities

One of Max Schur's first tasks in London was to make sure Freud could get proper medical help if an emergency should arise. Hans Pichler had referred Freud to a Dr. George Exner who had been his pupil, but Pichler was not sure Exner could cope with the complexities of Freud's nose and mouth. The lesions could easily turn malignant again and they were hard to operate on because they were high up in the nasal cavity. Exceptionally, the Home Office gave Schur permission to act as Freud's doctor before he had passed the examinations he needed to practice in Britain.

Being a young doctor in a foreign country required much tact. Max Schur had to struggle to learn how to work with Exner. Medical vanities were the problem. Exner would defer to Hans Pichler, his old teacher, but not to Schur. Early in August, Schur found a small lesion in front of the area where the last operation had been performed. This was worrying, but Exner "listened with a mixture of disbelief and annoyance to the statements of a foreigner." Very concerned, Schur wrote to Pichler to ask if he would come from Vienna. Pichler must have told Freud how worried Schur was. Freud was angry and accused Schur of being alarmist.

Freud himself told Marie Bonaparte the worrying medical news. On August 18 she replied that Professor Rigaud of the Marie Curie Institute advocated more electrocoagulation. Max Schur then found that a large area had lesions behind the place of the last operation; he thought that was ominous. Schur now again asked Hans Pichler to come to London and stressed it was urgent. Freud had every reason to live because his book on Moses would be published in August, thirty-seven years after he had first stood in front of Michelangelo's great statue.

13
Moses and Monotheism

On November 14, 1986, Professor Yosef Hayim Yerushalmi gave the Lionel Trilling lecture at Columbia University. He revealed that he had obtained from the Library of Congress a hitherto unknown version of Freud's *Moses and Monotheism* and that this original draft was "different in significant ways from the published version." Freud, it was clear, had been too anxious to state his real views on anti-Semitism while he was in Vienna.

In his 1937 article in *Imago*, Freud wrote: "To deprive a people of the man whom they take pride in as the greatest of their sons is not a thing to be gladly or carelessly undertaken—especially when one himself belongs to that people." There was no mention of the present dilemmas Jews faced. But Freud wanted to write something far more direct, Yerushalmi argued, as the unpublished version read: "*My immediate purpose was to gain knowledge of the person Moses, my more distant goal to contribute thereby to the solution of a problem, still current today.*"

Freud explained that his book had been written twice, "the first time a few years ago in Vienna where I did not think it would be possible to publish it. I determined to give it up but it tormented me like a ghost," a ghost that was still not at rest. Ironically the Nazi invasion that forced Freud to leave "freed [him] from any anxiety." In England he was at liberty to say what he thought without fearing that the authorities, Father Schmidt, or the pope would take revenge on psychoanalysis. The moment he crossed the Channel, Freud admitted, "I found the temptation irresistible to make the knowledge I held accessible to the world." Freud sometimes joked that he had Hitler to thank for forcing him to go to London. "Thank the führer," was the quip he often used.

Moses and Monotheism is a mixture of psychoanalysis, biblical criticism, and analysis of anti-Semitism. It is an examination by a Jew of why Jews have been hated through the ages. Freud explored three different threads. First, he believed that Exodus got it completely wrong; Moses was not a Jew but an Egyptian. Pharaoh's daughter did not find the baby floating in a basket amid the bulrushes and did not take him to Pharaoh's palace. That kind of fable was typical of many stories of the origins of heroes. In reality, the prophet was an Egyptian, probably a member of Pharaoh's court. There was a rumor that Moses might even have been a general who led Egyptian forces in Ethiopia, the Jewish historian Josephus claimed.

Second, the very name "Moses" was suggestive. Freud acknowledged his debt to a nineteenth-century Egyptologist, James Henry Breasted, who pointed out that Moses was a noun in Egyptian; "mose" meant "child." Little Egyptians had names like Amen-mose," meaning "Amon-a-child" or "Ptah-mose," meaning "Ptah-a-child." Moses was not a Jewish name at all. No author, Freud said, had even considered the obvious, that a child born in Egypt who had an Egyptian name might be Egyptian—and not Jewish at all. If Moses was not Jewish, just what religion did he belong to or believe in? Freud knew his answer would outrage Jews and Christians alike.

The third theme centered on the birth of monotheism. Ancient Egypt rejoiced in nearly as many gods as palm trees. There were gods of the moon, the sun, the earth, and stars; there were abstractions such as Maat the god of Justice and Truth, as well as animal gods. Cats and crocodiles were favorites.

Around 1370 BCE, the Egyptians were becoming skeptical about their all-too-blatant gods. The School of Priests in the Sun Temple at Heliopolis had been developing the idea that there was one universal god who was an ethical being, unlike the dog, cat, and fish deities. These reforming priests found a new Pharaoh who was sympathetic to their "heresy." Akenhaton's father allowed them to worship the sun god and spread the solar gospel. His son was even more of an enthusiastic sun worshipper but he was spiritually subtle. The sun was not just the brightest object in the sky but a symbol of the divine being whose energy glowed in its rays.

Freud quoted the German historian Adolf Erman who wrote in *Die Ägyptische Religion*, published in 1905: "There are . . . words which are meant to express in an abstract form the fact that not the star itself was worshipped, but the Being that manifested itself in it."

The novelty was that Akenhaton's God was exclusive, not one god among many. One of his hymns from 1370 BCE praised: "O Thou only God, there is no other God than Thou." There was not one God greater than other gods, but just one God.

Six years into his reign, Akenhaton left Thebes and built a new capital lower down the Nile at Tell el-Amarna. The move was symbolic of this profound change to the worship of the one true God. The site now is a desolate spot in the desert about three hours from Cairo.

In light of all this, and the word "light" is perhaps very appropriate, Freud argued that Moses was an important official, perhaps even a priest, at the time of Akhenaton. Moses was able, ambitious, and a devout believer in the new sun religion. When Akenhaton died, the traditional priests tried to bring the old gods back and outlaw monotheism. Moses had to choose, Freud said: abandon his new faith or do something dramatic. Here Freud offered a daring hypothesis. Moses decided that if his country was turning its back on the new—and true—religion, he would found a new empire with a new people who believed in a new religion—that of the one and only God. A new religion needed believers. But Moses did not have to seek too far because Egypt was full of Jews who were flattered that an important Egyptian took an interest in them. They listened and accepted Moses, who "placed himself at their head." Freud assumed that generations of slavery had made the Jews servile and supine, so no troublemaker asked Moses, "What makes you think you are a prophet?"

For his part, Moses insisted that the Jews adopt some Egyptian ways. The Greek historian Herodotus had noticed a telling characteristic on a visit to Egypt in 450 BCE. The Egyptians had a horror of pigs—eating pork is totally forbidden under kosher laws, too. It took a Jew to point out that kashrut was, in fact, an ancient Egyptian custom. Freud then suggested it was Moses who insisted that Jewish boys be circumcised. Forget the covenant with Abraham as recorded in Genesis; Moses the Egyptian made the Jews lose their foreskins. For Freud, this was highly significant: he had always believed that Jews were persecuted because they were circumcised and therefore reminded men of their fears of castration.

Freud then argued that the book of Exodus is partly right. Somehow Moses persuaded the Pharaoh to let his people go. But the forty years of wandering in the desert did not proceed as told in the Bible. There was no parting of the Red Sea. Moses simply waved good-bye to the Pyramids and marched his followers into Sinai. The new Pharaoh who had succeeded Akenhaton did not even bother to pursue them. According to Freud, written and archaeological evidence suggested that the Exodus from Egypt took place between 1358 and 1350 BCE, soon after the death of Akenhaton.

But the wanderings of the Jews did not end in the Sinai Desert, as Exodus claimed. They went to Meribah Kadesh—"Meribah" means a "place of the waters" and "Kadesh" means "holy." There they made an alliance with a tribe from the land of Midian. The priests of each tribe praised the superior qualities of their own God, Freud claimed, and they then agreed on a compromise. The Jews embraced the Midian god Jahve, who was a volcano god. There were volcanoes in Western Arabia, so it was sensible to worship and appease a volcanic deity. This God was rather primitive, belching flames and inclined to violence, but was just what the Jews needed to stiffen their resolve before marching into Canaan. In return, the Midianites accepted some Jewish practices, though it was unclear what these might be. Freud argued that this compromise did not please Moses, who did not believe in a god who was volcanic or even tribal. So what made him accept it?

Freud's argument then relied on the work of the German biblical scholar Ernst Sellin. Sellin claimed Moses never agreed to the compromise. He had never made it to the Promised Land not because God would not let him enter Canaan but because the prophet had been murdered—by the unruly Jews. Sellin based this sensational discovery on a reading of the book of Hosea. Sellin had been unable to explain why the Jews should do that; Freud could, however.

Moses would not compromise with the volcano god, so the Jews killed their "father" Moses, just as the Stone Age sons had killed their father in *Totem and Taboo*. But they could not escape feeling guilty. After the Neanderthal sons committed murder, they stuck their father on a totem; the Jews, being more advanced, proclaimed Moses the real father of their new religion.

Freud then made an extraordinary leap of the imagination. In the section of *Moses and Monotheism* called "The Analogy," he argued that there was a long gap between the Jews beginning to worship the volcano god and the emergence of monotheistic Judaism as we know it: about eight centuries, Freud reckoned. It was not just human children who had a latency period—this was Freud's "leap"—Judaism had one, too. Freud quoted the work of the biblical scholar Paul Volz who said in 1907: "The exalted work of Moses was understood and carried through to begin with only feebly and scantily till, in the course of centuries, it penetrated more and more and, at length in the great prophets it met with like spirits who continued the lonely man's work."

The different identities of the "advanced" Egyptian one God and the "primitive" volcano god affected the Chosen People ever since. "Jews are riven by an oscillation between Akenhaton's 'Universal' God and Yahweh/Jehovah the Tribal God." Suffering in biblical days made "their God became hard, relentless, and, as it were, wrapped in gloom. But the Jews had the consolation of knowing they were His chosen people." Though he was somewhat vague in describing the process, Freud claimed that over eight hundred years, the Jewish God came to resemble the Mosaic Egyptian God. But traces of the conflict between the tribal God and the advanced ethical deity can be found in the Second Commandment. It does not say there are no other gods, but *Thou shalt have no other gods before me.*" The implication is that there are minor gods behind Yahweh.

Freud then provided one of those case histories he could make so riveting, that of a little boy who, as so often happened, "in middle-class families shared his parents' bedroom during the first years of his life." This child had often observed sexual acts between his parents—seeing some things and hearing still more. He was very sensitive to noises, and once he had woken up he could not get to sleep again. The child became aggressively masculine and "began to excite his little penis with his hand and to attempt various sexual attacks on his mother." The mother then forbade him to touch his penis. Marthe Roberts argues that one reason Freud developed his ideas about Moses is that, at the end of his life, he was yet again trying to distance himself from his father and was finishing Jacob off—symbolically, at least.

In the third part of *Moses and Monotheism*, with considerable passion, Freud tried to understand why Jews had been hated and persecuted for centuries. He pointed out that "the poor Jewish people, who with its usual stiff-necked obduracy continued to deny the murder of their 'father,' were endlessly accused of killing the Christian

God. Being arrogant and stiff-necked, Jews denied it was their fault."

"You won't admit that you murdered God," screeched the anti-Semites.

Then the ones who were more honest said, "It is true, we did the same thing, but we admitted it, and since then we have been purified."

Freud believed this story had had a deep impact on Jews and argued that it was a characteristic of Jews that "there is no doubt that they have a very good opinion of themselves, think themselves nobler, on a higher level, superior to the others, from whom they are also separated by many of their customs. With this they are animated by a special trust in life, such as is bestowed by the secret possession of a precious gift." Freud, who claimed he was a pessimist, added, "It is a kind of optimism. Religious people would call it trust in God."

As the Chosen People, Jews felt especially close to God. Freud said they shared "in the grandeur of God," which made them proud and confident. This new God also blessed them above all other peoples. Moreover, Jews were forced to become more intellectual because they worshipped a God who could not be seen. As a result, Freud claimed, Jews were less slaves to their instincts than were other groups. The world, however, condemned their insufferable arrogance and made them suffer for it. Freud had managed the remarkable feat of writing a book that praised Jews and the Jewish heritage, at the same time outraging the rabbis, most Jews, and many Christians.

"The Christian religion did not maintain the high levels in things of the mind to which Judaism soared," Freud attacked. Christianity was not up to the challenge of monotheism and so it brought back many lesser gods "lightly veiled" and in subordinate positions; it also restored the great mother goddess to her pedestal, as Catholics especially adored the Virgin. Freud argued that the triumph of Christianity was a fresh victory for the priests of Amun over Akenhaton's superior god after an interval of fifteen hundred years. It's hardly surprising that Freud's argument was likely to upset just about everyone.

A number of rabbis learned what Freud was writing and begged him to stop. Wasn't Hitler making enough trouble for Jews? Did Freud have to add to their misery by denying the truths of the Torah?

Many Christian theologians were not keen on the Akenhaton thesis either, since the Gospels speak of a direct line of descent—fourteen generations from Moses to David and fourteen generations from David to Jesus. Those who urged Freud to keep quiet did not know him, a man who never considered keeping quiet about his ideas to spare others. The question of whether Freud was right or not about Moses is not possible to judge. But there is a consensus now that the Pharaoh Akhenaton "invented" monotheism. There Freud was right and well ahead of specialist scholars.

Freud published *Moses and Monotheism* in Amsterdam. It was, as he expected, very controversial and received with outrage. It had been a long while since one of his works had been so harshly criticized. Even many of his fellow analysts hated it. In London, the *News Chronicle* called for Freud to be sent back to Germany—the paper forgot he actually had come from Austria. There is no sign that Freud minded the row. The book sold eighteen hundred copies in two months and Freud was very happy with that. He wanted it to be translated quickly. He hesitated about who should do it, but Ernest Jones insisted that he would produce an English version immediately, with help from his wife.

Now, and virulently, Freud's cancer came back. Max Schur summoned Hans Pichler, who flew to London on September 7. It was a race against time; immediate surgery was needed and it would have to be radical. Pichler would have to cut in through the cheek and lips. He asked Schur if he thought Freud's heart could take the strain of an operation. Schur thought Freud would cope.

The two Austrian doctors arrived at the London Clinic on September 8. Neither was entitled to operate in Britain but Pichler had a European reputation and the British surgeon, George Exner, had been his pupil. Pichler took control in the operating theater. He split Freud's lip, carried the incision up the nose, and managed to excise a great deal of pathological tissue. Under the microscope the tissue did not seem to be cancerous. Pichler also had to perform another electrocoagulation.

Max Schur had been right about Freud's ability to cope. By the evening the patient was feeling well enough to read, Hans Pichler wrote in his notes. Anna Freud wrote to Marie Bonaparte that Pichler had behaved "exceedingly well," a phrase that makes complete sense when one realizes that Pichler was a member of the Nazi Party. Freud then had a good night's sleep, and after visiting his patient in the morning, Pichler flew back to Vienna.

On September 27, 1938, Freud moved into the house at 20 Maresfield Gardens. Paula Fichtl unrolled the Persian carpet, which had come from Vienna, and then she and Anna arranged the art objects in exactly the same positions as they had been in the Berggasse. Clearly Anton Sauerwald had managed to get the thousand antiquities out of Austria. Sauerwald claimed that he had had to pay for three carriages in a freight train to load all the Freud goods. Neither Ernest Jones nor Marie Bonaparte says a word about what was an astonishing piece of sly transportation across frontiers. Sauerwald had obviously crossed another line.

The antiquities made Maresfield Gardens seem very like 19 Berggasse. Freud's wife, daughter, and maid were trying to comfort Freud, and he needed comfort, as the latest operation had drained him. Freud complained to Marie Bonaparte: "I am abominably tired and weak in my movements although I began yesterday with three patients but it is not going easily."

Clearly, Freud's health was getting worse. He had walked up the stairs at the Hotel Esplanade. The house at 20 Maresfield Gardens was a detached villa with two floors. His sister-in-law Minna was confined to a bedroom on the second floor and Freud could not visit her because he could not manage the stairs. Soon after that, she had to be sent to a nursing home.

There was also aggravation about the English translation of *Moses and Monotheism*. Ernest Jones was slow, he did not turn up to discuss progress, and then he excused himself, saying that he had a cold; he warned Freud that he might not finish the translation until February or March. Jones had insisted on translating the book. Freud was sarcastic when he said, "[You have taken] this burden on yourself. I know that you have many things to do which are at least as important as this." Freud insisted he did not want to die before the book appeared in English.

There was some light relief in the shape of a too-eager disciple. Freud exchanged letters with the man who had hoped to organize a Festschrift for Freud's eightieth birthday. A. A. Roback sent some clippings to Freud in October 1938. A poem about Freud's escape to London had appeared in the Yiddish press in New York, a Mr. Twersky was bringing out a book called *The Young Freud*, and Roback enclosed clippings that purported to tell the story of Freud's escape. Freud replied that he was glad to forget the Nazi invasion and commented on a newspaper clipping Roback had sent. The story claimed Freud had been "ransomed." He shot back that it was "fabrication and lies. I often wonder about the mentality of American journalists who can get pleasure out of such performances." He asked Roback if he had seen people getting together a collection of funds in Boston to ransom him. "Probably no more than I have," Freud replied. The idiots of the press would distort his book on Moses and claim he was writing The Psychoanalysis of the Bible, Freud added.

Hilda Doolittle came to visit, but she was frustrated because she could get no time alone with Freud. It was quite different talking to him with others around. Marie Bonaparte came back on October 29 and stayed for five days. She had no positive news about making arrangements for Freud's four sisters to leave Vienna.

That same day Freud wrote a fulsome letter to a woman he did not know, Rachel Berdach. He had received her book *The Emperor, the Sages and Death*, which told the story of the Holy Roman Emperor Frederick II and Rabbi Jacob Charif Ben Aron. Frederick was a collector just like Freud, but he had the power to collect more than objets d'art. He collected wise men and their wisdom—Arabs, Jews, and Greeks—to exchange views on science, medicine, astronomy, and astrology. In Berdach's book there is a gripping debate between an Arab healer and a bishop. The Arab explains why he finds the story of the resurrection of Lazarus absurd and revolting. Lazarus suffered a vile ordeal. He died, was brought back to life just to make the point that Christ was a great healer, and then he died again.

In the book, Rabbi Ben Aron slowly becomes the dominant figure. He has a student who follows him to Frederick's court. The student dies, leaving behind writings that ask profound questions. Do animals have any sense of it when they are close to death or are only humans cursed with such awareness? Why does God inflict this insight on human beings? After his student dies, the rabbi becomes depressed. He wakes up one night and the silence seems uncanny. He runs through the town, which is eerily empty. He goes into the countryside. Nothing is left alive. The Angel of Death has swooped over the world but somehow forgotten the rabbi. He then dies, begging the Angel to return to take him away.

Freud wrote to Berdach that he had not read anything so "substantial and poetically accomplished for a long time." Its excellence made him wonder why she had written him such a diffident letter and he asked if that, as well as "the priority you grant to death," meant that she was very young. To the end he was something of a flirt on paper.

Years later, Max Schur met the author, who had been in analysis with Theodor Reik. With her permission, Reik told Schur that Rachel Berdach had lost someone very dear to her when she was very young.

In November 1938, Polly Hartwig wrote to tell Freud that her brother Morris had died. Morris had sent him a letter out of the blue and Freud had replied to it. Now Morris had died in a car crash near Port Elisabeth—yet another accident in the family.

On November 28 Freud wrote to Hilda Doolittle with a small mystery. A gift of gardenias—"by chance or intention, they are my favourite flowers"—had been delivered to Maresfield Gardens. He noted that these were the flowers that ancient Greeks used to mark the return of the Gods "or goods," he punned. He suspected she was responsible and thanked her for "so charming a gesture."

On December 18, Freud wrote to Arnold Zweig, whose son had been in a car accident. He was relieved that the boy was well and ended that life "would be quite comfortable if weren't for this and that and a lot of other things too." He was waiting for a second bone splinter to detach itself, which would make his mouth less painful. Max Schur felt this stubborn chip should come out and eventually managed to perform the small operation himself. "I shall not easily forget Freud's reaction of gratitude. Which needed no words but was expressed by the look on his face and an especially warm hand-shake," Schur recalled later.

The next day, Freud wrote sadly to Max Eitingon, "I am waiting like a hungry dog for a bone which has been promised to me only it is supposed to be one of my own." He was finding it hard to work more than four hours a day.

Polly Hartwig sent her famous uncle presents for Christmas. Freud was embarrassed that he had sent her none, and when he wrote to thank her, he apologized. He would make up for it, he promised; she would get a good reception when she came to visit them again.

Two days after Christmas Freud was well enough to write a long letter to Marie Bonaparte. They had been freezing, his garden was covered with snow, which looked beautiful but "we dare not imagine what London will look like when all the snow turns to water." There was no end to "the usual news of death and suicide from Vienna." Evidently there was no news about his four sisters.

Max Schur said that Freud was now too tired to do creative work but he was still tinkering with *An Outline of Psychoanalysis*, his final statement of his thoughts on his life's work. Visitors like Leonard and Virginia Woolf did sense Freud was not the force he had once been.

The Woolfs had been publishing English translations of Freud's works since 1924 when a discreet advertisement told the reading public they could buy Collected Papers by Sigmund Freud, M.D., vol. 1 and vol. 2, and that the complete set including three more volumes would cost 4 guineas. The Woolfs paid Freud £50 as an advance on each volume, but they had never met their author before.

Freud was, Leonard Woolf noted, not just a genius but also "as unlike many geniuses, an extraordinarily nice man." He had an "extraordinarily civilised temperament . . . which made every kind of relationship with him so pleasant."

Soon after Freud settled in Hampstead, Leonard Woolf had made "discreet inquiries as to whether he would like Virginia and me to come and see him. The answer was yes and in the afternoon of January 28, 1939, we went and had tea with him. I feel no call to praise the famous men I have known"—and Woolf had known more than a few. His acquaintances included Bertrand Russell, the poets W. B. Yeats, T. S. Eliot, Nehru, as well as the economist-hedonist, John Maynard Keynes. These celebrities had not left Woolf agog with admiration. "Nearly all famous men are disappointing or bores or both. Freud was neither; he had an aura not of fame but of greatness. The terrible cancer of the mouth . . . had already attacked him." Leonard Woolf then added, "Freud was extraordinarily courteous in a formal old-fashioned way—for instance he almost ceremoniously presented Virginia Woolf with a flower." It was a narcissus. "There was something about him of the half-extinct volcano, something somber suppressed, reserved," her husband added. "He gave me a feeling which only very few people whom I have met gave me, a feeling of great gentleness, but behind the great gentleness, great strength."

Freud was "a screwed-up shrunken very old man with a monkey's light eyes paralysed spasmodic movements inarticulate; but alert. Difficult talk. Immense potential, an old fire now flickering," Leonard Woolf also recorded.

Perhaps the most interesting remark is one that Virginia Woolf noted. Freud said to the couple, "It would have been worse if you had not won the war. I said we often felt guilty—if we had failed, Hitler would not have been. 'No,' he said with great emphasis, 'he would have been infinitely worse.'" Unfortunately Freud did not elaborate on this truly bizarre statement, and Virginia Woolf made no attempt to get him to explain it.

Freud and the Woolfs also had some fun. Leonard Woolf said that a few days before they went to visit he had read the report of a case in which a man had stolen books from Foyles famous bookshop on Charing Cross Road. Some of the books were Freud's. Leonard Woolf added, "The magistrate fines him [the thief] and said that he wished he could sentence him to read all Freud's books as a punishment. I told Freud about this and he was amused and, in a queer way, also deprecatory about it. His books he said had made him infamous, not famous. A formidable man."

Later in January, the persistent A. A. Roback wrote to say he had been in touch with Carl Jung. Freud warned him, "You would not heighten Jung's esteem for yourself through politeness." (This is one of the few times Freud wrote about Jung in the 1930s. Mostly he ignored him. Jung was much more apt to justify his differences with Freud.)

Roback asked Freud if he had really said that he had never charged as much when the Gestapo took his money. In a letter dated February 9, 1939, Freud responded. "I actually did make the remark you mentioned when the Nazis confiscated from me 6,000 schillings—not 8,000. It was something like 'I never walked off with that much after a visit.'"

Then came the most unexpected visitor of all.

Sauerwald Visits

Anton Sauerwald suddenly turned up in London to see Freud in the spring of 1939. At his trial, Sauerwald claimed Freud had written to him and asked him to come. The reason was purely business. Now that the antiquities had reached London, Sauerwald and Freud devised a plan for Marie Bonaparte to buy the remaining stock of books the publishing company still had in Germany. Sauerwald said Freud also wanted to discuss his bank accounts. But it was not only books and banks that the two men discussed.

Though Max Schur gave many details of Freud's illness and did mention Anton Sauerwald, Schur's account is vague after March 1939. The reason is simple. Schur had obtained a visa to go to the United States but felt he could not leave when his patient was so ill. But American visas had time restrictions. If Schur did not go by April 21, he would forfeit the precious right to live there. Freud understood and gave him his blessing to sail for New York.

In a letter to Marie Bonaparte written in April, Freud said that his handwriting was poor and that his pen "has left me like my physician." He added that things are "not going well with me." He felt that he was being deceived about the true state of his cancer. There was an attempt by George Exner to operate, but it seems to have been botched.

Freud was now dreadfully weak—and, more humiliating, he smelled disgusting. When his beloved dog Lun came out of quarantine, the dog refused to come near him because he stank so vilely. Freud now never ate in front of other people because the botched operation had made it impossible for him to eat without dribbling and making a mess. Paula Fichtl had to clean food off his trousers, jacket, and the floor. For a fastidious man like Freud, these were terrible humiliations.

Because Anton Sauerwald was in London, Freud seized the opportunity. He asked his old trustee to see if he could persuade his Viennese surgeon, Hans Pichler, to come to London again. Freud had faith that the surgeon could perform another operation that would buy him some more time.

Anton Sauerwald promised to do his best. The moment he got back to Vienna, he went to see Hans Pichler and explained the situation. Pichler was not Jewish, so there were no complicated exit formalities. As it was so urgent, Sauerwald drove Pichler all the way to London. The two men put Sauerwald's car on the ferry and hurried to Hampstead where Pichler examined his patient. Freud's instinct had been right. It was really a matter of life and death. Pichler again managed to persuade colleagues at the London Clinic to allow him to operate.

Anton Sauerwald said that Hans Pichler charged high fees, and he produced Pichler's bill, which said that it had been paid by Sauerwald. This raises another intriguing question. Sauerwald insisted he was a poor man and was getting a salary of 500 reichsmarks a month. How did he have the money to pay Pichler? Sauerwald claimed that he justified paying Pichler's fees as "moving expenses" and got the money from the Gestapo. This seems a little far-fetched. It seems much more likely that either Marie Bonaparte paid or, if Sauerwald had indeed received some cash for his help, he now used some of that to settle the fee for the operation. Pichler certainly got paid. His receipt is in the files in the Vienna archives at Gasometer D.

Later, Anton Sauerwald described himself as something of a savior, but that was not the way one member of Freud's family remembered it. His nephew Harry wrote: "The Gestapo had graciously left him in possession of a sufficient sum of money to tide him over the first days of his exile. Shall we call it naivete or shamelessness when a Nazi official visited him in London a long time afterward and demanded this amount back?" Paula Fichtl said long ago that Harry was the only member of the family she felt who was not that bright. There is no evidence that any Nazi other than Sauerwald came to see Freud in London, and Sauerwald never asked for the money back. Harry's mistake would cost the trustee dear.

Hans Pichler had done his best, but the greatest doctors in the world could not reverse the mouth cancer now. It was inoperable. Freud would have to live with it—and die with it. He would never see his last book published, but he was determined to make it part of his legacy. He had said his final word on Moses. It was now time to return to his ideas about sexuality one last time.

14
Last Works, Last Words

Freud now finished *An Outline of Psychoanalysis*, a short book but not one for beginners because it makes many assumptions about what readers know. At the start of chapter 5, "Explanatory Notes on The Interpretation of Dreams," Freud writes a sentence that reflects much of his beliefs and character: "States of conflict and turbulence alone can further our knowledge."

In much of the book, Freud used military metaphors. The task of therapy was to strengthen the ego, which has been weakened by conflict, and "we have to come to its aid." He compared the situation to being "in a civil war which has to be decided by the assistance of an ally from the outside." The ego could only accept help if it still had some "degree of coherence." The ego of neurotics often did still have that, which is why many of them managed to function in the real world; the psychotic ego, however, was just too chaotic to do that. So with the neurotics "we make a deal," Freud said. They had to speak with total honesty and the analyst would guarantee complete discretion.

Freud highlighted successes, failures, and worries about the future of the discipline he founded. He lamented that no philosopher or psychologist could begin to explain consciousness or how mind and body are linked. Nevertheless, he could provide "a first report on the facts that we have observed." Psychoanalysis had "proved fruitful after all" because it had found that the laws by which the unconscious worked differed from those of the conscious mind. He had not wasted his time.

Freud repeated one of his long-held ambitions—to make it possible for psychoanalysis to help human beings develop more maturity or as he put it that "where the id and the superego were, the ego will be." Freud's elegant sentence reveals how much he hoped psycho-analysis could transform people. If we recognize the forces in our unconscious, we are less at their mercy. If we know ourselves, we can control our chaotic, aggressive, and destructive impulses, to some extent at least. Self-knowledge is power.

Next, Freud returned to the sexuality of children. Some children were fascinated by their genitals at a very young age and even showed signs of arousal. Freud argued that such children "are said to be degenerate," but that was unjust, even though it was "understand-able" that psychoanalysis caused some shock and that many denied its truths. But Freud was dismayed that so many intelligent, even artistic, people still refused to admit the existence of the Oedipus complex. When Freud had suggested that Hamlet was an Oedipal drama, the "lack of understanding from the literary world demon-strated the huge extent to which the mass of humans were prepared to cling to their infantile repressions."

Patients used many tricks to hide what they could not face. They had to reveal not just the intimacies they knew they hid from others, but also those they did not know—the patient's unknown unknowns, so to speak. The only way analysis could succeed was for the patient to "tell us everything," even if it seemed trivial, stupid, or bizarre. Analysis had to create a space where the patient was not civilized, not inhibited, not self-critical. Only then would the analyst get truly valuable material.

To describe the role of the analyst, Freud used a striking image that for once was not military. The analyst was offering to play the role of a mountain guide on a particularly difficult mountain, but the patient wanted more than a mere guide. That role was too unemo-tional. This led Freud to the question of transference, that powerful unseen undercurrent in all therapeutic exchanges. The analyst had to be aware that the patient wanted his approval, even love. Freud, we should remember, was writing this almost certainly with the assis-tance of his daughter, whom he had analyzed. He may even have been dictating to her because he was now so weak.

If transference worked, the patient found that his ego got stronger and the analyst could reeducate him, but Freud warned against "misusing our influence." However much the analyst may be tempted to become a teacher and a role model, "to create humans in his own image," he must resist it. That is not his task in the analytic relationship. The patient did not need to be turned into a dependant child again.

The simplest cures happened, Freud claimed, when there was strong positive transference that let the analyst use his power to show the patient what caused his problems and persuaded him, or her, to be healed. But if negative transference became more powerful, the insights would be "blown away like chaff in the wind." The analyst found that painful, seeing months, even years, of work turn into hostility.

The analyst had to make the patient see both how real, and how unreal, transference was. It was best, Freud said, if neither the love nor the hostility became too extreme. "If we succeed as we mostly do," he added, "in making the patient see the nature of transference, then it gives him more power to feed to the ego." A strong ego can wallop the resistances into submission. Freud had no evidence for this other than his own assessment of how well his patients and those of his colleagues had fared. He never allowed any objective test of how well analysis succeeded, the legacy of Uncle Josef.

The ideal way for a patient to behave was to carry on as normal outside the analytic hour, but to let everything out within the hour. Analysis is a Wendy House for grown-ups, if you like, a safe space where one can play, pretend, and explore all kind of possibilities.

Freud stressed the importance of timing. A good analyst had to keep distinct "our knowledge and his knowledge"; the analyst might have deduced things very early on but the patient might not be ready yet for the revelations. The analyst had to judge very carefully when to reveal insights and deductions.

Under pressure the ego became defensive, which was no help. What we want, Freud, ever the armchair general, said, is for "the ego, emboldened by the security our help affords it, to venture to attack to recapture what it has lost." But the ego is often a bit of a coward and needs the analyst to stiffen it. With its loins girded and its ammunition provided by the analyst, the ego can advance. It has an unlikely ally, the id. "The battle that now develops if we achieve what we intend to achieve—namely to incite the ego to overcome its resistances—is carried out under our direction." Field Marshal Freud commanded the forces of the ego, ordering it to outflank the superego and the id, and he wrote that the mark of victory was if "a constant danger has been eliminated."

Sometimes real life did the trick. Many neurotics felt they deserved to be ill and refused to become healthy. Occasionally, Freud had noticed an extraordinary transformation in a patient after a real calamity. It was as if the catastrophe had made them suffer enough so they could at least send their neurotic symptoms packing. This led to the issue of suicide, which, I have argued, blighted the Freud family.

Two other themes are striking. Despite his dealings with Marie Bonaparte, Hilda Doolittle, and Karen Horney, Freud held to his theory that girls suffered from penis envy. They were wounded when they realized they did not have a penis but a clitoris instead. The clitoris was so much more discreet and girls certainly could not wave it around. This lack had "permanent consequences for her character development," Freud added. Many girls rejected sexual life as a consequence, he said.

Then, more diffidently, Freud claimed that suicide occurred when the self-preservation drive has undergone "a reversal in them." Suicidal patients could not endure being "restored to health by our treatment and resist it with every means at their disposal." Freud was sophisticated philosophically and would have known his argument was completely circular. Individuals killed themselves because their will to live was reversed. It is plausible to suggest that discussing suicide reminded him of his failure to help the members of his family who had killed themselves.

But the future was bright. Chemicals might provide cures. For now, however, Freud said, analysis offered the best hope for those who were in distress. Every day now, he was in great physical distress himself. It was clear to Max Schur that the cancer was inoperable and incurable. The best he could do was to alleviate Freud's pain. He had an obstinate patient, though, because Freud hated taking anything stronger than aspirin because it made him think less clearly.

The old bargain with Max Schur

In a newspaper interview in May 1939, Matthias Goering argued that as a Jew, Freud could not understand that the unconscious is not a domain of repressed sexual activity, but the "foundation of life," the source of creativity. The "new German psychotherapy" aimed to "strengthen belief in the meaning of life and reinforce the link with the higher world of values; it was to convey to the patient the consciousness of being bound and incorporated into the common destiny of the German people." Freud would have known what Goering said. Letters were still coming from Germany.

In May 1939, the lawyer Dr. Alfred Indra called on Freud on his way back to Vienna from America. Freud was in a flippant mood and said, "So you are going back to—I can't recall the name of the city."

According to Ernest Jones, Dr. Indra thought this showed Freud was losing his memory, but Jones was, for once, sharper when he said it was a deliberate mistake. Freud also replied to his sister Anna when she wished him a happy eighty-third birthday. He was grateful, but it was not really good fortune to live to be so old, he said. It seems to have been his last letter to her. Neither of them said a word about their four sisters left in Vienna.

Over the summer, H. G. Wells tried to get British citizenship for Freud, with the help of an MP, Oliver Locker-Lampson. Despite Freud's fame, Parliament rejected the proposal.

One of the last substantial letters Freud wrote was to A. A. Roback, who bizarrely sent him a dollar bill in the post. On July 10, Freud returned it, saying he had always been able to take care of his correspondence and a dollar was too small a sum to be distributed to refugees. Roback had asked how the American criticism of *Moses and Monotheism* had affected him. Freud assured him it would hardly affect his "frame of mind."

A month later, Roback sent him reviews of a play staged in Warsaw that was based on *The Interpretation of Dreams*. Freud does not seem to have replied. The pain was getting worse. Max Schur offered stronger sedatives, but Freud still refused to take anything more than aspirin. He would rather think in torment than not think at all, he told his doctor.

At one point, Ernest Jones told Freud there had been some discussion of not telling him how bad his condition now was. "By what right?" Freud demanded, as he had done in 1923. But there would be no reprieve now.

Marie Bonaparte came to Maresfield Gardens on August 6. Freud was still concerned about the fate of his four sisters in Vienna. Dolfi, Mitzi, Rosa, and Pauli Freud would never be allowed to leave Vienna. The Princess would have made some note of what she sensed was their last meeting, but I have not been able to get access to it. It is very likely in the restricted material in the Library of Congress.

Soon after Marie Bonaparte returned to Paris, Max Schur moved into Maresfield Gardens so that he could be with his patient all the time. This allowed him to see how Freud behaved in the shadow of death. Schur was full of admiration because he never heard Freud direct an "angry or impatient word" against anyone. Schur would now have to deliver on the bargain they had agreed to back in 1927 when he first became Freud's physician.

On September 3, Britain declared war on Germany. The next few days saw Freud's condition deteriorate. He was in more and more pain and he could not think well anymore, which he found utterly distressing. Suffering made no sense to him if his brain was not functioning normally.

In his last letter to Freud, dated September 14, 1939, nine days before Freud's death, Stefan Zweig wrote, "I hope that you are suffering only from the era, as we all do, and not also from physical pain. We must stand firm now—it would be absurd to die without having first seen the criminals sent to hell." Zweig does not seem to have realized how sick Freud was.

Maresfield Gardens was now a house in which a much-loved man was dying. He was tended by his wife, his daughter, and Paula Fichtl. As ever, it was Fichtl who spoke of the ordinary details, of the meals they tried to get him to eat, of the three women at his bedside. Freud did not write another word, it seems.

On September 21, in severe pain, Freud asked Max Schur to fulfill his side of the old bargain. The suffering did not make sense anymore. He asked Schur to ease him out of life. Freud said good-bye to his wife, to his daughter Mathilde, to his sons, and finally to his youngest daughter, Anna, his true heir. She did not want him to take the morphine. But Freud saw no point in prolonging his existence now and prepared himself lucidly. Schur gives a touching description. Taking the hand of the physician at his bedside, Sigmund Freud said, "My dear Schur, you certainly remember our first talk. You promised me then not to forsake me when my time comes. Now it is nothing but torture and makes no sense any more." Schur reassured his patient that he had not forgotten. "When he was again in agony, I gave him a hypodermic of two centigrams of morphine. He soon felt relief and fell into a peaceful sleep. I repeated this dose after about twelve hours."

Freud died toward midnight on September 23, 1939. He died in

Hampstead, in freedom, but a stateless refugee, not as the English-man of his "intense wish phantasy." He was cremated three days later at the Golders Green Crematorium. The family asked Ernest Jones to give the funeral oration and he rose to the occasion. "It had been hard to wish him to live a day longer when he was suffering so much." He said that he thought of friends who were far away, like Brill, Sachs, and Eitingon, as well as of Ferenczi and Abraham who had died. Jones paid respect to "what in others expresses itself as religious feeling" but in Freud was expressed "as a transcendental belief in the value of life and in the value of love." Jones recalled Freud's vivid personality and "instinctive love of truth." He added that he felt no one could ever have lied to Freud. "One can say of him that as never a man loved life more, so never a man feared death less." One should not speak ill of eulogies, but many people lied to Freud and, at times, he seems to have lied to himself.

Ernest Jones made the point that Freud had died in a country that had given him "more courtesy, more esteems and more honour than his own or any other land." He finished in some style. "So we take our leave of a man whose like we shall not know again. From our hearts we thank him for having lived; for having done; for having loved." Stefan Zweig then gave a speech in which he recalled their long friendship and Freud's courage and humanity. Martha Freud wrote to Jones to thank him and added that all the sympathy she had received made her forget she was among strangers in Britain.

There were many obituaries. The most original perhaps was a fine poem W. H. Auden wrote in memory of the man he called "an important Jew" who

> went his way down among the lost people like Dante,
> down to the stinking fosse where the injured
> lead the ugly life of the rejected.

The authoritative scientific journal *Nature* asked Cyril Burt, a psychologist who had made his name with studies of intelligence, to write an obituary. On October 28, 1939, Burt said: "His bold speculations and even bolder expression of them aroused initial opposition." But the traumas of the First World War "quickly convinced workers like Rivers, Myers and McDougall that there was a most important foundation of truth in the novel doctrines that Freud had advanced."

Thomas Mann said that "Freudian theory is one of the most important foundation stones for an edifice to be built by future generations, the dwelling of a freer and wiser humanity."

Freud had made a will in London and he left an estate of over $109,000—a very large sum at the time.

15
After the War: The Fate of Sauerwald and Others

As Freud was laid to rest, his unlikely helper, Anton Sauerwald, was called up by the Wehrmacht. With his academic qualifications, Sauerwald was drafted into the Luftwaffe and got a commission. In the summer of 1940, he became involved with the Nazi commune that had the motto "Together, for one another." Everyone involved was a member of the party. Members picked lots to decide who could build a house on what plot. There were strict rules about how much land was needed for each house, but the war made it impossible to build the houses because building materials were needed for the war effort. The twenty-nine families in the commune made the best of it and decided instead to lay out allotment gardens on the land. Sauerwald was responsible for landscaping. The twenty-nine families dwindled to fifteen over the next three years. The failure of the project mattered because soon after the war Sauerwald would find that he was homeless.

The death of Freud did not mean the end of Anton Sauerwald's involvement with the family or the publishing business. He still had to settle its affairs, and he finally achieved that in 1941.

The war changed the lives of many psychotherapists. Matthias Goering joined the Luftwaffe, as Sauerwald had done. The First World War had made his cousin Hermann Goering very aware of the pressures pilots faced in combat, and Hermann encouraged Matthias Goering to forge links between the Goering Institute and the Luftwaffe. Many officers attended seminars at the institute to learn how to handle their men better.

During the Battle of Britain, Matthias Goering even persuaded the Luftwaffe to set up mental health stations at airfields so pilots who survived dangerous missions could get immediate help in dealing with their anxieties. This was a perfect use for the short-term therapy Goering favored. In dealing with stress, the Royal Air Force deployed the stiff upper lip while the Luftwaffe deployed therapists who asked pilots how they felt after being shot at by Spitfires.

Working for the Luftwaffe, Matthias Goering could not maintain day-to-day control of the institute. The few Freudians still there exploited his absence, managing to continue training psychothera-pists, and even to stay in charge of the polyclinic. Some were partially Jewish even, according to the historian Geoffrey Cocks. The Freudi-ans even dared to make their patients lie down on the analytic couch to which Goering had objected so strongly. But there were limits. The Freudians had to compromise and use euphemisms, talking of "depth psychotherapy" instead of "psychoanalysis."

In these bizarre conditions Working Group A, as the Freudians were called, trained thirty-four analysts between 1938 and 1945. The psychoanalyst Gerard Chrzanowski interviewed some of them and wrote: "Neither the people inside the Institute nor organised German psychiatry outside of the Institute believed that psycho-analysis had been extinguished. Not one person interviewed by us expressed the slightest doubt that he had continued to function as a psychoanalyst throughout the Hitler years. We have no doubt as to their sincerity."

Both patients and analysts feared that what they said in treatment might be betrayed to the Gestapo or to the police. But "whether one likes what it became or not, psychoanalysis was going on, albeit in a most peculiar way," the analyst John Rittmeister said in 1939. He was later executed by the Nazis. The behavior of the analysts at the institute revealed "a degree of social blindness, moral cowardice and self-seeking," according to Cocks. Freud had said in *Analysis Ter-minable and Interminable* that many analysts had psychological problems. This was shocking confirmation of that.

None of the analysts protested as the Goering Institute became involved with and justified Hitler's "euthanasia" program. Leading members of the institute, including Felix Boehm, came to accept euthanasia as a solution for the "untreatable" patient. Europe would not just be rid of all Jews; it would also be rid of all so-called defec-tives. Carl Jung was also conspicuous by his silence on this point.

Death in the Camps

After Freud left his apartment at Berggasse, it was taken over by Nazi officials but the Race Institute did not move in, as Berlin had wanted. The position of his four sisters became increasingly desperate. They had spent the 160,000 schillings Freud and their other brother, Alexander, had left them. By late 1939, they were moved out of their homes. Nazi policy was to hand good housing over to good Austrians and put the Jewish families into very cramped apartments. Once-well-off families were forced to share bedrooms and toilets with many others. Alexander believed that the sisters would be safe as long as they were receiving money from abroad because the Nazis were desperate for dollars. His son Harry organized sending them $200 a month through an intermediary called Kafka. On June 14, 1941, Harry's father wrote to him: "the head must not abandon hope." But news was impossible to obtain. A few months later Alexander suggested to Harry that there had to be a way of contacting Anton Sauerwald, but by 1942 the United States was at war with Germany. There was no way of learning anything about the aunts.

As late as June 8, 1943, Anne Freud wrote to Harry that she had "the feeling" that the aunts were still alive, but she was wrong. There are conflicting accounts of the fate of Freud's sisters. Harry left details in his family history, which include many corrections that he scribbled over. Sir Martin Gilbert, Churchill's biographer, in his work on the Holocaust offers one account. Harald Leupold-Loewenthal, the Freud scholar, studied the fate of the sisters in detail and often differs from Gilbert.

We perhaps know most about the fate of Regina Deborah Graf-Freud (Rosa) who was seventy-nine years old in 1939. Freud liked her more than the other girls because he felt that, like himself, she had "a nicely developed tendency toward neurasthenia," he wrote back in 1910. Rosa did not have a happy life. After a traumatic love affair, she married a doctor, Heinrich Graf, who died in 1908. Their son, Hermann Adolf, died in action during the First World War. Their daughter Cäcilie committed suicide.

The last document from Rosa was a letter the International Red Cross sent to Maresfield Gardens. She only had the right to send twenty-five words; they were addressed to her sister-in-law. "Dear

Martha! Greetings with heartfelt emotion. Wondering about the state of your Alexander's family. Four alone. Sad. Painful. Health. Yours warmly." The words might be sad but Rosa's last phrase suggests she perhaps did not understand the terrible danger she faced. "Best furnishings in storage. Graf Rosa." The furniture would never come out of storage, of course.

Rosa was deported to Theresienstadt on August 28, 1942. The transcripts of the Nuremberg trials include a statement from a witness that describes the arrival of one of Freud's sisters at a camp—and it may have been Rosa. She introduced herself to the commandant as Sigmund Freud's sister. He examined her papers and "said that there was probably some mistake and showed her the railroad signs, telling her that there would be a train to take her back to Vienna in two hours. She could leave her belongings, go into the showers and, after bathing, her documents and her ticket to Vienna would be ready." Of course, the woman went to the bathhouse and never returned.

It shows the confusion that Gilbert cites an account in which it is claimed Rosa Graf asked to be given "lighter walk" where it seems the more probable phrase is "lighter work." The commandant of Theresienstadt camp, Siegfried Seidl, was charged with having been personally responsible for sixteen executions. He was found guilty and hanged.

Freud's second sister, Maria Moritz-Freud (Mitzi), had a tragic life before her tragic death. She worked as a governess and in 1887 married her Romanian cousin, Moritz Freud, who committed suicide in 1920. One of their four children, Lilly Marlé-Freud, became a famous actress and inspired the song "Lili Marlene." After Mitzi's youngest child, Theodor (Teddy), drowned in 1923 in Berlin, his mother came back to Vienna to live with her sisters. Her son-in-law killed himself and so did her daughter, Tom Seidmann, as we have seen. According to Leupold-Loewenthal, Mitzi Moritz-Freud was deported first to Theresienstadt on June 29, 1942, then to Maly Trostinec where she disappeared. It is likely she died in the gas chambers. Harry Freud's notes initially claimed she died in Treblinka, but he then scribbled that out and wrote in "Auschwitz."

Esther Adolfine (Dolfi) was seventy-seven years old in 1939. She never married and looked after her father when he fell ill, and then took care of her mother. Her nephew Martin Freud thought that caring for her parents would have been very hard. Dolfi "was not clever or in any way remarkable, and it might be true to say that constant attendance on Amalie (her mother) had suppressed her personality into a condition of dependence from which she never recovered," he noted. She was deported to Theresienstadt on August 28, 1942, where she died from "internal hemorrhages" on February 5, 1943. It seems likely that she died of malnutrition. There is unanimity on her fate.

Freud's youngest sister, Pauline Regine Winternitz-Freud (Pauli). was seventy-five years old in 1939. She married Valentin Winternitz and immigrated to the United States, where their daughter, Rose Beatrice, was born on March 18, 1896. After her husband's death in 1900, she returned to Berlin. Her daughter suffered a severe nervous breakdown. There are two differing accounts of her. Harald Leupold-Loewenthal, who became president of International Psychoanalytic Association, claims that in June 1942 she was taken first to the concentration camp of Theresienstadt, then to the extermination camp of Maly Trostinec. Martin Gilbert and Harry Freud believe she was taken to Treblinka on September 23, 1942. It is not certain in which of these camps she perished.

In 1945, in some despair, Anna Freud wrote to her nephew Harry wondering if they would ever learn what had happened to the sisters. He had received a letter from a bureau that was trying to discover what had happened to those taken to the camps. It said that no trace of the sisters could be found.

Freud had been lucky to die in his own bed at a time of his own choosing. Age took its natural toll of the loved ones he left behind. Minna Bernays died in London in 1942 after a long illness.

Stefan Zweig managed to achieve what Freud had not—he became a British citizen in 1940. But he left England soon after. He moved to New York and then settled in Brazil. In 1942, he and his wife committed suicide by taking poison. The Europe he had loved had destroyed itself and he refused to be a witness to the destruction. Arnold Zweig lived through the war and went to live in East Germany where he became friends with Bertolt Brecht. He died in 1968.

In 1942, the musicologist Max Graf surprised analysts by revealing that in 1906, perhaps to thank him for reports on his son "Little Hans," Freud had given him an unpublished paper. The subject reflected Freud's interest in theater and was called "Psychopathic Characters on the Stage." The text was never published in German, but Graf had an English translation published in 1942.

16

The Trials of Anton Sauerwald

At the start of my research, I got talking with a young Austrian woman on the No. 15 bus, which goes between Paddington station and the Blackwall tunnel in London. I explained I was writing about how Freud had escaped Vienna. She smiled. "Ah, you know I went to the Sigmund Freud High School but I have no idea if the school had any connection with Freud at all." The school had never bothered to explain to its pupils why it was named after him.

Such reticence was very Austrian. She told me, "In Austria they still don't talk about the war," as if she were not really an Austrian herself. She added, "It was a pity, as those who knew about it are getting old. My grandparents were part of it but you know they never say anything about it."

In trying to finish this story, I encountered a degree of reticence that I found astonishing more than sixty years after the end of the war. It has to be remembered, however, that Austria had a president, Kurt Waldheim, who became secretary-general of the United Nations until he was exposed as a former Nazi. And Austria's neo-Nazi Party consistently gets between 15 and 20 percent of the vote in elections.

In 1945, after Anton Sauerwald was released from the prisoner of war camp at Bad Heilbrunn, he went back to Vienna, which had been divided into British, French, Russian, and American zones. Much of it had been destroyed. Conditions were grim. Sauerwald could not find his wife. Marianne had worked in a factory toward the end of the war but had fallen ill. She was told to go and get some healthy mountain air. She left Vienna and her apartment. Sauerwald could not get back into his own home, and the new tenant had stolen many of his possessions, he claimed.

Eventually, Anton Sauerwald found out that his wife had gone to

Brixlegg in the Tyrol and he followed her. Brixlegg might also give him a chance to find work. For five hundred years Brixlegg had been an important mining area and there was a copper refinery there. He knew the place because he had gone hunting in the Tyrol and Brixlegg, which was why he had acquired a hunting rifle in 1937.

The place had an exotic history. The local castle, Schloss Matzen, had been restored by Fanny Reid Grohman, an Irish woman who claimed to be a relative of the Duke of Wellington. Her son, William Baillie-Grohman, became a celebrity; one of his books, published in 1878, has an irresistible title: *Gaddings with a Primitive People*. Like Sauerwald, William Grohman was a hunter and he also produced an authoritative edition of the *The Master of Game*, the second-oldest English book on hunting. He got his friend Teddy Roosevelt, who was an avid hunter, to write a foreword to it.

In Brixlegg, Anton Sauerwald was reunited with his wife and they decided to stay there. This change of address made him hard to find, but Harry Freud tracked him down and had him arrested. Sauerwald was sent for trial in the People's Court, the Volksgericht, which was set up in the summer of 1945 by two laws. The first, the so-called Nazi Prohibition Act, was passed by the Austrian Provisional Government on May 8, 1945, a few hours before the German Wehrmacht surrendered. The second, the War Criminals Act, passed on June 26, 1945, made it possible to indict Nazis and collaborators for a number of offenses: war crimes in a restricted sense and crimes against humanity; torture and acts of cruelty; violation of human dignity; and expropriation, expulsion, and resettlement.

Two professional judges and three lay assessors presided over the cases. There was a severe shortage of judges because so many Austrian lawyers had worked for the Nazis. But the courts also had to deal with a question that had never arisen in Germany: the guilt of those who had joined the Nazi Party after Dollfuss had banned it in 1934, the so-called illegals. It was an act of treason to belong to the clandestine Nazi Party. The laws passed after the war also made it an offense to have lied about one's role in the Nazi Party.

The People's Court launched preliminary proceedings in 137,000 cases and the records of these proceedings were kept secret for nearly fifty years, the Austrian Research Center for Post-War Trials complained. I was told I was very lucky to be given access to Anton Sauerwald's file. According to the librarian at the Vienna archives, if anyone else had been charged with Sauerwald the file would have to remain confidential and he would not have allowed me to read it. The vast majority of the 40,000 cases led to no legal action. In the end only 11,500 people were prosecuted, of whom around 6,000 were found guilty. Most got minor sentences, but 28 individuals were sentenced to death and 21 to life imprisonment.

Anton Sauerwald was accused of war crimes, of having been an illegal member of the Nazi Party, and of having profited by the "Aryanization" of Jewish property. The police interviewed a number of witnesses to decide whether or not he had been an active Nazi. Some of the questions asked were almost silly, such as: Had Sauerwald hosted rowdy parties at his apartment? The witnesses disagreed on the extent of his Nazi activities, however. Anna Talg, his mother-in-law, insisted she had no idea that he was a member of the party. One of Sauerwald's neighbors contradicted that; Sauerwald had started to wear the uniform of a political leader after the Anschluss. One neighbor insisted she had seen his devoted wife, Marianne, wearing party insignia. This evidence makes his behavior toward the Freuds all the more remarkable.

The behavior of the Freud family toward Sauerwald is also hard to explain. In October 1945 Anna Freud clearly knew of the plight of Sauerwald and wrote to Harry that:

> [the] truth is that we really owe our lives and freedom to Sauerwald since he used his position as Kommissar to protect our personal safety. Without him we would never have got away. It was he who saw to our safe travel, who got Dr. Stross her permit at the last minute so that Papa would not travel without a doctor. But much more than that. I suppose you know that Martin who was quite beside himself at that time had kept some very incriminating papers about our affairs in Switzerland in his desk. They were found there but Sauerwald kept them safely locked up until we were gone.

Having explained that her brother Martin hated being powerless and that made him unable to deal with Sauerwald, Anna Freud added that:

> Sauerwald was really my only friend and standby after Martin and all our Jewish friends had left. The Princess always knew and thought the same about him . . . so nothing should happen to Sauerwald. Or if he is arrested these things should speak in his favour. Papa always said that perhaps some-

day we should repay our debt to him. Even more, after we had left he used to visit the aunts and sit with them very much as you used to do on a Sunday. They were only without protection after he had gone into the army.

Harry Freud did not act on this letter. Once he returned to the United States, there is no evidence he did anything to help Sauerwald. Nor did Anna Freud, even though she visited Vienna soon after the war ended and could have at least visited him.

Political influences undermined the work of the People's Court from the start. It was very much a question of politics. Half a million former members of the Nazi Party were a significant constituency. In 1945, the Nazis had lost their right to vote, but they got this back before the elections of 1949. Austrian politicians began to compete for their support and were eager to show they had the interests of the "soldiers' generation" at heart. Typically there were long delays in settling claims for Jewish compensation. A British historian, Robert Knight, found a revealing sentence in the minutes of the government. The minister responsible for the settlement of Jewish claims stated: "*Ich bin dafür, die Sache in die Länge zu ziehen*"—"I suggest we drag out that issue."

Such attitudes make what happened to Anton Sauerwald all the more bizarre. No one ever accused him of violence against any Jew. Yet he spent some of the period between late 1945 and 1947 in jail, even though he was ill with tuberculosis. On June 28, 1947, he was so ill that he was taken to a hospital, where he stayed a month.

The Vienna police sent out a questionnaire as part of their investigation into Anton Sauerwald's Nazi past. Questions focused on these issues:

> Did the accused call himself an illegal Nazi?
> Did he take an active part in Nazi activities and political acts and commit actions against Jews?
> Did he denounce people for political reasons?
> Did he play an active role in the Nazi Party either while it was banned or after the *Anschluss*?
> Did he give money to Nazi Party funds?

Anton Sauerwald told the court a complicated tale about his membership in the Nazi Party. He had become a member but had never done anything much for the party. For about two months in 1938, his former employee, Emil Rothleitner, tried to train him to become a propaganda leader, but that petered out. The only work he did for the Nazis, Sauerwald claimed, was that he had distributed cinema tickets for propaganda newsreels!

Anton Sauerwald kept on insisting he had worked ceaselessly for Freud. No one took much notice, however. The long periods in jail, the separation from his wife, the tuberculosis took their toll. Losing the war did not seem to make the slightest difference to the way Vienna bureaucracy worked—very slowly. Sauerwald felt frustrated by the delays and by his illness. The truth was so simple. He had helped Freud and his family when they were desperately vulnerable.

The crucial evidence finally came from Anna Freud. She had replied to Marianne's desperate letter, but there was some confusion because Marianne could no longer get into her old flat to pick up mail. By the time she got Anna Freud's letter, Sauerwald had been in jail a long time.

Anna Freud's letter was dated July 22, 1947. It is worth quoting in full.

> My parents and I have in no way forgotten that we have every reason to be grateful to your husband in a number of regards.
>
> We were in a very precarious situation at that time and there was not any doubt that your husband used his office as our appointed commissar in such a manner as to protect my father. In his dealings with him he always showed great consideration and respect and did his utmost to prevent other functionaries of the regime bothering him. I well know that he kept documents which could have endangered our lives hidden in his desk for quite some time.

Anna Freud knew perfectly well which documents Anton Sauerwald had kept hidden in his desk: they were papers and statements relating to secret bank accounts. Anna's letter to Marianne Sauerwald was also careful. It did not draw attention to the fact that Sauerwald had probably managed to transport some of the thousand antiquities by less than legal means.

After the letter was admitted into evidence, Sauerwald was allowed out of jail, but he was not exonerated. He remained accused in a sort of limbo for a further eighteen months. The court justified that on the grounds that it was not satisfied that Sauerwald had been frank about his work for the Nazis.

Carl Jung, of course, did not spend one second in jail. In 1945 he wrote in the *Neue Schweizer Rundschau* (*New Swiss Observer*) that "the German catastrophe was only one crisis in the general European sickness." Like a Swiss Colonel Blimp, Jung railed, "What is wrong with our art, that most delicate instrument for reflecting the national psyche? How are we to explain the blatantly pathological elements in modern painting? Atonal music?" Jung defended his political record, too:

> It must be clear to anyone who has read any of my books that I have never been a Nazi sympathizer and I never have been anti-Semitic, and no amount of misquotation, mistranslation, or rearrangement of what I have written can alter the record of my true point of view. Nearly every one of these passages has been tampered with, either by malice or by ignorance. Furthermore, my friendly relations with a large group of Jewish colleagues and patients over a period of many years in itself disproves the charge of anti-Semitism.

But there were, in fact, only two Jewish colleagues he could name.

After the War

At the Nuremberg trials, Hermann Goering was found guilty of crimes against humanity and sentenced to death. Shortly before he died, his brother Albert promised to take care of Hermann's wife, Emmy, and their daughter, Edda. On October 15, 1946, two hours before his execution, Goering committed suicide in his cell; he had managed to acquire some poison. Despite his many acts of kindness to Jews, Albert Goering was also imprisoned after the war, but those he had helped did not forget what he had done; they helped him survive years of unemployment, which embittered him. He died in 1966.

Felix Boehm and Carl Müller-Braunschweig recovered and achieved professional respectability, though one report said of Müller-Braunschweig, "I believe his personality has deteriorated during the Nazi regime . . . and I think he is 'dark grey.'" Boehm was seen as possibly "black," meaning completely corrupted.

On October 16, 1945, Müller-Braunschweig was asked to reconstruct the German Psychoanalytic Association. He was appointed its president, though his 1933 paper had hailed the new true Nazi psychotherapy that became the official representative of orthodox psychoanalysis, the once vilified Jewish science. He taught psychoanalysis at the Berlin Free University.

Felix Boehm did not have it much harder. In 1950 he became president of the reconstituted German Psychoanalytic Association and was upset that it was refused admission to the International Psychoanalytic Association. Boehm did not lack insight before 1933, so he cannot have been surprised by that refusal.

After he got to Bolivia, the photographer Edmund Engelman, who took the last pictures of 19 Berggasse, managed to make it to New York. He had a hard time trying to establish himself. After the war, he went to Vienna to find August Aichhorn, who had asked him to take the pictures at 19 Berggasse. But Aichhorn was no longer at the same address and no one seemed to know where he lived. Vienna was chaotic and devastated. Engelman was overjoyed when he eventually tracked down a Miss Regale who told him that Aichhorn had somehow got the negatives to Anna Freud. Engelman had a successful career, not as a photographer but as an engineer.

Years later, Edmund Engelman managed to visit 19 Berggasse and was appalled by the state of the building. It was empty, dirty, and sad. He called the place an "abused premises." The outline of the analytic couch was still marked on the floor.

At the start of 1949 Anton Sauerwald was declared innocent of all charges, apart from that of having been an illegal Nazi. The court said it had been impossible to judge the charge and explained that that was why the case had dragged on for four years. But Sauerwald was free. He moved to Innsbruck in the next few years. He seems to have had no further contact with the Freuds. Anna Freud's last secretary, Gina Le Bon, had never heard of him. The Freud family had not repaid their debt to Sauerwald, it would seem.

The firm of Freud and Co. traded at 61 Bloom Street in Manchester until 1942. Then it moved to 2 & 4 Beever Street. Sam Freud died in 1945 at 35 Old Lansdowne Road, West Didsbury.

Martha Freud died in 1951 at the age of ninety, surrounded by her children and grandchildren. Of John Freud, her husband's playmate in childhood, no one has ever found a trace.

On December 20, 1955, the People's Court was dissolved by a constitutional law. The prosecution of Nazi criminals had ceased some years earlier. The Austrians were not alone in wanting to forget. The Americans pardoned a great number of German war criminals convicted by Allied courts. The reason for this was the Cold War. The Allies needed Germany as an ally when the Cold War started. Simon Wiesenthal, the famous "Nazi hunter," said there was only one real winner of the Cold War, namely the old Nazis.

Carl Jung died in 1961. One of his disciples, Laurens van der Post, would have great influence on Prince Charles, especially on spirituality and alternative medicine. Many of Charles's more controversial ideas owe much to van der Post and Jung.

Anna Freud became a formidable psychoanalyst. With Dorothy Burlingham, she ran the Hampstead Nursery. Gina Le Bon, who was her secretary from 1970 to 1982, described the way she and Dorothy Burlingham worked in "Memories of Anna Freud and of Dorothy Burlingham." (She published the article under the name Gina Bon rather than her full surname of Le Bon). After the British edition of this book appeared, she wrote to me and I went to visit her in Zurich. She is a bright woman in her seventies, showed me some of the photographs of the Christmas parties they held, and added, "Anna Freud had an amazing gift for dealing with children."

On the interminable question of whether Freud's daughter and the Tiffany heiress were lovers, Le Bon was noncommittal. "Does it really matter?" Le Bon said. The question tired her. She added that when Dorothy died, Anna Freud was distraught.

Le Bon smiled as she told me that Anna Freud was quite capable of noticing handsome men. Once when they were discussing Carl Jung, she smiled and said that he was a very good-looking man. Jeffrey Masson, the author of *Against Therapy,* who argued that Freud had cynically changed his ideas about the sexual abuse of children by parents, was also very handsome. Masson charmed Anna Freud, Le Bon insisted.

Fascism had left its mark on Anna Freud, Le Bon insisted. One case impressed her very much. Freud's daughter was asked to help in the case of a South African man who was imprisoned on terrorism charges. Under the law, his wife could come to visit him and bring their son along, until the boy was five years old. After that the child would not be allowed to visit. "Miss Freud felt that would be very damaging to the boy," Le Bon told me. She wanted to make sure the boy got to see his father. She spent a long time writing out a draft letter to the prison governor arguing that it would be inhumane to deprive the son of seeing the father.

"Did it work?" I asked.

"Yes." She smiled.

Anna Freud did not forgive the Nazis or Germany, which may explain why she seems to have not helped Anton Sauerwald after his trial. "Miss Freud would not have a Mercedes but drove a Volvo rather and she was a very bad driver as opposed to Miss Burlingham." When Anna Freud discovered that IBM typewriters were being made in Germany, she would not have one. But it was the best typewriter at the time, so she managed to persuade a Mr. Painter (who seems to have been in charge of typewriters for the Freuds) to find an IBM that had not been manufactured in Germany.

Paula Fichtl was awarded a medal by the Austrian government in 1980.

Anton Sauerwald was never honored as he should have been. After the war he was in poor health, but he returned to one of the least dangerous of his interests: he did some occasional work as a gardener. He did not try to contact the Freuds and they did nothing for him. The Jews Albert Goering had helped had been far more generous. Sauerwald died in 1970 in Innsbruck. He and his wife had no children.

It is ironic that it took longer to conclude the matter of the secret bank accounts than it took to conclude World War I, World War II, or the Cold War.

17
The Secret Bank Accounts

After the war, the World Jewish Congress claimed that, in their passion for protecting bank secrecy, Swiss banks had deliberately muddled the question of deposits made by Jews in the 1930s. Some Holocaust survivors even alleged that, when they asked about accounts set up by their long-dead relatives, officials told them to produce death certificates. Prove your families were gassed or you will not get a Swiss centime!

The World Jewish Congress was not going to accept interminable delays. It lobbied and harried; it persuaded pension funds to threaten economic sanctions against the Swiss and started proceedings in the United States where there was some hope of quicker action.

Forty-three years after the war ended, both sides decided to try to settle these issues behind closed doors. The American judge Edward Korman had some imagination. He took all the parties out to dinner in a Brooklyn steak house and then locked them in his courtroom to hammer out a settlement. It took only two days for the lawyers to achieve that. Swiss banks would have to come up with $1.25 billion by way of compensation.

But the Swiss government objected to the deal and pointed out that it had established two independent inquiries—the first a panel, under Paul Volcker, the former head of the Federal Reserve. Volcker would have access to all documents. The Swiss also set up a commission chaired by Jean-François Bergier to study these controversies. Both these initiatives needed time. The settlement in Brooklyn was too hurried; all the evidence had not been assessed. Korman ignored such arguments and told the banks to start paying.

Bergier's commission, in fact, provided some of the most damning evidence against their own banks. In 1954 the big Swiss banks made a secret pact, he discovered. They agreed with one another to refuse to divulge information about any transactions that were more than ten years old. Anything that had happened before the war would be kept secret. "The banks relied on a combination of discreetly playing down the problem and erecting barriers to investigation," the Bergier report said. The secrecy laws, the laws the Nazis had railed against, were used against Jewish depositors by the banks "to legitimize their reluctance to provide information while at the same time charging high search fees for conducting investigations." As a result of these fees, "unclaimed accounts, deposits and safe-deposit boxes could also disappear in the space of a few decades." Bergier found that when an account had very little money in it, "it could be cashed in," often by the bank itself. Some bank employees stole unclaimed assets. He concluded that "legal principles were exploited for corporate objectives."

After the compromise reached in Brooklyn in 1998, it took years before any victims got any money. It took three years, for example, for the banks to publish a list of twenty-one thousand "probable" victims who had lost their money through the delinquencies of the banking system.

It was another adminstrative nightmare; many claimants were old, poor, sick, and close to death. In 2000 Judge Korman decided the banks had to put up cash for an immediate aid program for needy Holocaust survivors. The funds would make most of a difference to survivors and their families in the former Soviet Union, who were the poorest of all the Jewish groups. This ruling incensed many Jewish survivors in the United States.

Naturally the people with the strongest claims for compensation were those who could prove they had had accounts and how much was in them. Korman decided they should be allocated $800 million of the settlement. Almost nobody involved in the investigations, on either the Swiss or the Jewish side, thought it would be possible to find claimants for anything like this amount of money.

One of the people who read the list of accounts the banks produced was Freud's grandson, Anton Walter Freud. He saw that there was more information on Freud's accounts than on most others. Anton Freud incidentally was unusually willing to be frank about family secrets. For instance, he had discovered that Eli Bernays, his great-grandfather, had been jailed in Hamburg in 1867. He published the fact.

When Anton Walter Freud came forward in 2001, no one was sure how much money Freud had. Because he was famous, his accounts were eventually one of the 2,597 claims that the tribunal set up by Judge Korman examined in detail. The lawyers found a customer card, which proved Freud had held one custody account and two demand-deposit accounts, one of which was denominated in Dutch guilders. Given the accounts I have traced that were set up in 1914, it is likely that some records had been destroyed. The card did not reveal either how much was in the accounts or to whom any monies had been paid.

The average held-in-custody accounts in 1945 was SFr13,000 and in deposit accounts SFr2,140 (in U.S. dollars terms roughly $8,000 and $1,500). As there was no specific evidence about how much money was in Freud's accounts, they were assumed to have held the average, a total of SFr17,280 in the three accounts. The Brooklyn court established a formula for dealing with interest rates and inflation since 1945 and ruled Freud would have had 216,000 Swiss francs by 2005 (U.S. equivalent: $231,000). His heirs were paid that amount, but it took time. Like thousands of Jews, Anton Walter Freud never saw his grandfather's stolen money repaid. He died, at age eighty-two, a few months before the tribunal finished work on his lawsuit.

Paul Volcker's report, published more than a year after the settlement, refrained from estimating the amount of Nazi victims' money the Swiss were still holding. He carefully worded his conclusion to appease the rival Jewish and Swiss members of the committee. It absolved the banks of "systemic disruption" and "organized discrimination."

In early 2004, Judge Korman held another public hearing. He wanted to consult about how money left over should be distributed. Jewish community workers pleaded for the money to be disbursed immediately as an act of charity, so that aged Holocaust survivors could be given a little dignity. Many argued that it was absurd to link every last penny in the Swiss banks to individual claimants.

Many survivors, however, were upset at the thought of the court distributing money before all claimants to Swiss accounts had come forward. "At our age, it's not easy to wait such a long time," said

Alice Fischer, whose family had been killed in Auschwitz and Mauthausen. "And now we are discussing what to do with leftovers? I did not see a penny of the money yet." Another survivor, Greta Beer, begged the judge not to disburse the $800 million until the search for true claimants was complete. "$800 million is a sacred amount of money, Judge Korman," she said. "It has survived the Holocaust. It has survived the bank manipulations and come here to this country. It belongs to souls who from their grave have made the money come here to the United States. And it has to be distributed among us." Despite such pleas Judge Korman allowed the emergency payments to go ahead.

The next twist came in 2007. Hans Baer, the head of the Julius Baer bank, published his memoirs. He was angry at what he discovered about the way Swiss banks had handled the issue of the accounts set up by desperate Jews in the 1930s. "All of us came too late to the conclusion that the real scandal was not the dormant assets but the closed accounts," said Baer. "It is true that nobody had organised any great plunder," he continued. "It was a Swiss variation—unorganised theft."

Baer was shocked to discover that his own bank had charged a $75 "search fee" to claimants who inquired about a relative's account. Other banks charged even more. "I could not have imagined discovering such improprieties. There was never a Jewish conspiracy. We simply became victims of our own smugness," Baer wrote. Smugness seems too soft a word. I called the Bank Julius Baer, who referred me to the Swiss Bankers Association, who told me the matter was still controversial. No one wanted to comment.

Epilogue

The descendants of Sigmund Freud and Martha Bernays have been extremely successful. They include Lucian Freud, one of the great artists of the twentieth century; the writer-politician Clement Freud; Lord David Freud, an authority on the politics of welfare; the writers Emma Freud and Esther Freud; as well as Matthew Freud, who followed in the footsteps of Edward Bernays and has become a major figure in public relations. Matthew Freud married Elisabeth Murdoch, Rupert Murdoch's daughter. One can only wait to see what their children achieve. In the 1920s Freud had boasted to his nephew Sam Freud, "What a thriving tribe we are." That boast-wish-consolation given the untimely deaths in the family between 1919 and 1930 has turned out to be very true.

A few years after Freud wrote that to Sam, Max Eastman told his readers that the founder of psychoanalysis had more of a sense of humor than his writings suggested. Freud "often threw his head back and laughed like a child," Eastman added.

That image comes back to me as I finish this book.

In the 1970s, Freud's grandson Clement was a Liberal MP as well as a TV personality and confirmed gambler on horses. During the Cultural Revolution in the 1970s, Clement traveled to China as part of a parliamentary group. One of his fellow travelers, as it were, was Churchill's grandson, who was also named Winston. The young Churchill was a Conservative MP.

On the last day of the visit, the Chinese minister for information asked Clement Freud if there was anything he would like to ask.

"Yes. Everything you do, you do with extreme care and precision. . . . Now I am in your country with a colleague, than whom I am older, have been in Parliament longer, have held higher positions in our respective political parties: we are both staying at the Peking Palace Hotel and his suite is bigger than mine. Why?"

The embarassed minister replied, "It is because Mr. Churchill had a famous grandfather."

"It is the only time that I have been out-grandfathered," Clement Freud wrote.

I venture to suggest that Freud would have thrown his head back and laughed like a child.

Appendix 1
The Cast List

FREUD FAMILY

Jacob Freud, father of Sigmund Freud: born in Galicia in 1815; died in Vienna in 1895.

Sylvia Kanner, first wife of Jacob Freud: born in Galicia in 1829; died in Freiberg in 1852.

Rebecca, second wife of Jacob Freud: born c. 1832. She is something of a mystery, appearing in hardly any texts. They married in 1852; by 1855 she was dead or had disappeared. There do not seem to have been any children.

Amalie Freud, third wife of Jacob Freud: born in Galicia in 1835; died in Vienna in 1930. They married on July 29, 1855.

Josef Freud, uncle of Sigmund Freud: born in Galicia in 1824; died in Vienna in 1897. He was sentenced in 1866 to ten years' imprisonment in Vienna for forging roubles.

CHILDREN OF JACOB FREUD AND
HIS FIRST WIFE, SYLVIA KANNER

Philip Freud, half brother of Sigmund: born in 1831 in Tysmenitz. He immigrated to Manchester around 1860. He died in August 1911 in Chorlton near Manchester.

Emanuel Freud, half brother of Sigmund Freud: born in 1833 in Tysmenitz in Galicia, part of the Austro-Hungarian Empire. He worked in his father's textile business in Freiberg. He immigrated to Manchester in 1860. He died in Parbold, a small village near Southport, on October 17, 1914.

CHILDREN OF JACOB AND AMALIE FREUD

Sigmund Freud: born in Freiburg on May 6, 1856. He married Martha Bernays. Freud died in London on September 23, 1939.

Julius Freud, brother of Sigmund: born in October 1857. He died at the age of eight months in April 1858.

Anna Bernays-Freud, sister: born on December 31, 1858, in Freiberg. She was her father's favorite daughter. Anna married Martha Bernays's oldest brother, on October 14, 1883. She died on March 11, 1955, in New York.

Regina Deborah Rosa, sister: born on March 21, 1860, in Freiburg. She married Hans Graf. She died in the Treblinka concentration camp in 1942.

Maria Moritz-Freud (Mitzi): born on March 22, 1861, in Vienna. In 1887 Mitzi married her Romanian cousin Moritz Freud (1857–1920). She died in a concentration camp in 1942.

Esther Adolfine Freud (Dolfi): born on July 23, 1862, in Vienna. She died in 1943 in the concentration camp at Theresienstadt. She was unmarried.

Pauline Regine Freud (Pauli): born on May 3, 1864, in Vienna. She married Valentin Winternitz and immigrated to the United States; their daughter, Rose Beatrice (Rosi), was born on March 18, 1896. Pauline returned to Berlin in 1900 and died in the Holocaust in 1942.

Alexander Gotthold Efraim Freud: born on April 15, 1866, in Vienna. He died in 1943 in Canada.

IMMEDIATE FAMILY OF MARTHA, SIGMUND FREUD'S WIFE

Berman Bernays, father: born in 1826 in Wandsbek, Germany. He died in 1879 in Vienna.

Emmeline Bernays, née Philipp, mother: born on May 13, 1830, in Hamburg. She died in Vienna in 1890.

Martha Freud, née Bernays: born on July 26, 1861, in Hamburg. She became engaged to Sigmund Freud in 1882 and married him in 1886. They had six children. She died in London in 1951.

Minna Bernays, sister-in-law of Sigmund: born in 1865 in Hamburg. She died in London in 1942.

Eli Bernays, brother of Martha Bernays, brother-in-law of Sigmund: born in 1860 in Hamburg. He died in New York in 1921 of appendicitis.

CHILDREN OF FREUD AND MARTHA

Ernst Freud, eldest son: born in Vienna in 1887. He worked as an architect and married in 1919. He died in London in 1970.

Mathilde Freud: born in Vienna in 1888. She married in 1909. She died in London in 1978.

Martin Freud: born in Vienna in 1889. He was a lawyer and publisher. He died in London in 1967.

Oliver Freud: born in Vienna in 1891. He was named for Oliver Cromwell who was one of his father's heroes. Oliver became a civil engineer and died in Williamsburg, Virginia, in 1969.

Sophie Freud: born in 1893 in Vienna. She married Max Halberstadt and died at the young age of twenty-seven, of pneumonia, on January 25, 1920, in Hamburg.

Anna Freud: born in Vienna 1895. She was one of the most important writers on child psychoanalysis. She died in London in 1982.

OTHER RELATIVES

Johann Freud, Emanuel's son and Sigmund Freud's oldest nephew: born in Freiberg on August 13, 1855. He was sometimes known as John. It is not known where or when he died. A true mystery.

Pauline Freud, Sigmund's niece: born in Freiberg on November 20, 1856. She died in Manchester in 1944. She never married.

Solomon Samuel (Sam) Freud, Emanuel's fourth son: born on June 28, 1860. He died in Didsbury in 1945.

Mary (Poppy), niece: born on October 23, 1873, in Manchester She married Frederick Oswald Hartwig. She preserved the letters Sam and Sigmund had written. She died in 1953 in Manchester.

Morris Herbert Walter, Philip's second child: born in Manchester on April 2, 1876. He died in Port Elisabeth, South Africa, in July 1938.

Edward Bernays, nephew: born in 1891 in Vienna. He was widely recognized as the founder of political public relations. He was an adviser to Woodrow Wilson and a major influence on the American neoconservative movement. Edward Bernays was in charge of Freud's works in the United States. The longest living member of the family, he died in 1995 in New York at the age of 104.

Harry Freud, son of Alexander Freud, nephew of Sigmund Freud: born in 1909. He died in 1968 in the United States.

The Early Group of Psychoanalysts Who Were of Some Significance in the 1930s

Ernest Jones: born in 1879. Nicknamed the Welsh Wizard, he was a Welsh doctor and was the authorized biographer of Freud. He died in 1958.

Carl Jung: born in 1875. He was the son of a Swiss pastor. A psychiatrist and analyst, he founded his own school after a bitter quarrel with Freud. Freud saw him as his successor, but the two men never had any contact after 1914, when they had their rift. Jung died in 1961.

Wilhelm Reich: born 1897. Reich was one of the most brilliant and provocative of Freud's disciples. He was found guilty of offenses under the Food and Drugs Act and committed suicide in an American jail in 1957.

Otto Fenichel: born in 1897. During the war he organized contact among psychoanalysts by means of secret circular letters. He died in Los Angeles in 1946.

August Aichhorn: born 1878. Aichhorn was an analyst and authority on juvenile delinquency. He died in 1949 in Vienna.

Freud's Patients Who Are Relevant to This Period

William Bullitt: born 1891. He was an American diplomat, and coauthor with Freud of a book on President Woodrow Wilson. He died in 1967.

Princess Marie Bonaparte: born in 1882. She was the great-granddaughter of Napoleon. Like Freud, she was an analyst, and a dog lover. She died in 1962.

H.D. (full name, Hilda Doolittle): born in 1886. She was an American poet and the author of the best book on the experience of being in analysis with Freud. She died in 1961.

OTHERS

Dorothy Burlingham: born 1896. She married one of the heirs of Tiffany's. She was a close friend of Anna Freud. She died in 1989 in London.

Paula Fichtl: born in Salzburg in 1902. She was the Freuds' housekeeper. She died in Salzburg in 1987.

FREUD'S DOCTORS

Hans Pichler: born 1877. He was an oral surgeon who handled Freud's cancer from 1923 onward. He died in 1949.

Max Schur: born in 1897. He was Freud's personal physician. He died in 1977.

THE NAZIS

Dr. Felix Boehm: born in 1881. He was a psychoanalyst. He died in 1951.

Dr. Anton Sauerwald: born in Vienna in 1903. He was a chemist. He died in Innsbruck in 1970.

Dr. Carl Müller-Braunschweig: born in 1881. He was a psychoanalyst. He died in 1958.

Hermann Goering: born in 1893 in Rosenheim in southern Germany. He was Hitler's deputy and head of the Luftwaffe. He committed suicide in 1946, two hours before he was due to be executed.

Dr. Matthias Goering: born 1879. He was a psychoanalyst, though not a Freudian, and he was the cousin of Hermann Goering. He died in 1945.

Appendix 2
The Restricted Files

In addition to the files outlines in chapter 2, the following files are restricted:

Restricted until 2050, correspondence with Felix and Helene Deutsch. The couple were analysts and Felix Deutsch was also Freud's doctor until 1923, when he was dismissed.

Restricted until 2057, correspondence with Elsa Foges; she was a cousin of Dora's, one of Freud's cases that has caused endless controversy. Foges was interviewed in 1979 when she was ninety-seven years old by Anthony Stadlen. He wrote: "Dora had always got on particularly well with her and had shared all sorts of secrets with her." Frau Foges told Stadlen that she had asked Dora at the time of her analysis in 1900: "Who is this Freud?" Dora replied: "He asks me lots of questions, and I want to make an end of it." Elsa Foges was never a patient of Freud's and the files may well contain material critical of Freud because Dora certainly felt she had been poorly treated by him.

Restricted until 2057, correspondence with Clarence Oberndorf, an American psychoanalyst Freud treated in 1923 and 1924. They quarreled about the meaning of a dream. When Oberndorf dreamed of a black horse and a white horse, Freud argued it showed he had inhibitions about wanting to marry a white or black woman. Freud eventually became annoyed with Oberndorf, who did not accept this interpretation.

Restricted until 2057, correspondence with Edoardo Weiss, the psychoanalyst who founded the *Italian Journal of Psychoanalysis*. Freud corresponded with him about his analysis of his daughter, Anna Freud.

Restricted until 2057, correspondence with Ernst Kris, a psychoanalyst who was part of the team that analyzed the character of Hitler for the Office of Strategic Services in 1943.

Restricted until 2057, correspondence with Oskar Rie, a psychoanalyst, the doctor of Freud's six children.

Disputes About Access

In 1982, a historian of analysis, Phyllis Grosskurth, accused James Hutson, head of the Manuscript Division of the Library of Congress, of favoritism. One author, Celia Bertin, had been allowed a peep inside the Bonaparte files. Hutson denied the charge, saying, "Neither Ms. Bertin . . . nor any other scholar has received access to the Bonaparte Papers since they have been in the custody of the Library of Congress." He went on to justify that "donors of collections of psychoanalytic materials, in the interest of guarding the confidentiality between analyst and patient, tend to suggest restrictions for longer periods of time to protect the privacy of descendants and others who might be involved."

Phyllis Grosskurth was not convinced and replied that it was strange that she had not been told she might have access to these materials in Paris. There were copies in the papers of the Bonaparte family, so perhaps the Library of Congress exaggerated the confidentiality. In that vein Grosskurth also accused the Library of Congress of ignoring the wishes of some donors. When Diana Riviere, daughter of Joan Riviere, one of Freud's translators, sold correspondence between her and Freud to the Sigmund Freud Archives, Ms. Riviere said this material should be made available to serious scholars. When Grosskurth said that to Dr. K. R. Eissler, secretary of the Sigmund Freud Archives, it did not help. Eissler replied that "the Sigmund Freud Archives had acquired the letters through purchase, not donation." Because the archives now owned them, the archives controlled them and "had deposited them in the Library of Congress while restricting them until the year 2000."

Grosskurth was angry. Other scholars also complained that Dr. Eissler allowed some favored individuals access to some documents, while denying it to others. Eissler sometimes even refused to let donors themselves see their own material once they had given it to the archives.

References

Works by Sigmund Freud

All references are to the Standard Edition (hereafter, SE), edited by Strachey and Strachey with the help of Anna Freud. It was published by The Hogarth Press of London, which was run by Leonard and Virginia Woolf.

1899 *The Interpretation of Dreams*, SE 4–5, 8.

1903 *Jokes and Their Relation to the Unconscious*, SE 8.

1913 *Totem and Taboo*, SE 13, pp. 1–161.

1914 *The Moses of Michelangelo*, originally published in *Imago*, SE 13, pp. 211–38.

1920 *Beyond the Pleasure Principle*, SE 18, pp. 7–64.

1923 *The Ego and the Id*, SE 19, pp. 3–66.

1925 *An Autobiographical Study*, SE 20, pp. 3–70.

1925 *Resistances to Psycho-Analysis*, SE 19.

1927 *The Future of an Illusion*, SE 21, pp. 3–56.

1930 Preface to the Hebrew Translation of *Totem and Taboo*, London: Hogarth Press, 1955.

1932 *Why War*, pamphlet for the League of Nations, SE 22, pp. 197–215.

1937 *Analysis Terminable and Interminable*, SE 23, pp. 209–53.

1937 translation of Marie Bonaparte's *Topsy*, Brussels: Allert de Lange.

1938 *Moses and Monotheism*, SE 23, pp. 3–137.

1940 *An Outline of Psychoanalysis*, SE 23, pp. 141–207.

1966 with William Bullitt, *Thomas Woodrow Wilson, Twenty-eighth President of the United States*, Boston: Houghton Mifflin.

Letters

Freud, S. (1960). *Letters*. New York: Basic Books.

———— (1961). *Letters of Sigmund Freud 1873–1939*. Edited by E. Freud. London: Hogarth Press.

———— (1989). *Letters of Sigmund Freud and Eduard Silberstein: 1871–1881*. Cambridge, MA: Harvard University Press.

Freud, S., and Freud, S. *Letters (1914–1938)*. MS collection in John Rylands Library, University of Manchester. The collection includes letters from Polly Hartwig and Anna Freud.

Freud, S., and Rolland, R. (1993). *Correspondence, 1923–1936*. Edited by Henri and Madeleine Vermorel. Paris: Presses Universitaires de France.

Works by Relatives and Friends

Bernays, Edward (1929). *Crystallizing Public Opinion*. New York: Boni and Liveright.

———— (2004). *Propaganda*. Brooklyn, NY: Ig Publishing.

Bernays, Jacob (1861). *Ein Lebensbild in Briefe*. Republished, Breslau M & H Marcus, 1932.

Bernays-Freud, Anna (1940, November). "My Brother Sigmund Freud." *American Mercury 51*, no. 203, 335–42.

———— (2005*). Eine Wienerin in New York*. Berlin: Aufbau Verlag.

Bernays-Heller, Judith (1973). "Freud's Mother and Father." In *Freud as We Knew Him*. Edited by H. M. Ruitenbeck. Detroit: Wayne State University Press.

Berthelsen, D. (1991). *La Famille Freud au jour le jour; souvenirs de Paula Fichtl*. Paris: Presses Universitaires de France.

Freud, A. (1949). "Report on the Sixteenth International Psycho-Analytical Congress." *Bulletin of the International Psychoanalytic Association 30*, 178–208.

Freud, Martin (1958). *Sigmund Freud: Man and Father*. New York: Vanguard Press.

H.D. (Doolittle, H.) (1984). *Tribute to Freud*. New York: W. W. Norton.

Mann, Thomas (1930/1942). "On German Fascism, in 'An Appeal to Reason'" ["Deutsche Ansprache. Ein Appell an die Vernunft"], *Berliner Tageblatt*, October 18. In *Order of the Day, Political Essays and Speeches of Two Decades*, translated by Helen T. Lowe-Porter. New York: A. A. Knopf.

———— (1936/1957). "Freud and the Future" ("Freud und due Zukunft"),

Imago 22, 313-5. In *Essays*, translated by Helen T. Lowe-Porter. New York: Vintage.

Zweig, Arnold (1936). *Education Before Verdun*. New York: Viking Press.

Zweig, Stefan (1929/1933). *Mental Healers*. London: Cassell and Co.

———— (2000). *The Royal Game*. New York Holmes and Meier.

Biographies and Aspects of Freud's Work

Bakan, D. (1958/1990). *Sigmund Freud and the Jewish Mystical Tradition*. London: Free Association Books.

Baur, E. (2008). *Freuds Wien*. Munich: Verlag C. H. Beck.

Bertin, C. (1987). *Marie Bonaparte*. New Haven, CT: Yale University Press.

Bettlelheim, B. (1982). *Freud and Man's Soul*. New York: A. A. Knopf.

Cioffi, F. (ed.) (1973). *Freud: Modern Judgements*. London Macmillan.

Dilman, I. (1984). *Freud and the Mind*. Oxford, UK: Blackwell.

Edelson, M. (1984). *Hypothesis and Evidence in Psychoanalysis*. Chicago: University of Chicago Press.

Edmundson, M. (2006). *The Death of Sigmund Freud*. London: Bloomsbury.

Fancher, R. (1973). *Psychoanalytic Psychology: The Development of Freud's Thought*. New York: W. W. Norton.

Farrell, B. A. (1981). *The Standing of Psychoanalysis*. New York: Oxford University Press.

Ferris, P. (1997). *Dr. Freud*. London: Sinclair-Stevenson.

Forrester, J. (1998). *Dispatches from the Freud Wars*. Cambridge, MA: Harvard University Press.

Gay, P. (1988). *Freud: A Life for Our Time*. London: Dent.

Gilman, S. (1993). *Freud, Race and Gender*. Princeton, NJ: Princeton University Press.

Hayman, R. (1999). *A Life of Jung*. London: Bloomsbury.

Hofstader, G. B (1994). *Jung's Struggle with Freud* Wilmette, IL: Chiron.

Hook, S. (ed.) (1959). *Psychoanalysis: Scientific Method and Philosophy*. New York: New York University Press.

Jones, E. R. (1953–1957). *Sigmund Freud*. 3 vols. New York: Basic Books.

Malcolm, J. (1983/1984). *In the Freud Archives*. New York: A. A. Knopf.

Masson, J. (1984). *The Assault on Truth: Freud's Suppression of the Seduction Theory*. London: Faber & Faber.

Rand, N., and Torok, M. (1997). *Questions for Freud*. Cambridge, MA: Harvard University Press.

Ricoeur, P. (1970). *Freud and Philosophy: An Essay in Interpretation*. Translated by Denis Savage. New Haven, CT: Yale University Press.

Robert, M. (1976). *From Oedipus to Moses: Freud's Jewish Identity*. Garden City, NY: Anchor Books.

Roith, E. (1987). *The Riddle of Freud*. London: Tavistock.

Sharaf, M. (1983). *Fury on Earth: A Biography of Wilhelm Reich*. London: Hutchinson.

Sulloway, F. (1979). *Freud, Biologist of the Mind*. New York: Basic Books.

Timms, E., and Segal, N. (eds.) (1988). *Freud in Exile: Psychoanalysis and Its Vicissitudes*. New Haven, CT: Yale University Press.

Whyte, L.L. (1960). *The Unconscious Before Freud*. New York: Basic Books.

Wollheim, R. (1971). *Sigmund Freud*. New York; Viking Press

———— (ed.) (1974). *Freud: A Collection of Critical Essays*. Garden City, NY: Anchor Books.

Wollheim, R., and Hopkins, J. (eds.) (1982). *Philosophical Essays on Freud*. New York: Cambridge University Press.

Young-Bruehl, E. (2006). *Anna Freud: A Biography*. New Haven, CT: Yale University Press.

Other Works

Adams, L. (1952–1955). Letters relating to Freud in City of Manchester Library Archives.

Aichhorn, A. (1935). *Wayward Youth*. New York: Viking Press.

Auerbach, E. (1975). *Moses*. Translated and edited by Robert A. Barclay and Israel O. Lehman. Detroit: Wayne State University Press.

Authers, J., and Wolffe, R. (2002). *The Victim's Fortune: Inside the Epic Battle over the Debts of the Holocaust*. New York: HarperCollins.

Baillie-Grohman W.A (1878) *Sport in the Alps in the Past and Present*. An account of the chase of the chamois bouquetin, capercaillie, and black-cock with personal adventures and historical notes and some sporting reminiscences of H.R.H. the Late Duke of Saxe-Coburg-Gotha.

Berdach, Rachel (1962). *The Emperor, the Sages and Death*. Translated by William Wolf. New York: Thomas Yoseloff.

Bibring, Grete (ed.) (1951). "Report on the 17th International Psychoanalytical Congress." *International Journal of Psychoanalysis 33*, 249–51.

Blüher, H. (1922). *Secessio Judaica: philosophische Grundlegung der historischen Situation des Judentums und der antisemitischen Bewegung*. Berlin: W. Ritter.

Boehm, Felix (1931). On the History of thew Oedipus Complex, *International Journal of Psychoanalysis* vol 12, 431–51.

Boehm, Felix (1978). *Schriften zur Psychoanalyse*. Munich: Ölschläger.

Brecht, K., Friedrioch, V., Hermanns, L., Kaminer, I., and Juelcih, D. (eds.) (1985). *"Here Life Goes On in a Most Peculiar Way": Psychoanalysis Before and After 1933*. Hamburg: Kellner Verlag; London: Goethe-Institut.

Brook-Shepherd, Gordon (1996). *The Austrians: A Thousand-Year Odyssey*. London: Harper Collins.

Burt, C. (1939). Obituary of Freud. *Nature* issue of 28 October.

Chrzanowski, G. (1975). "Psychoanalysis: Ideology and Practitioners." *Contemporary Psychoanalysis 11*, 492–99.

Churchill, W. (2005). *The Gathering Storm*. London: Penguin Classics.

Clare, George (2007). *Last Waltz in Vienna*. London: Macmillan.

Cocks, G. (1997). *Psychotherapy in the Third Reich*. 2nd ed. New Brunswick, NJ: Transaction Publishers.

——— (2001). "The Devil and the Details." *Psychoanalytic Review* 88, 225–44.

Danto, E. A. (2003). "Death of a 'Jewish Science'—Psychoanalysis in the Third Reich." *Journal of Interdisciplinary History 34*, no. 1, 90–91.

Díaz de Chumaceiro, C. L. (1993). *Freud and Music: What Freud Knew*. Psychoanalytic Explorations in Music, 2nd series. Edited by Stuart Feder, Richard L. Karmel, and George H. Pollock. Madison, CT: International Universities Press.

Diller, J. (1991). *Freud's Jewish Identity: A Case Study in the Impact of Ethnicity*. London: Associated University Presses.

Eastman, Max (1926). *Heroes I Have Known*. New York: Simon and Schuster.

Eder, M. D. (1917). *The Psycho-neuroses in War Shock and Their Treatment*. Philadelphia: Blakiston.

Eickhoff, F. (1995). "The Formation of the German Psychoanalytical Association (DPV): Regaining the Psychoanalytical Orientation Lost in the Third Reich." *International Journal of Psycho-Analysis 76*, 945–56.

Engelman, Edmund (1998). *Sigmund Freud: Vienna IX, Berggasse 19*. New York: Universe Pub.

Erman, Adolf (1905). Die Egyptisch Religion Berlin: George Reimer.

Fenichel, O. (1953). "On Social Anxiety." In *The Collected Papers of Otto Fenichel*, edited by Hanna Fenichel and David Rapaport. New York: W. W. Norton.

———— (1998). *119 Rundbriefe*. Two volumes. Edited by Johannes Reichmayr and Elke Mühlleitner. Frankfurt: Stroemfeld.

Garscha, W. R., and Kuretsidis-Haider, C. (1995). *Justice and Nazi-Crimes in Austria 1945–1955 Between Self-Purge and Allied Control*. In 1945: Consequences and Sequels of the Second World War. *Bulletin du Comité international d'histoire de la Deuxième Guerre mondiale, nos. 27/28*, 245–55.

Goggin, J. E., and Goggin, E. B. (2001). *Death of a "Jewish Science"—Psychoanalysis in the Third Reich*. West Lafayette, IN: Purdue University Press.

Goering, M. (ed.) (1940). *Sonderheft der Deutschen Institut fur Psychologisch Forschung und Psychotherapie*. Leipzig: S. Hirzel.

Grosskurth, P. (1982, December 6). "The Shrink Princess." *New York Review of Books*.

Heidemarie, Uhl (2001). "Transformations of Austrian Memory: Politics of History and Monument Culture in the Second Republic." In *Austrian History Yearbook*, edited by the Center for Austrian Studies, vol. 32, 149–67. Minneapolis.

Heine, H. (1821/2001*). Almansor*. In *Collected Works of Heinrich Heine*; Boston Adamant Media Corporation.

Hitler, A. (2007). *Mein Kampf*. Mumbai: Jaico Publishing House.

Holpfer, E., Loitfellner, S., and Uslu-Pauer, S. (2003, February). "Wiener Urteile wegen NS-Verbrechen. Abschluss der Erfassung des hauptverhandlungsregisters des Volksgerichts Wien (1945–1955)." *Justiz und Erinnerung*, no. 7, 29–30.

Jacoby, R. (1975). *Social Amnesia*. Sussex, UK: Harvester Press.

———— (1983). *The Repression of Psychoanalysis*. New York: Basic Books.

James, W. (1985). *The Varieties of Religious Experience*. New York: Penguin Books.

Jones, E. R. (1931). *Elements of Figure Skating*. London: George Allen and Unwin.

Keneally, T. (1993). *Schindler's List*. New York: Simon and Schuster.

Klein, D. (1985). *Jewish Origins of the Psychoanalytic Movement*. Chicago: Chicago University Press.

Knight, R. (2000). *"Ich bin dafür, die Sache in die Länge zu ziehen."* Die Wortprotokolle der österreichischen Bundesregierung von 1945–1952 über die Entschädigung der Juden. 2nd edition. Vienna: Bohlau Verlag.

Krüll, Marianne (1979). *Freud und sein Vater. Die Entstehung der Psychoanalyse und Freuds ungelöste Vaterbindung*. Munich: Beck.

——— (1986). *Freud and His Father*. Translated by Arnold J. Pomerans. New York: W. W. Norton.

Langer, Walter; Murray, Henry; Kris, Ernst; and Lewin, Bertram (1943). *A Psychological Analysis of Adolf Hitler: His Life and Legend*. Washington, DC: Office of Strategic Services.

Langer, W., and Gifford, S. (1978). "An American Analyst in Vienna During the Anschluss, 1936–1938." *Journal of the History of Behavioral Sciences 14*, 37–54.

Lawrence, D. H. (2004). *Psychoanalysis and the Unconscious; and Fantasia of the Unconscious*. Edited by Bruce Steele. Cambridge, UK: Cambridge University Press.

Léon, M. (1946). *The Case of Dr. Carl Gustav Jung: Pseudo-scientist Nazi Auxiliary*. Report to U.S. Department of State and Nuremberg Tribunal.

Leupold-Löewenthal, H. (1989). "Die Vertreibung der Familie Freud 1938." *Psyche-Zeitschrift für Psychoanalyse und ihre Anwendungen 43*, no. 10, 908–28.

Lewis, D. (2003). *The Man Who Invented Hitler*. London: Headline.

Lobner, H. (1975). *Bulletin of the Sigmund Freud Museum*, vol 1, 18–29.

Lockot, Regine (1985). *Erinnern und Durcharbeiten: Zur Geschichte der Psychoanalyse und Psychotherapie im Nationalsozialismus*. Frankfurt am Main: S. Fischer.

——— (1994). *Die Reinigung der Psychoanalyse: die Deutsche Psychoanalytische Gesellschaft im Spiegel von Dokumenten und Zeitzeugen (1933–1951)*. Tübingen: Diskord.

Loitfellner, S. (2002). "Aryanisation 1938/39 in Vienna and the People's Court Trials After 1945." In *Austria in the European Union*, edited by Günter Bischof, Anton Pelinka, and Michael Gehler. Contemporary Austrian Studies, vol. 10. New Brunswick, NJ: Transaction Publishers.

Maddox, B. (2006). *Freud's Wizard: The Enigma of Ernest Jones*. London: John Murray.

Mahony, P. J. (2006). The Moses of Michelangelo; *Canadian Journal of Psychoanalysis* Vol 14, 11–43.

Morton, Frederic (1962). *The Rothschilds*. London: Secker and Warburg.

Moses, R., and Hrushovski-Moses, R. (1986). "A Form of Group Denial at the Hamburg Congress." *International Review of Psycho-Analysis* 13, 175–80.

Müller-Braunschweig, Carl (1933, October 22). "Psychoanalyse und Weltanschauung." *Reichswart*.

——— (1948). *Streifzüge durch die Psychoanalyse (Welche Position vertritt der Psychoanalytiker heute)*. Hamburg: Reinbeck.

——— (1955). Zur Menschlichen Grundhaltung, Psychologie und Technik der Psychoanalytischen Therapie, *Psychologische Beitrage*, vol 2, 56-69.

Nitzschke, B. (1999). "Psychoanalysis during National Socialism: Present-Day Consequences of a Historical Controversy in the 'Case' of Wilhelm Reich." *Psychoanalytic Review* 86, 349–66.

Oberhummer, W. (1969). "Herzig, Josef." In *Neue Deutsche Biographie*, vol. 8, p. 735. Berlin: Duncker & Humblot.

Olden, R. (1936). *Hitler*. New York: Covici, Friede.

Pollak, J. (1925). "Josef Herzig." *Berichte der Deutschen Chemischen Gesellschaft 59*, A, 55–75.

——— (1923). "Josef Herzig zum siebzigsten Geburtstag." *Österreicher. Chemiker-Zeitung 26*, 139f.

Reich, W. (1970). *The Mass Psychology of Fascism*. Edited by Mary Higgins and Chester M. Raphael. 3rd ed., rev. and enl. New York: Farrar, Straus and Giroux.

Rittmeister, J. (1939, October 15). *Letter to Alfred and Edith Storch*. Münsingen.

Roazen, P. (1973). *Brother Animal: The Story of Tausk and Freud*. New York: A. A. Knopf.

——— (2003). *On the Freud Watch: Public Memoirs*. London: Free Association Books.

Roback, A. A. (1940). *The Story of Yiddish Literature*. New York: Yiddish Scientific Institute.

Rosenberg, A. (1939). *Der Sumpf [The Swamp]*. 2nd ed. Munich: Eher Nachf.

Rückerl, A. (1979). *Die Strafverfolgung von NS-Verbrechern: 1945–1978: Eine Dokumentation*, 125. Heidelberg: C. F. Müller Juristischer Verlag.

Rüter, C. F., and de Mildt, D. W. (1998). *Die Westdeutschen Strafverfahren wegen nationalsozialistischer Tötungsverbrechen 1945–1997: eine systematische Verfahrensbeschreibung mit Karten und Registern*. Amsterdam and Maarssen: APA-Holland University Press; Munich: K. G. Saur.

Sanford, Bell (1902). "A Preliminary Study of the Emotion of Love Between the Sexes." *American Journal of Psychology* 2, 325–44.

Sauerwald, A., and Muller, A. (1927a, July). "Neue Synthese des 1,6-Dibrom-n-hexans und seine Einwirkung aufp-Toluolsulfamid." *Monatshefte für Chemie / Chemical Monthly 48*, no. 7, 521–27.

——— (1927b, September). "Neue Synthese und Reindarstellung des Hexamethylenimins." *Monatshefte für Chemie / Chemical Monthly* 48, nos. 9–10, 727–32.

——— (1927c, September). "Über das Verhalten des Aluminiumtriäthyls am Nickelkatalysator bei höherer Temperatur." *Monatshefte für Chemie / Chemical Monthly* 48, nos. 9–10, 737–39.

Schur, Max (1972). *Freud: Living and Dying*. London: Hogarth Press and the Institute of Psycho-Analysis.

Skellett A.-M., Millington, G., and Levell, N. J. (2008). "Sudden Whitening of the Hair: An Historical Fiction? *Journal of the Royal Society of Medicine* 101, 574–76.

Steffek, A., and Uslu-Pauer, S. (2000, October). "Die Kartei der Wiener Volksgerichtsprozesse 1945–1955. Die EDV-Erfassung und wissenschaftliche Auswertung der Kartei der am Volksgericht Wien zwischen 1945–1955 geführten gerichtlichen Voruntersuchungen." *Justiz und Erinnerung*, no. 3, 3–6.

Steiner, R. (2000). *"It Is a New Kind of Diaspora: Explorations in the Sociopolitical and Cultural Context of Psychoanalysis*. London: Karnac.

Thurber, J. (1939). *Let Your Mind Alone*. London: Readers Union.

Thurber, J., and White, E. B. (1952). *Is Sex Necessary?* or, *Why You Feel the Way You Do*. London: Hamish Hamilton.

Vasari, G. (1971). *Life of Michelangelo Buonarroti*. Translated by George Bull. London: Folio Society.

Wegscheider, R. (1925). "Josef Herzig." In *Almanach der Akademie der Wissenschaften* vol 75, 194–98.

Wiesenthal, S. (1991). "Speech on the Occasion of the Annual General Meeting of the Documentation Centre of Austrian Resistance (DÖW) in the Old City Hall of Vienna, March 11, 1991." In Jahrbuch 1992, edited by the Dokumentationsarchivs des österreichischen Widerstandes, p. 10. Vienna.

Wylie, J. (2006). *The Warlord and the Renegade: The Story of Hermann and Albert Goering*. Gloucestershire, UK: The History Press.

Yerushalmi, Y. (1991). *Freud's Moses: Judaism Terminable and Interminable*. New Haven, CT: Yale University Press.

Acknowledgments

I owe much to Brian Farrell who taught me about Freud years ago at Oxford. Interviews with Viktor Frankl (who felt Freud ignored him) and Harald Leopold Loewenthal made me all the more interested. I have continued to be surprised by the way "normal" psychiatrists (who believe in medication) keep on being interested in—and influenced by—Freud and "the talking cure." My good friends, the late Dr. James MacKeith and the thankfully very alive Dr. Harvey Gordon are among those. Both encouraged me in this project.

Many libraries and librarians have been helpful—the John Rylands University in Manchester, Manchester City Reference Library, the Institute of Psychoanalysis Library, Swiss Cottage Library in London, the Royal Society of Medicine Library, the Librarian of Vienna city archives, the Austrian State archives, the National Library in Vienna as well as the usual suspects—the Library of Congress in Washington, DC, the Wellcome Library, and the British Library. The Freud Museums in London and Vienna remain inspiring, as does the Jewish Museum in Manchester. The Vienna Criminal Museum which contains many exhibits relating to forgery is fun to visit if forgers and murderers are of interest.

I am grateful for very useful discussions on Freud with Dr. Riccardo Steiner, with Dr. Lesleey Sohn who is still practicing analysis at the age of 88 and with Michael Molnar, the Director of Research at the Freud Museum in London.

Professor R. Werner Soukup of the Technical University, Vienna, explained to me what Sauerwald's chemical work was all about. Jonathan Edwards of the Royal Society of Chemistry was also most helpful with that.

My thanks to my friend and agent Sonia Land for believing in this book, to Jeremy Robson for the very constructive criticism, to Peter Mayer for more ideas and constructive criticism, to Dan Crissman, to my dear son Reuben, to Aileen La Tourette, to Dr. Murray Hall in Vienna for sharing his information about Freud's publishing activities and Sauerwald, to Kurt at Vienna's engaging Lhotzky's Literaturbuffet for his help, to Brian Levene and to Martin Hay for comments, to Hantie, to Daniel Sisspella and Dr. Gabriele Kohlbauer-Fritz of Vienna's Jewish Museum, to Julia Ross, to my cousin Anita Frank and to Meike Currie who helped me make sense of some of the documents relating to the Sauerwald trials.

Index